HOW SOON IS NOW?

Darley-Del.   HENRICK SC

HOW SOON IS NOW?

Medieval Texts, Amateur Readers, and the Queerness of Time

CAROLYN DINSHAW

DUKE UNIVERSITY PRESS DURHAM & LONDON 2012

© 2012 Duke University Press

All rights reserved

Printed in the United States of America

on acid-free paper ♾

Designed by Jennifer Hill

Typeset in Garamond Premier Pro

by Tseng Information Systems, Inc.

Library of Congress Cataloging-in-

Publication Data appear on the last

printed page of this book.

FOR MARGET

TIME AND TIME AGAIN

CONTENTS

started thinking about this book over a decade ago now, but I experienced a defining moment in its composition at the Medieval Festival in New York in the fall of 2008. The Medieval Festival is the enormous annual festival held around the Cloisters — the branch of the Metropolitan Museum of Art dedicated to Western European medieval art and architecture — in Fort Tryon Park, drawing thousands of people, many in elaborate costume. "Take the A-train to the 14th Century," a sign in the subway urged. I boarded the train and rode to the far north of Manhattan to find the park filled for the day with toddlers bearing plastic swords, men in chain mail, women in lace-up wench outfits, and food stalls selling roasted turkey legs and Ye Fried Dough.

Many of the costumes were extravagant and fabulous. But the one that proved revelatory to me was hardly a costume at all: I saw a young man, softly playing the recorder while walking alone, wearing a

Preface 1. Young man in bathrobe
with recorder. © *Marget Long, 2008.*

terry cloth bathrobe. It was dark blue, with a monogram that I didn't quite
catch. What struck me immediately upon seeing him was that he must
really have wanted to go to the festival that day, so that even in the absence
of a costume he did his best and left the house in this makeshift garb. My
students later suggested, upon seeing his photograph, that he had glanced
around his house and grabbed something that looked like a monk's robe
or that otherwise signified "medieval" (see preface figure 1). Haphazard as
the gesture might have been — and in keeping with the long tradition of
fashioning a costume with whatever is at hand — the dressing gown signi-
fies "medieval" for a reason. The design, with its enveloping drapery and
broad sleeves, brings to my mind an illumination from a fifteenth-century
manuscript showing a man (Tobit, of the Book of Tobit) sleeping by a fire
in a similar-looking garment (see preface figure 2).[1] The bathrobe style is
old but still with us because it has proven continuously useful. The past
is present in this intimate, mundane element of undressed everyday life.

The young man threw on a bathrobe because he wanted to go to a fair.
In that single gesture he simultaneously drew together past (medieval style
of robe), present (what was in his closet that day), and future (the goal

Preface 2. Tobit sleeping by the fire in a bathrobe-like garment.
© *The British Library Board, MS Royal 15 D I f. 18.*

of attending the festival in the park). Michel Serres and Dipesh Chakrabarty help me theorize this gesture — "Pasts *are* there in taste, in practices of embodiment, in the cultural training the senses have received over generations," writes Chakrabarty — but it was the festivalgoer himself (seeking pleasure, as I understood him to be) who enacted this expansive *now*, knew it in some sense.[2] The festivalgoer's medievalist act urges me to think further not only about multiple temporalities but also about the sources of scholarly research and knowledge, and the potentials for opening them up beyond the paradigm of professionalism that has rigorously delimited scholarship from any other more explicitly affective enterprise.

The Medieval Festival, in its twenty-sixth year in 2008, included tours of the Cloisters and a gallery workshop for families, as well as a wide array of activities throughout the adjacent grounds: music, theater, jousting, artisan demonstrations. This was some serious fun. The labor expended in amateur medievalism was everywhere evident: in handmade garb, in the regulated play of the tournament, in manually forged weaponry. It was different from scholarly labor, but it was indubitably labor — detailed, thorough — and, importantly, not sealed off or separated from pleasure. Indeed, as Aranye Fradenburg points out, "the transition from popular to scholastic medievalism takes work, but it is not the work of acquiring a taste for the work involved in producing knowledge." Among the artisans and players that day at the fair was pulsing a love of knowledge.[3]

In fact, I felt a vibrant resonance between this amateur medievalism and professional medievalism, and the location of the festival contributed to this sense. The contiguity of popular festival and high-culture museum (the Cloisters is one of the premier locales in the United States for pursuing scholarly research into Western European medieval art and architecture) — and the element of interpenetration, as festival attendees entered the gates of the museum for tours — embodied a linked relationship between amateurs and professionals. The two are hard to separate entirely, and that is of course a big part of the point: I have put the Cloisters on the side of scholarly medieval studies because of the holdings it offers for research, but the museum building itself is an eclectic creation incorporating medieval cloisters, medieval chapter houses, and other architectural elements from the Middle Ages into an early-twentieth-century structure. The purpose behind the design was not to copy a specific medieval building but rather to create an "intimate" and "contemplative" atmosphere — related to that of the original spaces — in which the works of art can be viewed and studied now.[4] This architectural jumble presents a high-culture version of the temporal heterogeneity that I recognized in the guy wearing the dressing gown.

In reality, not so very high. "To culture snobs, the Cloisters is disgusting," writes Thomas Hoving, the former curator of the medieval department and subsequent director of the Metropolitan Museum of Art, as he explains the horrified reaction of a scholar of medieval history. "To them it's nothing more than a hodgepodge of ancient European architectural history, ripped out of context, pasted together to form a dreamlike but haphazard ensemble." But Hoving loves the place, and he counters that scholarly disdain with his own affectionate time-travel fantasy: "If you dream a little, you can float through time to the eleventh century in southern France, through twelfth-century Spain and all the way to the beginning of the sixteenth century in Germany."[5] In Hoving's account, professional and amateur medievalist gestures are held in tension, simultaneously.

In the 1960s and early 1970s the Medieval Festival was in fact "held within the museum's walls," according to the 2008 printed program, and was aided in its beginnings by the Cloisters' educational director. The festival in its current form no doubt helps the museum by bringing a large population to the Cloisters' doors, perhaps to return later for a visit dedicated solely to viewing the museum's rarities. The museum, in turn, grounds the festival (literally, as the architectural high point around which the activities are oriented, and figuratively, as the repository of medieval materials). But it doesn't limit the festival: on that day in the fall of 2008 the festive proceedings stretched into the park, which became a re-creational in addition to a recreational space.

Seeing the festival attendee in that profoundly unprogressive garment, the bathrobe, was a revelation to me, the ever-so-professional medievalist. Anyone who has studied the Middle Ages in an academic setting knows that medieval (and Renaissance) fairs are, to say the least, frowned upon as resources or venues for serious research. They are patronizingly dismissed or laughed at. And yet the profession has not always been so distanced from amateurs. In his 2009 annual Medieval Academy of America presidential address, Patrick Geary looked back at the professional organization's origins in the first quarter of the twentieth century and discovered "architects, businessmen, and educated amateurs" among its founders, and noted the early assumption that "the Academy should be an organization of professionals and enthusiasts alike." Charles Collens, the archi-

Preface 3. Young man in bathrobe taking notes. © *Marget Long, 2008.*

tect of the temporal mishmash that is the Cloisters, was an early member. Geary observed as well that in those early years the scholars might not have agreed with the nonscholars' approaches — he referred to one non-scholarly founder's "desire to bring back the Middle Ages" — but they determined that both should have a place in the organization. Anyone who has attended the academy's annual meetings will know that this balance has not been achieved of late. Geary exhorted the membership in 2009 to think about the price of professionalization and to conduct research that connects "in significant ways the deep past of medieval culture and contemporary social and cultural challenges."[6] Engaging this train of thought about the profession's exclusions, I suspect that amateurs have something to teach the experts: namely, that the present moment is more temporally heterogeneous than academically disciplined, historically minded scholars tend to let on, and that some kind of desire for the past motivates all our work, regardless of how sharp-edged our researches eventually become: love and knowledge are as inextricable as the links in chain mail. I don't know what brought the bathrobe guy to the Medieval Festival, but perhaps he was there for his own research; I saw him at one point taking notes, which dispelled any idea I might have had of him as a simple, unconscious naïf loose in the park, the merely passive object of my professional gaze (see preface figure 3). Perhaps those notes were on me.

This book is about nonmodern temporalities, both the times that are operant in the literature of the Middle Ages as well as the expansive *now* that can result from engagement with that literature. These are temporalities that are not laminar flows of some putative stream of time, not historicist, not progressive or developmental in the modern sense. This book discusses the spatialization of time that underlies the subway poster's wit. It takes nonprofessionals and dilettantes seriously as they operate in nonmodern temporalities of their own. Indeed, it takes the intimacy of that bathrobe seriously — as seriously as it takes the root of the word *amateur*: *love* — in its exploration of amateur medievalists as a bit queer in a professionalized, detached modernist world.

ACKNOWLEDGMENTS

'␣ve certainly taken my own sweet time with this
book. Many colleagues and friends participated
with me in this temporally extended enterprise. I
delivered numerous talks that helped me define my
project, beginning with a lecture in 2000 to the New
Chaucer Society and continuing for more than a decade; I warmly thank my colleagues, whose invita-
tions proved so useful — and so pleasurable, to boot.
To the varied, inquisitive, generous, and especially to
the disgruntled audiences of these talks, I give particular thanks. Pivotal to my thinking were lectures
at the University of Illinois at Urbana-Champaign
(thanks to Lisa Lampert-Weissig); King's College,
London (Robert Mills, Simon Gaunt); Cambridge
University (Christopher Cannon); University of
Pennsylvania (Jessica Rosenfeld, Robert Perelman);
University of Manchester (David Alderson, Anke
Bernau, David Matthews); University of Colorado
at Boulder (Elizabeth Robertson, William Kuskin);

University of Tasmania (Jenna Mead); University of Utah (Kathryn Bond Stockton); Smith College (Carolyn Collette, Nancy Bradbury); University of Iowa (Jonathan Wilcox, Kathy Lavezzo); Cornell University (Masha Raskolnikov, Andrew Galloway); University of Virginia (Gabriel Haley, Bruce Holsinger); Yale University (James Knabe, Alastair Minnis); and Bristol University (Ika Willis, Anna Wilson). Presentations at the New Chaucer Society Congress in 2006 and 2008 were important in shaping my thinking; I thank my fellow panelists and the audience members in New York and in Swansea. I was privileged to deliver the 2012 Alexander Lectures at the University of Toronto, in which I presented materials from almost the entire manuscript; I thank Donald Ainslie for his gracious hosting, and Michael Cobb, Suzanne Conklin Akbari, and Simon Stern in particular for making that visit so fruitful.

To name everyone involved in such a lengthy writing process is of course impossible — so many people contributed in large and small ways. Nevertheless I want to try to acknowledge the generosity shown to me over the long haul. The sustained interest in and support of this project shown by Paul Strohm and by Christopher Cannon — extraordinary intellectual generosity, from beginning to end — cannot go without mention. Elaine Freedgood offered crucial conceptual insight as well as lively and welcome support. To those who read articles or chapters and offered valuable thoughts I give heartfelt thanks: Lisa Cohen, Susan Crane, Ann Cvetkovich, Kathleen Davis, Elizabeth Freeman, Phillip Brian Harper, Amy Hollywood, Jennie Jackson, Annamarie Jagose, Arthur Lindley, Heather Love, Maureen MacLane, Mimi McGurl, Kellie Robertson, Martha Rust, Kay Turner, David Wallace, Deanne Williams, the Penn Medieval and Renaissance Group, the Ladies Composition Society (especially Tavia N'yongo, José Esteban Muñoz, Janet Jakobsen, and Gayatri Gopinath), and, further back in time, the queer reading group at NYU. For provocative and thoughtful bibliographical references, thanks to Jeffrey Jerome Cohen and Eileen Joy. For ideal collegial generosity, thanks to John Hirsh. For stimulating prompts and significant details, Christopher Baswell and Jonathan Alexander. Wonderful graduate students in my "Time and Temporality" seminars in fall 2007 and spring 2011, "Medieval Women's Writing" seminar in spring 2009, and "Ecological Approaches to Medieval Literature" seminar in fall 2009, spurred me on; a special shout-out to Liza Blake, who sent me a reference at a propitious moment. To my peerless graduate research assistant, Sarah Ostendorf, go abundant thanks. For support beyond textuality I thank many of those listed previously, plus Gretchen Phillips, Lee Wallace, Alisa Solomon, Marilyn Neimark, Sharon Marcus, Ellis Avery, Lisa Duggan, Ann Pellegrini, Sandy Silverman, Marty Correia, Kate Conroy, and our neighbors and friends back in the day, up in the Catskills. I thank my parents for their beautiful love and constancy, and my sisters, their spouses, the Janssens, the Rosens, and the Longs for their generosity and loving support.

Portions of chapter 2 appeared in early form in "Pale Faces: Race, Religion, and Affect in Chaucer's Texts and Their Readers," *Studies in the Age of Chaucer* 23 (2001): 19–41. An earlier version of chapter 3 appeared as "Temporalities" in *Middle English*, edited by Paul Strohm (Oxford University Press, 2007), 107–23. Parts of chapter 3 got their start in "Margery Kempe," *The Cambridge Companion to Medieval Women's Writing*, edited by Carolyn Dinshaw and David Wallace (Cambridge University Press, 2003), 222–39. In chapter 4 I have reused some material from "Are We Having Fun Yet? A Response to Prendergast and Trigg," *New Medieval Literatures* 9 (2007): 231–41. Portions of chapter 4 appeared in early form in "Born Too Soon, Born Too Late: The Female Hunter of Long Eddy, *circa* 1855," in *21st-Century Gay Culture*, ed. David A. Powell (Cambridge Scholars Publishing, 2008). I thank Wilbur Allen for permission to quote unpublished materials from the Hope Emily Allen papers at Bryn Mawr College.

I benefitted enormously from the work of the readers for Duke University Press—Kathryn Bond Stockton and anonymous readers—to whom I give thanks. I feel lucky to have had, again, the guidance and support of Ken Wissoker and the expert help of the staff at the press. I thank David Prout for compiling the index. This book is for Marget Long, with whom I have discovered the queer magic of the long term.

How Soon Is Now?

take my title from the 1984 song by the legendary Manchester band The Smiths. If you know only one Smiths song, this is probably the one: it's instantly recognizable to anyone who lived through '80s club days or listens now to that soundtrack in the current '80s revival. The song's massive, quivering guitar sound and its length (over six and a half minutes) make it different from the band's other briefer and more melodic songs, but its lyrics and vocals are classic Smiths, featuring the lovelorn, melancholy persona of the lead singer, Morrissey. As so often in the Smiths songbook, he poses a question with a particularly desirous urgency: "When you say it's gonna happen now, / Well, when exactly do you mean?" Evoking the impatience, frustration, and desperation engendered by yet another lonely night at a dance club, Morrissey wails, "See, I've already waited too long, / And all my hope is gone."[1]

The song's title, "How Soon Is Now?," plays off the shifty meanings of those ordinary words *soon* and *now*. They are deictic, to use the linguists' term: their meanings depend on context; they denote times that are relative to the moment of their utterance.[2] Morrissey addresses a "you" (another deixis) who has tried to give him some advice and assuage his despair: "There's still hope, Morrissey," we infer the friend has said in the imagined backstory of the song; "You're going to meet someone great. It really is going to happen now." But Morrissey won't be appeased, can't be appeased by this flimsy encouragement. The problem with "now" is that it's . . . *now*. Or it's *now*. Or it's right *now*. The denoted moment shifts, it slips, it is deferred, potentially infinitely, along an endless timeline of moments. For the voice in this song this situation is unbearably wearisome, each moment more hopeless than the last, opening onto a future that is nothing but one newly empty *now* after another. The word *soon* only makes things worse, shifty and resistant as it is to fix a definite time.[3]

This is not merely a linguistic issue. It gets at a larger problem concerning the present, one that has dogged all theorists of time and history in the Western tradition, starting perhaps with Aristotle and certainly including Saint Augustine: *now* has no duration, so how can you talk about its being, how can it be said to exist at all? As soon as you fix on it, it's gone, it's a has-been, and we're onto the next *now*. In fact the *now* is never purely there at all: it is a transition, always divided between no longer and not yet; each present *now* is stretched out and spanned by a past *now* and a future *now*.[4] When, WHEN, *when*? Morrissey needs to know because he wants, and he wants *now*: that is, he desires *in* the present moment, and for that reason he desires *the present moment*. And because the present moment never comes — never *is* — longing in or for the present never can be fulfilled. Thwarted desire is inevitable for Morrissey: the chipper reply to his agonized "When?" can never be satisfying because "Now" cannot specify a determinate moment after all.

In "How Soon Is Now?" this temporal conundrum is exasperating and depressing, and Morrissey conjures up a vision of time that emphasizes relentless blankness, forward plodding, and never ending. And further, he's isolated within this temporality: you'd think that "now" is something that everybody understands as the same time, as the same moment, even if everyone has a different way of dating it (depending on each person's situation and interests). But Morrissey seems to doubt that presumption of shared present time, that presumption that *now* is the same moment for everyone: "When you say it's gonna happen now, / Well, when exactly do you mean?" *His now* is irremediably estranged from his interlocutor's; his yearning is so acute that the possibility of a common present is ruptured. Instead, he lashes out at the one who would counsel him to wait: "You shut your mouth. / How can you say / I go about things the wrong way?" And he cries alone. Vacuous formalities in an apparently causal sequence threaten to go on endlessly without any effect: you go to a club where "You could meet somebody who really loves you"; you stand there, you go home, you sob hopelessly, you do it all again tomorrow, and then the next day, and the next. The meaningless little cycles succeed one another along an endless timeline into a blank future.[5] This *now* is empty; this *now* is never *now*.

The song presents this whole temporal situation not only verbally but also sonically. The sound reinforces the strangely evanescent, vanishing quality of the present. Johnny Marr's rhythm guitar is heavily processed in a vertiginous tremolo produced with four reverb speakers playing back in sync; the result is a shimmering, oscillating deferral. Laid over that is a slide guitar part — "mesmerizing," as one critic put it — as well as "a separate guitar melody played in harmonics."[6] Because of these formidable — and completely analogue — technicalities, the song was rarely performed live by The Smiths, which seems entirely appropriate to its problematization of when *now* is. And also appropriate is the fact that it has been covered and sampled numerous times, perhaps most memorably in 2002 by the Russian duo t.A.T.u.

The sound of desire in "How Soon Is Now?" is restless, but through this impatience even bigger questions press forth: is there any other way to understand time, or a *life*-time, beyond this vacant sequence of isolated, and isolating, present moments? Is there another way to value waiting, other than as exasperating and without promise? Is there any way to participate in a public, communal present, something shared, something together, *now*? Of course Morrissey hardly intends to pose a philosophical problem or theorize Being and Time: he just wants to meet someone. "Now" actually means "when I meet somebody who really loves me," somebody who is unlikely to be Martin Heidegger. But this practical way of understanding *now* in fact points us to different ways of thinking about time beyond our worst visions of a mechanistic and constricting linearity that leads bleakly, infinitely onward. Time is lived; it is full of attachments and desires, histories and futures; it is not a hollow form (not a "hatful of hollow") that is the same always. The desolate image of time conjured by Morrissey is of a succession of moments, free floating and empty; but in contrast and in actuality, his *now* is really not empty at all: it is constituted by his "purposes and activities," needs and attachments.[7] "When I meet somebody who really loves me": this *now* is linked indissoluably to other moments past and future, and thereby to other people, other situations, other worlds; this *now* is impossible to delimit as a single discrete unit, yes, but exactly because it is so complex and vascular, it can prompt us to think and experience time differently. My broadest goal in this book is not only to explore but also to claim the possibility of a fuller, denser, more crowded *now* that all sorts of theorists tell us is extant but that often eludes our temporal grasp. This means fostering temporalities other than the narrowly sequential. This means taking seriously lives lived in other kinds of time.

It is no mere coincidence that a group with a sexually ambiguous aura would release their own version of "How Soon Is Now?" — t.A.T.u. made the song part of its small oeuvre of girl-on-girl performances. The Smiths' original version expressed the feel of the '80s gay club scene, particularly in their hometown, Manchester, England.[8] This voice, wanting and unfulfilled in the *now* as it is conventionally construed, this voice whose desire requires, even demands, another kind of time beyond such linearity, empty and homogeneous, is a queer voice. Queerness, I maintain in this book, has a temporal dimension — as anyone knows whose desire has been branded as "arrested development" or dismissed as "just a phase" — and, concomitantly and crucially, as I hope to show, temporal experiences can render you queer. By "queer" I thus don't mean only "gay" or "homosexual," though this song is about gay clubbing in the first instance. And I don't mean just "odd" or "different," though there's inevitably some of that here, too. In my theorizing of temporality I explore forms of desirous, embodied being that are out of sync with the ordinarily linear measurements of everyday life, that engage heterogeneous temporalities or that precipitate out of time altogether — forms of being that I shall argue are queer by virtue of their particular engagements with time. These forms of being show, in fact, that time itself is wondrous, marvelous, full of queer potential. The interrelations between desire, bodies, and the *now* create a broad framework for my concerns in this book.

Smiths fans know that desire can — and sometimes must — create its own time. How to describe the *now* of a show by the Sweet and Tender Hooligans, a Smiths tribute band, where audience members hug lead singer José

Maldonado as they would Morrissey? It's not that they actually believe the Hooligans are "the real thing," but rhythm guitarist Jeff Stodel speaks of "this sort of ritual thing" wherein "people will come up and people will do the same things that they would do to Morrissey at a live Morrissey performance if they had the opportunity."[9] This is ritual that conjures Morrissey's enduring persona—in which adolescence is a permanent condition, not a passing stage of life—loved by his fans with a commensurate, unchanging devotion that is the same now as it ever was.[10] Or how to describe the temporality of the personal tribute by Janice Whaley called "The Smiths Project"? This intricate "true labor of love," in which Whaley painstakingly layered her voice to create every sound of each Smiths song, was created in the span of a year in the interstices of her regulated days, "fitting the music time in around parenting, working, commuting, etc.," finding new time, in fact, within the measured, regulated time of paid work and the time-intensive labors of the home.[11] After all, "Work Is a Four-Letter Word," as Morrissey sings; the time outside of those normative spheres is a different kind of time in which one labors, but labors for love. I shall dilate on the idea throughout *How Soon Is Now?* that amateurs—these fans and lovers laboring in the off-hours—take their own sweet time, and operating outside of regimes of detachment governed by uniform, measured temporality, these uses of time are queer. In this sense, the act of taking one's own sweet time asserts a queer force. *Queer, amateur*: these are mutually reinforcing terms.

The observation that the present moment of *now* is full and attached rather than empty and free-floating is a general one, and my attendant claim—that desire can reveal a temporally multiple world in the *now* (a queer world, that is)—is also very broad. I offer this theoretical framework and some examples of heterogeneous temporal experiences not as definitive models of queer or alternative temporalities and experiences; I offer them as provocations that will, I hope, help readers of *How Soon Is Now?* to develop other frameworks and find other examples. My own resources for exploring queer ways of being in time and, indeed, the potential queerness of time are medieval: the frame of reference in *How Soon Is Now?* is late medieval English texts and their postmedieval readers, and the specific temporal theme upon which I focus is *asynchrony*: different time frames or temporal systems colliding in a single moment of *now*. Such medieval texts are especially interesting in this regard because there were numerous powerful temporal systems operant in the Middle Ages: agrarian, genealogical, sacral or biblical, and historical, according to Russian medieval-ist Aron Gurevich.[12] Medieval Christianity provides the framework for heterogeneous and asynchronous temporalities on the macro scale — in all of world history — as well as on the micro scale, such as in the operations of the individual human mind, as we shall see further on in this introduc-tion. But my interest lies as well in secular temporal conceptualizations and, most particularly, in dissonance between and among all such views. Medieval narratives of people swept into another temporal world reveal with unusual clarity the constant pressure of other kinds of time on the ordinary, everyday image of one-way, sequential temporality: in chapter 1 short "Rip van Winkle" stories from the twelfth through fifteenth cen-turies, stories in which other temporal realms are visited and reveal a keen desire for another kind of time, are the medieval textual focus; in chap-ter 2 the *Book of John Mandeville*, a fictitious fourteenth-century travel narrative replete with different times and desire for different temporal ex-periences, is the medieval text under discussion; the multifarious early-fifteenth-century *Book of Margery Kempe*, intimately engaged with earthly and heavenly temporal schemata, is featured in chapter 3; and both the late-fourteenth-century English translation of a philosophical dialogue, called *Boece*, and the early-fifteenth-century Scottish poem that refers to *Boece*, called *The Kingis Quair* (The King's Book) — each intensely preoccu-pied with the nature and passage of time — are the texts read in chapter 4.

The effects of these representations of medieval temporal worlds on their postmedieval readers form a further, major concern of this book: I argue that exposure to, or contact with, such temporalities can expand our own temporal repertoires to include extensive nonmodern — okay, call them queer — temporal possibilities. The particular readers I discuss in *How Soon Is Now?*, from the nineteenth through the twenty-first centuries, are in fact already inhabitants of different temporalities: I shall introduce them below, but in a word here, they are all amateur readers — amateur medievalists — who are by definition nonprofessional, non-"scientific," and thus nonmodern in a modern world defined by "scientific" profes-sional expertise. Clearing space for such amateurs, hobbyists, and dabblers is an important goal of this book: I offer this book as a contribution to a broad and heterogeneous knowledge collective that values various ways of knowing that are derived not only from positions of detachment but also — remembering the etymology of *ama*teur — from positions of affect and attachment, from desires to build another kind of world.

But I get ahead of myself. (Which seems unavoidable in a book dedicated to asynchrony.) My concern in this book is *now*: I look at various examples to ask, with and beyond Morrissey, what is it, when is it, who gets to live in it, and who decides? The present moment is more heterogeneous and asynchronous than the everyday image of *now* — the ordinary view of measured temporal unfolding that panics Morrissey — would allow. Even Aristotle knew this — Aristotle, who is so strongly associated with the image of time that implies a sequence of identical punctual moments, singular and empty *now*s. In this introduction I want first to take up Aristotle's description of time in the *Physics*, for it turns out that even here, as Heidegger saw, linear sequential temporal measurement is dependent on asynchrony, and everyday life is profoundly asynchronous. Saint Augustine's theorization of time has proven as foundational as has Aristotle's in the Western tradition; he "retain[s] in principle the Aristotelian concept of time,"[13] and indeed provides another take on human life as asynchronous. It is to Augustine's analysis — very negative about asynchrony as it turns out — that I shall look next. Finally, having presented these two approaches to time and asynchrony and then briefly reviewing a hypothesis concerning the modernist impediment to our apprehension of such heterogeneous temporalities, I shall introduce the readers of those texts, the nonmoderns, the asynchronous amateurs, whose queer spirit presides over this book. The chapter subheadings bear little messages for Smiths fans.

ASLEEP: ARISTOTLE'S *PHYSICS*

Early on in his scientific explanation of reality, of what time is, in the fourth book of the *Physics*, Aristotle refers to a legendary tale of extraordinary temporality. Aristotle opens his analysis of time in the *Physics* — one of the "four things that are fundamental to the study of nature" along with change, the infinite, and place[14] — with several puzzles about time: can it be said to exist, since it is composed of parts (a past and a future) that do not exist? What relationship does time have to the *now*, which seems *not* to be a part of time?[15] His method in the *Physics* — a text made of accumulated lecture notes, closely reflecting what he actually taught and at times with an unedited and "rag-bag" feel — is dialectical: he begins with "commonsense intuitions, previous opinions of philosophers, and observed facts," as Edward Hussey describes the process, and moves through a rational consideration of them toward what he determines is an accurate account and definition of the subject.[16]

In pursuing time's definition, Aristotle first briefly dismisses Platonic and Pythagorean opinions about the nature of time, then moves to arguments proving that time is not change itself (or motion, another translation of both *kinesis* and *metabole*, two words Aristotle uses more or less interchangeably in book 4) but is nonetheless related to change: it cannot exist apart from change. "We assume, that is," as Ursula Coope puts it, "there can be no time without change," for if we don't change or perceive that we have changed, we don't perceive the passage of time.[17] Aristotle illustrates this common-sense assumption with a story of magical sleep:

> When we ourselves do not alter in our mind or do not notice that we alter, then it does not seem to us that any time has passed, just as it does not seem so to the fabled sleepers in [the sanctuary of] the heroes in Sardinia, when they wake up; they join up the latter now to the former, and make it one, omitting what is in between because of failure to perceive it. So, just as, if the now were not different but one and the same, there would be no time, in the same way, even when the now *is* different but is not noticed to be different, what is in between does not seem to be any time.[18]

Repeating and looping back several times, the passage then continues with a reference to something like a dream or reverie, making the opposite point, that when we do perceive change, we do sense time: "We perceive change and time together: even if it is dark and we are not acted upon through the body, but there is some change in the soul, it immediately seems to us that some time has passed together with the change."[19] In sum, writes Coope, "there is time *when* there is change and *only when* there is change."[20] Aristotle continues to refer to ordinary experience and assumptions—common expressions (221a31–221b1), an example of dogs and horses (223b5), even a reference to Homer (221b32) and the Trojan War (222a25–222b16)—as he moves forward to his famous definition of time as "a number of change in respect of the before and after" (219b2–3).[21]

But who are these fabled sleepers in Sardinia? Aristotle doesn't elaborate. Typically in the *Physics*, he is brief and allusive: he uses analogy as familiar illustrative material for his students—material not necessarily true (such as the *Iliad*, whose narrative events are also alluded to) but vivid and pointed, perhaps notorious or at least interesting for its supernatural claims. Two Greek commentators on the *Physics*, Philoponus and Simplicius, help clarify the fable of the sleepers to which Aristotle was referring. Simplicius (writing more than eight hundred years after Aristotle) is particularly useful for his lengthy expatiation. He begins to explain the myth: "For Hercules was said up to the time of Aristotle and perhaps of Alexander the commentator on Aristotle's works to have had nine sons by the daughters of Thespius the son of Thespieus, who died in Sardinia; their bodies were said to continue whole and uncorrupted, and to give an appearance of being asleep. These are the heroes in Sardinia." So they are supernaturally preserved heroes, gods or god-like and asynchronously lying there as if they've just died. Then comes the heart of the legend, with Aristotle's point made clear by Simplicius: "It is likely that people slept long sleeps besid[e] them, for the sake of dreams or through some other need, in imitation of them. These people joined the now at the beginning of sleep to that at the end, making them one now, because they were unconscious of change between the two nows; and they joined their notion of time to this now and obliterated the time, because they were unconscious of the change between."[22] These are the sleepers who — desiring prophetic dreams or a cure — sleep long sleeps, alongside and looking like the heroes themselves. They have no consciousness of time's passing because they are unaware of any change between the beginning of their long dormition and the end: thus Aristotle, according to Simplicius.

Aristotle's use of such a tale of asynchrony here is striking because it reveals ways of thinking beyond what is ordinarily attributed to him, beyond, that is, what Michel Serres calls "classical time" (linear, laminar, measurably constant).[23] And in fact, commentator Simplicius elaborates on the potential for asynchronous experience in the everyday in his observation that when we sleep undisturbed, or when we are engrossed "in intense thought or action . . . we think that no time has intervened, even though often a long time has passed." Conversely, "one can see it also from the opposite case, since people in pain and distress or in need and want, thinking that such a change is great, think that the time also is great." Simplicius exemplifies this latter point with quotations from Aristophanes's comedy *Clouds* ("Will day never come? / For I heard the cock ages ago") and from Theocritus ("Those who yearn grow old in a day").[24] Often, apparently, our experience departs from the metrical clocking of time that measures a succession of moments one after another.

Sleep and sorrow exemplify that our lived sense of time can differ from the measured time of successive linear intervals. As does drunken partying:

Simplicius refers to Eudemus's earlier, fourth-century commentary on the *Physics*, wherein Eudemus reports in detail a different sepulchral episode of asynchrony. He tells of an occasion in which revelers, very drunk in a deep cave at the religious celebration of Apatouria at Athens, slept soundly through two nights and a day. "'On the following day, when they woke up, they celebrated the Koureotis [the third day's festival] a day later than the other people [who were in the fourth day's celebration], which is how they discovered what had happened.'"[25] The asynchrony of the sleepers—their temporal displacement in relation to the clocked series of *now* moments on a line—results from their *not* having experienced all those moments sequentially. Supernatural sleep, ordinary sleep, absorption in deep thought, intense longing, inebriation—a wide range of conditions in fact brings out life's essential asynchrony. Simplicius embraces Aristotle's mythic example and sees its temporality in ordinary life: he interprets the fable and finds asynchrony in the everyday.[26]

This example in the *Physics* of the nine heroes in Sardinia is very brief, and it is pedagogical, but it is not merely heuristic. It contributes to what Heidegger, in fact, picks up as the doubleness of Aristotle's treatment of time: Aristotle's discussion of time as a measurement of change, a succession of numbers counting t_1, t_2, t_3, on the one hand, and his suggestion, on the other hand, that "our everyday experience of time . . . is not linear at all."[27] The linear, classically scientific concept of time as a series of punctual moments indeed depends on our more complex temporal experience ("lived" time, what Heidegger calls "existential time"), according to Heidegger. This scientific image of time, as William Large explains it, "smuggles in this everyday experience without drawing attention to it, constructs an image of time from it, and then explains our everyday experience with the image of time rather than the other way around," convincing us that experience is false and measurement is true.[28] That's how we have come to think of time as a line, by forgetting experience: "We can ignore the fact that we were measuring in order to carry out practical projects in the world, and come to think of time as a mere timeline," Richard Polt explains.[29] But the important point is, as Heidegger sees, that Aristotle—by defining time as a measurement but also using experience in order to come to that definition—has both closed down *and opened up* the question of temporality.[30] Drawing on that basic Heideggerian understanding that the lived present is constituted of (practical relations to) different times—the past and future—I want in this book to keep open that question and explore the multitemporality of the *now*.

The medieval Aristotelian interpreter par excellence, Saint Thomas Aquinas, it should be noted, keeps the fable of the nine heroes at arm's length. Aquinas is seven centuries and at least one language barrier further removed from the *Physics* than Simplicius.[31] Aquinas maintains his distance, carefully explaining the mythical culture as something that is, quite literally, foreign. He presumes, even assumes, distance from the legend in his dutiful exposition of "those who are fabled to have slept among the Heroes, or the gods, in Sardos, a city in Asia [*in Sardo, quae est civitas Asiae*]. The souls of the good and the great are called Heroes, and men revered them as gods, such as Hercules and Bacchus and others."[32] Aristotle's heroes are not themselves named by Aquinas as offspring of Hercules; Hercules is mentioned, rather, as an example of a hero, whose soul was revered as a god in this Asian city, Sardos. It's not certain what version of the *Physics* Aquinas was working with—probably a combination of various translations (there were five Latin versions, from both Arabic and Greek)[33]—and this location of the heroes in "Sardos, a city in Asia," doubtless originates in Aquinas's source manuscript. The effect, though, is detachment, which continues alongside a bit of confusion about the legend as Aquinas goes on to explain that "through certain incantations, some were made insensible, and these, they said, slept among the Heroes. For when they had awakened [*excitati*], they said they had seen wonderful things, and they predicted future events. However, when they returned to themselves, they did not perceive the time that had passed while they were so absorbed [*Tales autem ad se redeuntes, non percipiebant tempus quod praeterierat dum ipsi sic absorpti erant*]."[34]

If we press the logic here, it appears that these dreams must have occurred without the sleepers' conscious awareness of them as change. Or do the sleepers recount their visions and predictions without having come back to their senses? This is difficult to interpret, and may have something to do with uncertainty about where Aristotle locates the change (in our own minds, as eminent natural philosopher Galen understood Aristotle to have been saying, or in the events themselves).[35] Aquinas of course derives the correctly Aristotelian point from the example: "Therefore when we do not perceive some mutation, time is not thought of [*ergo tunc accidit non opinari tempus, cum non percipimus aliquam mutationem*]."[36] But the example in Aquinas's hands does not function quite as smoothly, and its temporality is not domesticated as it is in Simplicius's. The tale may be exoticized; is there a hint here of an effort to offshore such magical asynchronies to some other culture, pagan and far away in the East?[37] That is no doubt too much to assert about Thomas's very brief engagement with this myth. But traveling east into more heterogeneous temporalities is a powerful medieval and postmedieval theme in *How Soon Is Now?*, a spatiotemporal trope always infused with ideological potency. Such a space-time conceptual maneuver may be hinted at here; at the least, this moment serves to emphasize for us that time and space are inextricably linked, and that temporal disjunctions implicate the disposition of bodies in space. The political ramifications of this spatiotemporal trope I shall discuss in detail in chapter 2 in reference to the *Book of John Mandeville*.

In any case, in the midst of scientific analysis an illustrative tale of asynchrony reinforces how we ordinarily experience time and in so doing heightens our awareness of gaps in temporal consciousness and the everyday fact of asynchrony. Smooth sequential measurement may be the ordinary, default presumption about time when we're asked about it, but as Aristotle's teaching suggests, our temporal consciousness is tied to our experiences, attachments, and surroundings. Time is more heterogeneous than any ordinary image of time allows: Aristotle, father of "classical" scientific time, the measured clock time to which modernity "promoted" a particular "sensitivity" (as T. J. Jackson Lears puts it), in fact affirms what nonmoderns — medieval tales and their postmedieval readers — insistently represent.[38]

STRETCH OUT AND WAIT: AUGUSTINE'S *CONFESSIONS*

When Aristotle introduces the magical or supernatural as analogy in the *Physics*, the commentaries both acknowledge the supernatural as such but also have the effect of naturalizing it in the orderly everyday, the scientifically, natural-philosophically explicable world. But the mention of the gods in this context, with their own extraordinary temporalities, must alert us to the fact that time is not only, or not purely, secular. Aristotle's deepest interest was in the observable world of nature, of course — defined in terms of change or motion — rather than in any eternal invisible world of forms, which was in contrast Plato's ultimate concern. But it was Plato's thought, taken up by the Neoplatonists, that informed Saint Augustine's "profound concern for the world of the spirit," and it was the Christianized Neoplatonic Supreme Good that ultimately created and controlled time in Augustine's view.[39] For Aristotle, the universe itself was infinite; for Augustine, time is created and bounded by the infinite, the eternal, God

Himself. For Augustine, time is a good, because created by God, but is also associated with life on earth, which is ultimately an exile from the timeless divine realm, eternity. Augustine's unease about being in time is soothed by his belief in eternity: he firmly holds that time, associated with change (thus accepting that element of Aristotle's analysis), is directly regulated by God.[40] Keeping that in mind, I want to turn now to the *Confessions*, to understand Augustine's disquieted view of the profound asynchrony of human life: in this searching exploration his understanding of the relationship between time and eternity was much more ambivalent than that of his earlier writings, where he expressed the view that time is an image of eternity.[41] Augustine's understanding of time will add to our sense of the range of temporal versions beyond classical linearity. He, too, like Simplicius on Aristotle, is a theorist of the essential asynchrony of life; but unlike Simplicius, or Aristotle, he views this as a tragic condition.

If time is an image of eternity there is resemblance between the two but also difference, distance, and it is difference that is felt most keenly in the *Confessions*. Augustine's overall treatment of time in book 11, as Paul Ricoeur points out, gives an experiential, phenomenological response to the ontological question, "What is time?"[42] In this phenomenological emphasis, Augustine's analysis resembles Aristotle's.

Augustine uses ordinary human experience in his argument against the skeptics about the existence of time.[43] Like Aristotle, he accepts as true certain everyday temporal assumptions. With reference to whether time *is* at all, he asserts commonsensically: "We certainly understand what is meant by the word both when we use it ourselves and when we hear it used by others" [*et intellegimus utique cum id loquimur, intellegimus etiam cum alio loquente id audimus*]; moreover, "we are aware of periods of time" [*sentimus intervalla temporum*], and we deploy temporal concepts as we recount past things and predict future things.[44] Indeed, our ordinary experiences of memory and expectation contribute to a sense of the present that is complex and multifold.[45] Augustine determines that "it might be correct to say that there are three times, a present of past things, a present of present things, and a present of future things [*praesens de praeteritis, praesens de praesentibus, praesens de futuris*]. Some such different times do exist in the mind, but nowhere else that I can see. The present of past things is the memory; the present of present things is direct perception; and the present of future things is expectation [*praesens de praeteritis memoria, praesens de praesentibus contuitus, praesens de futuris expectatio*]."[46]

Augustine's present, his *now*, is in fact infused with temporalities: his is a stunningly *now*-oriented understanding of the past and the future as they manifest themselves in the present, in memory and anticipation. As Mary Carruthers comments about the past in particular, Augustine "had no interest" in it "except as it provides him with a way and a ground for understanding his present."[47] His *now* is not only spanned by the past and future but also in this different sense constituted by them.

And, as is adumbrated in that last quotation from the *Confessions*, that *now* is *in us*. Aristotle importantly sees that time is a number that depends on someone's consciousness to count. There is no time, in Aristotle, if there is no soul, and when time is understood to depend on human consciousness, temporal heterogeneity is the inevitable condition of human life. But Augustine goes further in construing the relationship of time and human consciousness: time, Augustine determines, is the activity of the mind as it shifts in the present between those temporal modes of memory, attention, and expectation. It is itself *distentio animi*, the distention of the mind, what Ricoeur calls the "contrast between the three tensions" of memory, attention, and expectation.[48] And it is woefully, existentially painful.

The mind is stretched out in opposite directions: this is time. Augustine provides an example of the complex temporal workings of the mind — the recitation of a song, the *Deus creator omnium* by Saint Ambrose — and here we can sense how tense and dialectical the operation of time is, in his view.[49] Augustine's is a phenomenological account of the *now*, as problematic and paradoxical as the *now* of which Morrissey complains:

> Suppose that I am going to recite a psalm that I know. Before I begin, my faculty of expectation is engaged [*tenditur*] by the whole of it. But once I have begun, as much of the psalm as I have removed from the province of expectation and relegated to the past now engages [*tenditur*] my memory, and the scope of the action [*actionis*] which I am performing is divided [*distenditur*] between the two faculties of memory and expectation, the one looking back to the part which I have already recited, the other looking forward to the part which I have still to recite. But my faculty of attention [*attentio*] is present all the while, and through it passes [*traicitur*] what was the future in the process of becoming the past. As the process continues [*agitur et agitur*], the province of memory is extended in proportion as that of expectation is reduced, until the whole of my expectation is absorbed. This happens when I have finished my recitation and it has all passed into the province of memory.[50]

What is striking here is Augustine's intense focus on the mind's differ-ence from itself as it shifts from one modality to another: time is disten-tion, and distention is the "noncoincidence" of memory, attention, and expectation.[51] The language Augustine uses to express this lack of coher-ence is very vivid. *Distentio* is in fact Augustine's own coinage: it denotes a stretching asunder, stretching out — "a stretching out on a rack," as Henry Chadwick translates it.[52] The same word is used a little further on in book 11 of the *Confessions* when Augustine, trying to locate himself in human time, entreats God to "see how my life is a distension in several directions" [*ecce distentio est vita mea*], a wasteful distraction by all this multiplicity: "The storms of incoherent events tear to pieces my thoughts, the inmost entrails of my soul, until that day when, purified and molten by the fire of your love, I flow together to merge into you" [*tumultuosis varietatibus dilaniantur cogitationes meae, intima viscera animae meae, donec in te con-fluam purgatus et liquidus igne amoris tui*].[53] The very language here — *dilaniantur, viscera* — gives a corporeal feel to this process of spiritual (i.e., in the mind, spirit) distention.

Augustine continues to puzzle out the experience of time by provid-ing a description of physical as well as spiritual effects, using yet another example to explain the feeling of time and contrasting this to God's way of knowing. "It [i.e., God's way of knowing] is not like the knowledge of a man who sings words well known to him or listens to another singing a familiar psalm. While he does this, his feelings vary and his senses are divided, because he is partly anticipating words still to come and partly re-membering words already sung" [*neque enim sicut nota cantantis notumve canticum audientis expectatione vocum futurarum et memoria praeteri-tarum variatur affectus sensusque distenditur*].[54] This active experience of the *now*, this mind enlarging, this *distentio* "is a vital activity of the human spirit," Aron Gurevich summarizes. This vital activity, though, consists in a chronic push and pull, a shredding disruption of personal — physical as well as spiritual — integrity more and more disorienting the more Augus-tine thinks about it.[55]

Human time is radically dissimilar to God's. As opposed to our own sublunar existence, God's eternal being is in a timeless *now* that is without before or after, past or future. Even the six days in which God created the heavens and the earth are not six days as humans would know them but are a "single atemporal instant," as Charlotte Gross puts it, a *modicum* that is in fact eternal.[56] And this fundamental dissimilarity provokes human sorrow: "the absence of eternity is . . . a lack that is felt at the heart of temporal experience," Ricoeur observes.[57] As Chadwick puts it, "This psychological experience of the spreading out of the soul in successiveness and in diverse directions is a painful and anxious experience, so that [Augustine] can speak of salvation as deliverance from time."[58] Ricoeur stresses that the framework of eternity in book 11 is necessary "to push as far as possible the reflection on the *distentio animi*."[59] Time, in Augustine's view in the *Confessions*, is an index of human existence as itself, grievously, asynchronous.

While Aristotle's exposure of humankind's experience of time as asynchronous deepens our understanding of the ordinary and can aid in opening up the heterogeneous possibilities in the *now*, the — or at least one — emphasis in Augustine's disquisition on time in the *Confessions* is to direct attention away from the everyday toward the eternal.[60] Asynchrony is a painful and unhappy condition; his desire for a remove from time, indeed for the unity that is eternal and totally out of time, is searing. Augustine's affective response to time informs some versions of temporality in the chapters that follow. Human life is lived in exile from Eden, an inaccessible region where, as we shall see in relation to the *Book of John Mandeville* in chapter 2, Augustine said time began, but where mundane temporality nonetheless touches on eternity. And again according to Augustine, the unique temporality that is Christian scriptural history multiplies the significance of all times past, present, and future in relation to Christ's incarnation; as we shall see, this can be thrilling, as in the accounts of the Holy Land in the *Book of John Mandeville* discussed in chapter 2, or it can cause acute pain, as in Margery Kempe's experiences, recounted in her *Book* and analyzed in chapter 3. Finally, in chapter 4, we shall see a similarly negative view of time in the vastly influential work by Boethius written a century and a quarter later than the *Confessions*, the *Consolation of Philosophy*.

WHAT DIFFERENCE DOES IT MAKE?
TIME-AS-MEASUREMENT AND AMATEUR HOUR

Those two theorists of time and asynchrony, Aristotle and Augustine, open the questions and provide powerful nonmodern frameworks for thinking the *now* in this book. They put us, or keep us, in mind of very long traditions in the West of construing time in ways other than as the measurement of discrete and identical forward-moving points on a line. Michel Serres finds in Lucretius a nonlinear, topological theory of time rather than a rigidly metrical or geometrical one. As Serres puts it, theories of turbulence in twentieth-century physics allow us to look back at Lucretius and see that "yes, in fact, there is already in Lucretius this kind of thing."[61] And certainly by our present moment in the early-twenty-first century, theories of nonlinear time are the rule, not the exception.

My discussion in *How Soon Is Now?* thus joins powerful intellectual currents. Even a cursory glance across the disciplines will locate relevant and provocative discussions of the *now*: the ongoing philosophical debates, for example, about tense, temporal relations, and presentism — a theory adopted out of the desire (among at least some of its adherents) "to do justice to the feeling that what's in the past is over and done with, and that what's in the future only matters because it will eventually be present"; or the crucial disciplinary conversation among anthropologists about contemporaneity, the *now* of ethnographic encounters — a conversation opened most explicitly by Johannes Fabian in *Time and the Other* and taken up by ethnographers such as Anna Lowenhaupt Tsing, who grapples with the "intellectual and political significance" of grammatical tense; or the remarkable dialogue between physicist Martin Land and anthropologist Jonathan Boyarin in *Time and Human Language Now*, which takes up (among other things) Émile Benveniste's theory of enunciation, the linguistic "now," and explores implications in an ethical realm as well as in physics.[62]

Yet Martin Land in that same book notes that "the success of Newtonian physics, and the authority awarded its method by Enlightenment thinkers, continues to exert undue influence on our view of reality and our use of language, imposing unnecessary restrictions on what we consider to be a reasonable interpretation of everyday experience."[63] Time-as-measurement suits a modernist view of the world — suits what Bruno Latour neatly calls the "modernist settlement" — that was always at most partial and indeed is by now discredited, but that nonetheless persistently exerts its shaping force. Let me briefly rehearse Latour's analysis, sketching the contours of this modernism; I shall then note the persistence of the "settlement" even now in the ways we think of historical time. From there I shall mention one trenchant strand of critique of this modernist settlement and the temporal divide it imposes between the premodern and modern periods. And finally I shall steer into my own critical path through this modernist thicket, exploring specifically the nonmodern times of amateurs.

Latour's "settlement" refers to a Western cultural formation that segmented the world into discrete realms — philosophical, psychological, political, and moral. He explains that it partitioned off an "out there" separate from a knower; an "in there" unconnected to an outside world; a "down there" of an unruly society "stigmatized as inhuman," distinct from a more elite human individual; and an "up there" of human morality cut off from the nonhuman world. What Latour calls, with his usual witty bravado, the Cartesian "brain-in-a-vat" was detached from a world conceived of as "outside."[64] In this Western modernism the observing subject was to be distinguished from the objective world "out there": "the classic relations between subject and object" in fact provided the feature that separated past from future, since more objectivity was always the goal for the future. The subject/object split thus characterized progress, a direction forward — in fact, the direction of time's arrow. "For the moderns," writes Latour, "without the hope of a Science at last extracted from the social world, there is no discernible movement, no progress, no arrow of time, and thus no hope of salvation" from a premodern "matrix of desires and human fantasies."[65] Latour argues that the separation between society and Science (the initial capital indicating a polemical formation), human and nonhuman, subject and object, was a modernist plot that created the image of time as moving relentlessly forward in a constant, measured flow and promoted the related, specious chronology of modernity with its abjected premodernity.[66]

Although time is now as a rule theorized more expansively, vestiges of that modernist settlement remain potent. No historian believes that time moves punctually forward, for example, emptily, evenly, and always progressively toward a single goal. Yet as Dipesh Chakrabarty discerns, in the work of historians some version of an abstract, a priori time still ticks on, time that is independent of, unaffected by, and prior to "any particular events." "The naturalism of historical time lies in the belief that *everything* can be historicized," Chakrabarty asserts. Conventionally trained historians, he writes, proceed in the assumption that "it is always possible to assign people, places, and objects to a naturally existing, continuous flow of historical time" which is "independent of culture or consciousness."[67] Cycles or different varieties of time — economic cycles, domestic time, work time, fast time, slow time — may well be differentiated, but all will nonetheless be temporalized, he maintains, into a natural, continuous historical flow that is also, crucially, secular. Think of those encyclopedic charts that graph world events onto a single timeline: the eighteenth-century "Chart of Biography" and "Chart of History" by Joseph Priestley might be the most famous, but even recent work that is fully informed by postmodern critique begins with a timeline — a carefully cross-cultural timeline. So naturalized is this concept of historical time: it is a methodological building block that "aims to function as a supervening general construction mediating between all the particulars on the ground."[68] But this time is not natural at all, argues Chakrabarty; it "stands for a particular formation of the modern subject" — the modern Western subject, Latour's brain-in-a-vat. "Godless, continuous, empty and homogeneous," this historical time cannot allow for "the presence and agency of gods or spirits" — a necessity if non-Western apprehensions of the world are going to be able to enter historical discourse.[69] The classically scientific time of historians, Chakrabarty argues, the time that operates as a "general construction mediating between all the particulars," must yield to the nonlinear, the post-Einsteinian — which Lucretius, if not Aristotle, can tell us about.

Ongoing critiques of such historical time — most trenchant for my purposes here are critiques by medievalists of the premodern/modern divide — intend to enable and put into practice the more radical claims of temporal heterogeneity. These medievalist arguments do not simply push back the modern period boundary; such critiques intend to facilitate — among other far-reaching potential projects — the consideration of diverse temporal regimes operating here and now. Bracing and multifarious, these analyses demonstrate that period boundaries are inadequate in the face of the complexity of temporal and cultural phenomena: among other things, they reveal periodization functioning in the interest of contemporary Western European (or Westernized) concerns — that is, as ideologically and politically interested — and they present arguments that periodization is not only philosophically challenging but may be in fact impossible.[70] Thus one study, for example, irrefutably demonstrates that French critical theory of the mid- to later twentieth century was itself obsessed with the Middle Ages, so that this quintessential avant-garde must always be understood in relation to the medieval.[71] Another scrupulously reveals the dependence of several of "our most basic historical and political assumptions" — namely, about the "'modern' sovereign state and secular politics" — on the Middle Ages viewed as period.[72] Another related, powerful strand focuses on the complex functioning of period concepts of medieval and modern in a global framework, working to understand intricate and various interrelations between medievalism, modernity, racialization, and colonialism.[73] The attempt to demarcate "the past as civilizations whole unto themselves" is itself a modernist gesture: "when we draw lines sharply between periods whole unto themselves, *wherever we draw the line*, we are already falling victim to the logic of the revolutionary moment," writes James Simpson. "It's the revolutionary moment that needs the sharp breaks in history to define itself. Wherever we draw the line to create a world whole unto itself, the wholeness of the world demarcated by that line is *already* informed by inevitable consciousness of what's on the other side."[74] Periodization itself is seen as logically impossible: "In an important sense," Kathleen Davis writes, having maintained that periodization is "a fundamental political technique" that undoes its gesture of chronological separation by its own contemporary interestedness, "we cannot periodize the past."[75]

But alongside such acknowledgment of philosophical inadequacies and political liabilities we still periodize—we cannot not, contends Fredric Jameson as he describes this inevitability.[76] And some such version of linearity still exerts a hold in academic institutions, still broadly organized by divisions flowing from this modernist settlement. The "hard" sciences (and "harder" social sciences) continue to be generally cordoned off from other disciplines both intellectually and fiscally. Curricula in humanities classes and departments are still built along the intellectual spine of historical chronology: the curriculum for the English major, Jennifer Summit notes, "is still structured historically, even if it remains unclear what historical vision or objects that structure manifests." And in such an intellectual terrain the gods and spirits of whom Chakrabarty writes can only be treated as "signifier[s] of other times and societies," objectified by the historian's or anthropologist's gaze; real consideration of divinities as active subjects or agents today can only be made in the institutionally far-flung context of theology.[77] Because of such modernist tenacity in the organization and production of knowledge, temporal critiques remain urgent. Such institutional divisions as these restrict possibilities for thinking more broadly—for thinking more democratically, for including a broader range of participants in the common good.

My own route through these temporal dilemmas proceeds by exploring not only nonmodern times in medieval texts but also the nonmodernity of certain readers of those texts. I cut my own queer critical path in *How Soon Is Now?* by invoking the concept of amateurism. For modernist time, time-as-measurement hitched to Western European concepts of progress toward a singular goal is also, I maintain, the time of specialization, expertise, professionalization; amateurism is everything the professional leaves behind on the modern train of forward progress.[78] Max Weber argued long ago that a secularization of spiritual asceticism created a modern ethos in which labor became an end in itself and "limitation to specialized work . . . is a condition of any valuable work in the modern world." Modern middle-class life entailed a "renunciation," a "departure from an age of full and beautiful humanity." The secularization thesis is deeply problematic in view of the critiques of periodization just outlined; furthermore, Weber is not referring to exactly the kind of culture of expertise that concerns me.[79] But what still proves generally useful here is Weber's pinpointing of specialized work as the engine of modernity—a vehicle of the modernist settlement—with time as its linchpin, and "beautiful humanity" as its cost.[80]

Professionals are paid for their work, and their expert time can be seen to share characteristics with money: it is abstract, objective, and countable. Professional work time is clock-bound and calendrical, regulated abstractly and independently of individuals, and the lives of professionals conform to this temporality.[81] Measurement—that one side of the Aristotelian temporal problematic—is the essence here. Consider the sequence of school nights and workdays, weeks, weekends and vacations, fiscal quarter following fiscal quarter, semester following semester, year following year. Such time is homogeneous and empty. It is secular: Weber's analysis, for example, contended that the "rational" scheme of monastic hours was the precursor of secularized Protestant time-consciousness.[82] And, like money, it is to be saved, budgeted, and spent.[83] A life regulated in this way is marked by significant milestones: on the quotidian scale, there are deadlines to be made; on the scale of the life course, there are schools, higher education, early apprenticeship, employment with benefits including life insurance, then promotions and eventual retirement, with the shining gold timepiece at the end.

Constitutively disenchanted, fully Enlightened, the modern expert that is my focus is a "scientific" creature.[84] Expertise—any and all modern-day expertise, I maintain, in literature and history as well as in, say, groundwater hydrology—is regarded as such because of the mystique of scientific method: experts' analyses are mystified as objective and disinterested; such analyses are believed to observe a clear and unbroachable separation between the researcher and the objects of study. Their narrow and delimited foci are understood as part of this objective paradigm, producing falsifiable assertions and replicable results. In this way expertise is understood to build up a "body of knowledge," as Peter Walsh points out, that exists precisely in order to be mastered.[85] Such analyses are part of a larger field, whence their authority derives and to whose specific methods—rules of evidence and analytical protocols—they adhere. These are the rules for "the access to, and the use of [their] base of knowledge" of which Walsh speaks. Thus delineated, the work of specialists is not answerable to nonspecialists; neither is their work necessarily comprehensible to them. Indeed, the opposition between expert and the general public, the one and the mob, as Latour might say, or the "interior" and the "exterior" (in Walsh's terms) is what makes the expert an expert.[86] Specialized languages and other ritualistic markers define the group; Erving Goffman pointed years ago to the performative aspects of professionalism.[87] The intended audience for their work consists of others like them or aspiring to be like them; they themselves have been trained, after all, in the fields that they are now furthering. And finally, a salary cements experts' membership in the group of specialists, rendering them professionals.

If amateurs are not paid—and defined as such they are not remunerated for work—what do they get at the end of their efforts? What, indeed, defines the end of amateurs' labors? Operating on a different time scheme from professional activities, amateurs' activities do not require punching a time clock and do not follow a predestined career path, since they are not wage labor. Amateur temporality starts and stops at will; tinkerers and dabblers can linger at moments of pleasure when the professionals must soldier duly onward.[88] Professionals must bring all elements of an operation into place in order to complete a replicable task—say, the making of a perfect omelet—but amateurs can enjoy the chance irruptions that occur when all is not synched up. Amateur time is not dictated by a mystified scientific method that requires not only a closed system and the elimination of chance but also, and most fundamentally, the separation of subject from object. In fact, not "scientific" detachment but constant *attachment* to the object of attention characterizes amateurism.[89]

Amateurism is personally invested; dilettante activities can be all over the map or minutely focused—or both—depending on particular interests. The modernist brain-in-a-vat was invented out of a fear of mob rule, Latour contends, a threat to Reason putatively posed by the supposedly brutish masses.[90] But amateurism is by definition multiplicitous: so much for the "bounded body of knowledge," the rules of access and processing, the expert credentializing.[91] There is more than one way to skin a cat; amateurism is bricolage, bringing whatever can be found, whatever works, to the activity. And even as it acknowledges many possible ways of proceeding rather than just one, it also values particularity over generality; it is sui generis, not intended to replicate itself in other activities, that is, in a field. In all his intimate particularity, as Roland Barthes muses about the possibility of his writing a novel, he "confron[ts] generality, confron[ts] science." Barthes goes on to suggest that in his creative activity he would be "scientific without knowing it"; in producing a novel rather than merely writing about one, "the world no longer comes to me as an object but as a writing, i.e., as a practice. I proceed to another type of knowledge (that of the Amateur), and it is in this that I am methodical." Such is his method: "I venture a hypothesis and I explore . . . I postulate a novel to be written, whereby I can expect to learn more about the novel than by merely considering it as an object already written by others."[92] Ika Willis analyzes how fan fiction — not writing about other fiction but writing fiction in response to fiction — is just such a practice that yields "another type of knowledge (that of the Amateur)": it makes legible "difficult negotiations between subjectivity and textuality," she argues, not only "complicated subject/text/world relations" but also what Barthes in another essay calls "the 'immoral right' to make and circulate meanings."[93]

Lest this description of amateurism seem purely idealizing, let me acknowledge that amateurism is not miraculously free of the shaping institutions of modernity; it may indeed be a kind of ruse of late capitalism. Amateurs might have wealth enough so that they don't need to work; that hardly puts them outside capitalism. Or they may be out of work and so have plenty of time for their hobbies. Amateurs might embody traits that are a neoliberal fantasy: they may be not only creative, but flexible and adaptable, too. They might be especially celebrated in a recessionary economy for being able to convert their passions into pounds sterling — all the while still staying passionate. They might be complicit in a culture and economy of deskilling. While acknowledging that amateurism cannot be celebrated naively — indeed, while wary of enacting the consummate professionalism of the critique of professionalism (than what is more academically rewarded?) — I am at the same time deeply and positively impressed by the increasing impact that amateurism is having on sacred professional arenas, intensely specialist preserves such as, say, archival transcription.[94]

By shifting the boundaries of knowledge production in this way amateurism shows the potential for shifting the whole system of credentializing, of judging who gets to make knowledge and how. This perception leads to my broad viewpoint in this book: that amateurism's operation outside, or beside, the culture of professionalism provides an opening of potentials otherwise foreclosed. It offers what Fred Moten and Stefano Harney call "the strangely known moment" that disturbs the critical academic and professional activity going on "above" and "without it."[95] It offers glimpses of "another type of knowledge," as Barthes puts it — different ways of knowing and sources of knowledge, and even (an aspiration I share with many others working in this vein, as I shall suggest below) a consequent broadening of the public sphere.

I focus in particular on amateur *reading*, while acknowledging that readers can and do engage in amateur reading at some times and professional reading at other times — scholarly argument by day, say, and fan fiction by night.[96] Amateur reading is not professional reading or criticism *manqué*. Some amateurs do indeed become professionals — André M. Carrington has documented early science fiction fandom in the United States and discusses several well-known fans who became professional editors — but *as* amateurs they can work to impose the opposite trajectory, making the professional mainstream itself more open, more multiple. Amateur literary activities can expose and critique professional literary activities.[97] Amateur readings, participating in nonmodern ways of apprehending time, can help us to contemplate different ways of being, knowing, and world making.

THESE THINGS TAKE TIME: FREDERICK JAMES FURNIVALL AND OTHER AMATEURS

I shall briefly introduce the medievalists to be discussed in *How Soon Is Now?*, but first I want to give some context for such amateurs in nineteenth- and early-twentieth-century England and the United States by taking up the story of one famous amateur medievalist: Frederick James Furnivall, the legendarily indefatigable Victorian editor and man of letters whose literary and linguistic activities were prodigious and whose engagement with life enormous. Born in Surrey in 1825 and educated at Trinity College, Cambridge, he left the British Isles only once in his life (to go to France) and died in 1910, until the very end "rowing, walking, chair-

ing committees, dashing off postcards to everyone, sending his daily pack-
age of cuttings to [James] Murray at the *Dictionary*, presiding over his
open house at the ABC tearooms [in London], and checking transcriptions
every day at the British Museum," as Derek Pearsall chronicles.[98] Furnivall
was editor and then one of the principal contributors to the *New English
Dictionary* (eventually to become the *Oxford English Dictionary* [OED]);
his chief accomplishment was, in fact, the founding of the Early English
Text Society (EETS) to supply reliable texts for the *Dictionary*'s vast historical lexicographical enterprise. Furnivall also founded the Chaucer Society, the Wyclif Society, the Ballad Society, the New Shakspere Society,
the Browning Society, and the Shelley Society;[99] he actively participated
in educational and social reform by, among other things, his involvement
with the London Working Men's College — not to mention his founding
the Girls' Sculling Club, as Derek Brewer notes, "for working girls to enable them and eventually men to scull on the Thames on Sundays."[100] Furnivall edited about a hundred texts himself and oversaw the immense out-
put of the EETS, which is still going strong today.

By the turn of the twentieth century, in England, professional disciplinary historicism — more and more specialized, with historical knowledge increasingly fragmented — had definitively separated itself from amateur antiquarianism, with its untrained, largely upper-class participants,
local enthusiasms, soft sentiments, and proclivity for mixing literary with
material evidence. Antiquarians, Philippa Levine documents, "were as
comfortable editing medieval poetry as they were inspecting Roman re-

Furnivall thus vigorously participated in the birth of early English
studies, but his role in the emergent field was ambivalent. He never held a
university post, and his editing was ridiculed by medievalists more firmly
ensconced in the professional establishment: Sir Frederic Madden of the
British Museum called him a "jackanapes," saying he should not be allowed
"to edit any works," since his writing style was "disgusting" and his igno-
rance "on a par with his bad taste."[101] In its early years the Chaucer Society,
despite its concern with English literature's highly revered and culturally
legitimated figure, was almost completely ignored by the "establishment
academy," as David Matthews documents.[102] And the rejection was mutual:
having had some independent wealth and then having been granted a government pension — in addition to financial aid from his friends — Furnivall
for all intents and purposes shunned the profession, disdaining its scholarly elitism.[103]

mains."[104] But specialization was required of the professional. Academic history had tentatively arrived "in the ancient universities" by the 1830s and continued to develop into full-fledged disciplinary arenas through the century.[105] From the 1830s, too, on the literary and linguistic side, a specialist approach to English vernacular studies was developing in England and distinguishing itself from antiquarianism, as Haruko Momma chronicles; the Rawlinsonian Chair in Anglo-Saxon studies was restructured as a modern chair at Oxford in 1858, and the chair of comparative philology at Oxford was established in 1868 for Max Müller.[106] I analyze something of the intimate relationship between philology and the British colonial enterprise in South Asia in chapter 2; suffice it here to say that philology was implicated in Orientalist and racialized projects. Philologists trained in this German academic tradition dismissed the editing efforts of Furnivall as mere enthusiasm, irrational and undisciplined, as Richard Utz documents. About some of the editing for the Early English Text Society, Arnold Schröer, professor of English philology at Cologne University, shook his head: "how lamentable it is," he wrote, "that these Englishmen have no strict philological education; they are kind amateurs, often of astonishing versatility and considerable knowledge." Possessing considerable knowledge, but still amateurs — with perhaps even greater intellectual range than the scholars ("astonishing versatility") but not enough distance, Utz argues, from their objects of attention.[107] Before the advent of professional philology, one would be hard-pressed to trace a firm distinction in attitudes between, on the one hand, those editors whose work is regarded now as protoprofessional (Thomas Tyrwhitt, for example, as David Matthews argues) and amateur antiquarian readers and editors (Thomas Percy is Matthews's contrasting example), on the other.[108] But once the historical and linguistic and literary professions emerged, those working in the shadow of professionals would ever be regarded as underdeveloped. The distinction was "value-laden," as Levine demonstrates, and it was also temporal:[109] amateurs, with their passions on their sleeves, had not yet achieved — and never wanted to, so never would — full detachment from the objects of their study, which was the goal and hallmark of the professional.

Of course this term *amateur* has to be used advisedly for Furnivall. For he can certainly be seen in important genealogical relation to the *profession* of medievalist as we know it now. After all, he made possible the field of Middle English Studies, having edited and published such a huge range of texts, and his publishing agenda, as John M. Ganim has pointed out, drew on the scientific philological model.[110] But Furnivall just as certainly worked outside the academic system and with distinctly different goals in mind. Subscribing neither to the elitism of the academy nor the elitism of a now-marginalized antiquarianism, and with considerable gusto, Furnivall recruited nonspecialists to work on his editions. The work he oversaw was often shoddy. Yet its purpose was not to elaborate a linguistic science, as would be the goal of the proper philologist (even if his publishing efforts drew on it, he "never cared a bit for philology," Furnivall commented toward the end of his long career); his goal was to make early English texts available for a wide range of readers to enjoy.[111] Those texts had the power, he believed, to transform lives.[112] Furnivall sought to connect Englanders to their past, to their "forefathers," and, looking across the Atlantic, to connect "the Chaucer-lovers of the Old Country and the New."[113] He involved different kinds of people—accordingly, the members of the Early English Text Society were "banded together"—to do this. When he worked in the archive his "high color" distinguished him from the pallid professionals around him and associated him with the laboring masses and colonized others. In the Manuscript Room of the British Museum, as observed by an American scholar, he worked zealously, alertly, eagerly: "His colour was high and his forehead and neck showed evidence of recent sunburn, a contrast to the pale, dull-eyed elderly men about him."[114] A fellow editor wrote to Furnivall, "your 'go-a-head-itiveness' puzzles me sometimes, but it's *an element of success*."[115] This correspondent is pointing to Furnivall's amateur style—pushing forward vigorously with whatever resources he had, bringing people together in order to create even broader attachments, all on his own, sui generis, and in his own time—and wondering at its efficacy.

The prefaces to Furnivall's editions convey a sense of the person behind them, the body that strained under the burden of this enormous entrepreneurial enterprise. He writes in the first person, colloquially. In one preface, he explains that he felt compelled to edit some sixteenth-century Scottish minor works, "notwithstanding a vow to edit no more texts for the Society for a year," he admits, "and thus get a rest for my right eye weakened by long night-work." He just had to edit them because the Scottish works so resembled complaints against the state of England in more or less the same time, and thus gave a sense of the voice of the people.[116] It was such a sense of pleasure borne of connectedness to the people (or just to people), not some narrowly chronological urgency, that impelled him to edit — or to take a break from editing.

Thus some editions were delayed. His edition of *Robert Mannyng*, for example, was twenty-two years in the making: "I took all my books to Yorkshire but never opened them," he wrote to the publisher who implored him to get the manuscript in. "Lawn tennis, cricket, walks, picnics, getting up a Concert and Dances, occupied all the holiday. Then since my return, there's been the practice for our Sculling Four Race next Saturday."[117] The edition eventually was finished, but in Furnivall's own time. Also produced in his own time was *Trial-Forewords to My "Parallel-Text Edition of Chaucer's Minor Poems"*; as he wrote at the end of that volume's part 1, "Here for the present I must break off, as I haven't time to study further the rest of the poems just now, and have been for six weeks, and am still, away from almost all my books and literary friends, among bluebells, honeysuckles, laburnums, cuckoos, and nightingales . . . [Chaucer would] have given us all a holiday, I'm sure: so, reader, let me put off Part II . . . for a time. . . ."[118] Intimately attached to his object of study, he nonetheless takes a break, in the comforting knowledge that his author, Chaucer, would want him to. Part 2, indeed, does not seem ever to have been completed (if, in fact, ever started). The Chaucer Society, notes Matthews, for which Furnivall edited part 1, had some early success in bringing about the "enlightened public sphere rather than an academic discipline" that Furnivall so passionately desired — and notably it was American interest in Chaucer that seems to have buoyed up the society, almost from the first in financial straits. But eventually the landscape changed. The "professionalization of literary teaching in the early twentieth century" brought with it a shift away from individuals toward institutional subscribers — and a shift away, too, as Matthews puts it, from "love."[119]

IS IT REALLY SO STRANGE? THE QUEER AMATEURS OF THIS BOOK

As I've already suggested, this binary opposition — amateur versus professional — is all too abstract and schematic. I use it to set up a general framework for more nuanced looks at engagements with medieval texts; many factors (social, political, economic, and psychological) conspire to hold this dualism in place, or make it more complex, or break it down completely. But I start with the premise that the postmedieval engagements of medieval texts featured in *How Soon Is Now?* are all amateur, in some definitive way. These engagements take a variety of forms — retellings of tales, parodies, editions, and commentaries on medieval texts undertaken outside the academy, nonscholarly accounts of medieval authors and works — and that heterogeneity is part of the point about the nature of amateurism; for convenience only, therefore, I refer to them as "readings," and their agents as "readers." Technically, these readers either lived before the profession of medievalist emerged or never held a university faculty position. (Henry Wadsworth Longfellow — professor of languages at Bowdoin College, then at Harvard University — is the exception that proves the rule, as I shall elaborate below in this introduction and in chapter 1.) But the amateurism of the medievalists in this book goes deeper than any technicality: it bears on their affections, their intimacy with their materials, their desires. These readings clarify that intimate longings — desires for authenticity, for origins, for meaning, for connection — motivate all turnings toward the past, however austerely impersonal the studies eventually become, however much such longings might themselves protect against more threatening psychic dissolution.[120] Amateur medievalist readings bring out or enact temporal multiplicities found in the medieval texts that are the foci of their affections: they make manifest that in the present we have not left the past entirely behind. And they point to or even create completely other kinds of time as well, be they Edenic, for example, or other supernatural temporalities, or the noncontemporaneous contemporaneity of the moment of reading, or the spectral asynchronies of the present.

Henry Wadsworth Longfellow read, wrote about, and taught a wide range of medieval literature in English and in Western European languages; I discuss his retelling of a medieval tale in chapter 1. Old languages, he argued, give us a sense of the strength and stature of people from the past. But in the classroom at Harvard this approach was sometimes belittled as decorative and entirely out of style;[121] it was not philological in the Germanic mold and in fact resembled Furnivall's amateurism (enacted at about the same time), which served an interest in connecting people, past and present. Longfellow's was a temporally multiple consciousness, amateur in its absorption into the Middle Ages. In chapter 2, I take up Andrew Lang, a highly educated and well-connected late-Victorian man of letters who was dubbed the "divine amateur" by Oscar Wilde, and who, as we shall see, deployed the language of the Middle Ages in — indeed, as — the legitimation of Empire in a parody of the *Book of John Mandeville*; yet he also, alongside this distanced use of the medieval, expressed affective attachment—melancholy for the past, and for Empire's evident passing. Fellow late-Victorian reader M. R. James, eventually an eminent professional medievalist, in a piece of juvenilia created a fake "lost chapter" of the *Book of John Mandeville*; in its merciless parody of a German self-described "amateur" philologist, it underscores the melancholy affect that links the colonial, the amateur, and the philological.

Hope Emily Allen, coeditor of the first modern edition of the *Book of Margery Kempe* (1940) is the reader in chapter 3. Allen was academically trained and highly regarded for her work on the literature of early English spirituality. Independently wealthy—she was a member of the Oneida Community in upstate New York after its dissolution as an organized spiritual community and reconstitution as a business corporation—she pursued her research outside, or at least alongside, the professional academy. Her magnum opus was never finished, because, I shall argue, of her absorption in the object of her study (characteristic of amateurism as I analyze it here), a proliferation of connections to and among past phenomena that finally overwhelmed her. Washington Irving's fictive persona, Geoffrey Crayon, is an American bachelor and amateur antiquarian, enthusiastic reader of early English literature and traveler to England. In chapter 4 I discuss his early-nineteenth-century account of visiting places significant to early English literary culture, analyzing the affective intensity of his medieval reenactment. Finally, in my epilogue, I take up the fictive figure of an amateur medievalist and local historian in *A Canterbury Tale*, the 1944 film by Michael Powell and Emeric Pressburger. Thomas Colpeper, a "loony English squire," loves his ancestral land so much that he not only wants to share its history with others but also believes people should be *forced* to engage the past. His bizarre strategy to compel temporal desire proves in fact to be criminal. The film, quite ambivalent in its depiction of Colpeper, exposes his approach as maniacal and an impediment to vibrant living on, but it also reveals that his amateur attachment to the land infused with the past is—if only momentarily—a medium of positive social connection.

About his partnership with Powell, Pressburger himself reflected once, "I always had the feeling that we were amateurs in a world of professionals. Amateurs stand so much closer to what they are doing, and they are driven by enthusiasm, which is so much more forceful than what professionals are driven by."[122] As I have suggested, amateurs wear their desires on their sleeves. The concepts that typically characterize amateurism—immaturity, belatedness or underdevelopment, inadequate separation from objects of love, improper attachment, inappropriate loving—sound just like what a developmental psychologist trained within the paradigm of a normative life course might say about the sexual "deviant."[123] (The normative life course is what José Esteban Muñoz calls "straight time," what Morrissey refers to when he sings of "unruly boys" and "unruly girls.")[124] Amateurism, I want to argue, is itself a bit queer, defined by attachment in a detached world. Amateurism in fact condenses a whole range of abjections from the normative modernist life course, including ethnicity and race, economic class, and sex and gender; any category that draws on distinctions in "work" will engage all such social and cultural dynamics, and I attempt to touch on a range of social and cultural formations. But for starters, I focus on sex, gender, and desire: the amateurism of my readers in *How Soon Is Now?* is explicitly associated with some form of sexual or gender queerness. They are "belated" or "underdeveloped" in relation not only to the profession but also to the reproductive family.

All these readers were of ultimately Western European extraction, middle to upper-middle class, and in this way inside normative social frameworks, but their relations to the reproductive family are compromised in some way. Thomas Colpeper in *A Canterbury Tale* is certainly the most egregious example: his amateurism is almost a sexuality itself. A cheerless misogynist, he lives alone with his mother and desperately seeks out male soldiers to listen to his historical lectures, punishing women for even potentially distracting the men he so desires as audience. (Moreover, Powell and Pressburger's relationship was a queer collaboration if there ever was one, described once by Powell as "like a marriage without sex.")[125] Hope Emily Allen, never married, seems to have been romantically as well as domestically linked to another woman, and her close circle of friends in England—which included an accomplished local historian and antiquarian—was female and marriage resistant, as Deanne Williams observes.[126] Geoffrey Crayon, like his creator Washington Irving, is a committed bachelor, an outsider to normative heterosexual love and family domesticity. M. R. James operated in the exclusively male homosocial environs of British higher education in the late-nineteenth and early-twentieth centuries, with a particular enthusiasm in his student days for "ragging," one of its more vigorous physical rituals.[127] But even Frederick Furnivall, robustly heterosexual, married out of his social class, shocking others with his amorous liaisons, and I have already suggested as well that his amateurism associated him with classed and racialized others—further distancing him from the normative family of his times. Henry Wadsworth Longfellow's contemporary critics observed gender ambivalence in his work: he had "a fancy for what is large and manly, if not a full sympathy with it," sniped one hostile observer. The gender crossing, the redefinition of sentimental manhood, the homosociality in his poetry all did delicately subversive cultural work, according to recent criticism, in the "feminizing" culture of antebellum America that rapidly became "pathologiz[ed] and belittl[ed]" by modernists.[128] If Longfellow and, further, Andrew Lang were not queer in ways that resemble the sexual or gender queerness of other amateurs in *How Soon Is Now?*, each one in his work expresses a desire that is part and parcel of his amateurism. As amateurs, I argue, these medievalist readers are queered; as queers, I maintain, they are ever and only amateur, not participating in the serious, fully developed social business of family reproduction.

And though I feel I have achieved my fullest incarnation here as professional, writing a book with reams of endnotes, I also feel a kinship with the amateur that I can only call queer. I know, I know: I have been professionally trained as a medievalist, have taught full time for more than thirty years, and have been recognized and well rewarded. So why should I ever feel myself to be an amateur in a world of professionals, ever lacking, ever behind? Because I am a queer—a dyke and only sort of white. Because I am a medievalist, and studying the Middle Ages is, finally, about desire—for another time, for meaning, for life—and desire, moreover, is so particularly marked for queers with lack and shame. These feelings are not simply personal insecurities. Like my queerness, my feelings of amateurism aren't a stage of development, aren't ever going to go away; as in the case of queerness, too, my goal is to contribute to the creation of conditions in which an amateur sensibility might be nurtured and its productivity explored.

It might be protested that it's easy for me to say that I feel like an amateur; I'm not only employed but in fact tenured, and thus I enjoy an increasingly rare form of job security. I take the point, certainly: I don't hereby risk my job. But even given my secure position, it's not so easy for me to say in the current atmosphere of professionalization in the university, on the one hand, and suspicion of a "creeping anti-intellectualism" in the affective turn in medieval studies, on the other.[129] In the hope that my reflections might help in the development of different conditions, I tell the story of my uncertain progress and uneven development as medievalist and queer in chapter 2 (parents and childhood home), chapter 3 (college days), chapter 4 (country home in the Catskills), and the epilogue (lecturing on Chaucer), as I explore my too-close, anything-but-disinterested, subjective connections to medieval texts and desirous amateur readers.

Aiding me in this exploration, close to hand as I have worked on this book, have been recent queer temporal critiques. Judith Halberstam's *In a Queer Time and Place: Transgender Bodies, Subcultural Lives* (2005) demonstrates that Western European middle-class norms have determined a normative life course but that "once one leaves the temporal frames of bourgeois reproduction and family, longevity, risk/safety, and inheritance"—a modernist framing of the life course—queer time brilliantly erupts, and the "death of the expert" is not far behind. That mortality, indeed, opens up the realm of low theory and popular knowledge featured in Halberstam's book, *The Queer Art of Failure* (2011). Lee Edelman, in *No Future: Queer Theory and the Death Drive* (2004), bracingly rejects the temporality of the normative life course—what he calls "reproductive futurity"—along with its investment in the Child as its guarantor; he dismisses the future as mere "kid stuff," while Kathryn Bond Stockton, in *The Queer Child, or Growing Sideways in the Twentieth Century* (2009), turns away from the normative vertical line of "growing up" to focus on nonlinear growth, finding "queer temporalities haunting all children" and the peculiar asynchronies of "the ghostly gay child . . . whose identity *is* a deferral . . . and an act of growing sideways."[130] José Esteban Muñoz opposes not only dreary "straight time" with its reproductive mandate but also the queer refusal of futurity: in his *Cruising Utopia: The Then and There of Queer Futurity* (2009) Muñoz insists that queerness is "an ideality that can be distilled from the past and used to imagine a future"; queerness engages temporal modes such as waiting, anticipation, and belatedness to open up the potentialities of what Ernst Bloch calls the no-longer-conscious and the not-yet-conscious. Queerness is "primarily about futurity and hope."[131] The contrast between Muñoz's focus in *Cruising Utopia* on queerness as emphatically *not now* and my own focus on the *now* points to a difference between my contention that queerness is potential in the everyday, on the one hand, and Muñoz's argument on the other hand that it cannot be achieved in everyday "straight" time frames; both works, nevertheless, are committed to a temporal politics that would bring about a full and varied temporal realm: Muñoz's by rejecting ordinary time frames; mine by opening them up to the multiplicities within. Elizabeth Freeman's conceptualization of "temporal drag" in her *Time Binds: Queer Temporalities, Queer Histories* (2010) — referencing the "classically queer practice of drag performance" and pointing to ways bodies find usable pasts — has stuck with me as I theorize how people play out temporal clashes. The deeply affective dimensions of historical belonging — and not belonging — are explored by Christopher Nealon in *Foundlings: Lesbian and Gay Historical Emotion before Stonewall* (2001), work that resonates with my own analyses of queer desires for other kinds of time, as does Carla Freccero's intensive engagement with the spectral in the context of desire and identification, past and present, in her *Queer/Early/Modern* (2006). The recent temporal turn in queer studies has been widespread; temporality is problematized significantly even in work whose central object is not explicitly temporal, and I have benefited from the growing range of queer studies that seek to extend possibilities for living *now*.[132]

Though the ultimate intention in my temporal explorations is to extend such possibilities, I do not mean to claim that there is anything inherently positive about the experience or the condition of multiple temporalities. Tim Dean has recently discussed the kinds of anxieties that can attend the experience of "temporal contingency" in the context of HIV/AIDS.[133] As I demonstrate in the course of this book, the condition of being asynchronous or being outside a normative or dominant time-scheme can prevent desired projects from ever coming to fruition; it can threaten to destroy sexual or social reproduction; among classes of people, among races, among nations, it can be deployed as a rationale for political subjugation. I shall examine cases of individual alienation, as well as broader cultural ambivalences and political subjugation; but I shall show, too, that asynchrony, in the form of restless ghosts haunting the present, can be the means of calling for justice for past exclusions and injustice; such a *now* is not only full and various, but it is also more just.

BACK TO THE OLD HOUSE: A FEW WORDS ABOUT NOSTALGIA

Amateur medievalists are routinely derided — by historically minded scholars or even by the general public, under the sway of modernist ideals of historical expertise — as merely nostalgic, naively, uncritically, and irresponsibly yearning for an idealized past as escape from a present felt to be dismal and unpromising. And amateurs are clearly aware of the negativity of such a dismissal: one re-enactor in the Society for Creative Anachronism, for example, uses the language of guilty confession as he acknowledges that some people use the society as an escape from a "real life" that "sucks."[134] But I want to join in a "creative rethinking of nostalgia" precisely because it can be a much-needed survival strategy for those for whom a relationship to "home" is disrupted: those displaced from their homelands either literally or figuratively, including queers of all stripes. Rethinking nostalgia will take it beyond a judgment as "'merely' personal, apolitical, trivial, or transitory," as Gayatri Gopinath writes.[135] Recent work on medievalism has undertaken to make nostalgia a subtle and complex instrument of historical and cultural analysis — rather than the punitive bludgeon that it has been — by demonstrating its complexities and not shying away from paradox or conceptual incoherence.

Let me return to the discussion of amateur antiquarian societies for a moment, both because it provides useful context and because it exemplifies a use of the term that I want to trouble a bit. Concerning the growth of these societies, Philippa Levine argues strenuously that "romantic nostalgia played no part" in the veneration of local place that was a major motivation of these organizations. But she nonetheless notes that that localism "was the expression of an overpowering sense of loss" in the face of the urbanization and centralization characterizing British modernization. Levine documents very precisely antiquarian pride in possessions, in property, and in "modern achievements," maintaining that antiquarians did not depend on "the Romantic movement fleeing from utilitarianism."[136] But this does not mean that these antiquarians did not mourn lost past times; it means that their understanding of and desire for the past were not uncomplicated or unconflicted.

"Nostalgia," writes Svetlana Boym about this historical juncture, "was not merely an expression of local longing, but a result of a new understanding of time and space that made the division into 'local' and 'universal' possible." That new understanding is framed by modernism: in an oft-quoted formulation, she argues that "nostalgia is rebellion against the modern idea of time, the time of history and progress." And according to Boym it is not always simple; in the tradition she calls "off-modern," "reflection and longing, estrangement and affection go together."[137] Helen Dell has recently emphasized the difficulty and pain of the experience of such contradictions, pointing out that it is "the being pulled apart by the continued, relentless co-presence of oppositional tendencies in the complex of nostalgia which is so hard to bear." The complexity of response of the amateur antiquarians suggests something of this ambivalence: they both rejoiced in progressive elements of modern life and also longed for forms of belonging and roots of identity lost in the process of modernization. Dell would encourage us not to ease the tension inherent in "the complex of nostalgia": "perhaps, in fact, it is the instability of nostalgia, its refusal to settle as either singular or plural, simple or complex, that makes it a productive site for discussion."[138]

The presence of affect cannot alone delegitimize an engagement with the past on the grounds of insufficient objectivity. In the context of medievalist practice Aranye Fradenburg has demonstrated over the course of her writings "the importance of passion to rigorous practices of knowledge," and in making this demonstration she specifically has brought together amateur and professional medievalism.[139] Any hierarchy of professional over amateur engagements with the past on the basis of the former's "*dis*-interestedness" must be debunked, and an understanding of the fundamental connectedness of the enterprises embraced.[140] But what is this past era? A further problem with the conventional understanding of nostalgia emerges from the uncomplicated linearity that is implied by the idea that we nostalgically desire to go *back* to a time and place that are no longer. Andrew Lynch points out that a past-oriented insistence on linearity and on the deficiencies of the present smoothes out other varieties of nostalgia.[141] My point is more basic, and it flows from the analysis of time that I have been highlighting: as I argued in relation to Morrissey, the present is ineluctably linked to other times, people, situations, worlds. Thus anything we might as a matter of course call "nostalgic" is inevitably more temporally complex than the usual deployment of the term allows. The reductiveness of the conventional term "confines the past and removes it from any transactional and material relation to the present," anthropologist C. Nadia Seremetakis writes.[142] But nostalgia rethought has to take account of these heterogeneous temporalities. It may seem contradictory, as Dell suggests, to insist that longing for another kind of time beyond linearity (such as for the return of the past, a longing which implies the past's inaccessibility due to its loss or lack) can coexist with a conviction that there are many possible times in the now, including many possible pasts. This apparent contradictoriness may be evidence of the instability that renders nostalgia, as she puts it, a "productive site for discussion." Indeed, the workings of the relationship between temporal desire and temporal multiplicity are what I seek to explore in this book.

Temporal desire can be wry, ironic, both mournful and melancholic—melancholic in its enactment of ambivalence, mournful as the work of grief moves the griever forward into the future.[143] And as I hope to show, even the most cloying of affective responses to the past—Henry Wadsworth Longfellow's multiplicitous temporal consciousness, "habitually dwelling . . . among vanished generations," in chapter 1, for example, or Geoffrey Crayon's saccharin but estranged celebrations of merrie old England in chapter 4, or Thomas Colpeper's queer attachment to the land of his forefathers in my epilogue—are rarely without their reflective, critical dimensions, not only because of the temperaments of the readers in question but also, and primarily, because of the nature of time itself.[144] Because of their reflective dimensions, these nostalgias so understood can lead us through the narrowly defined "personal" to a broader understanding of the shared, collective possibilities of life *now*.

FRANKLY, MR. SHANKLY: PROFESSIONAL PROBLEMS, AMATEUR SOLUTIONS

The young artists' collective called the Bruce High Quality Foundation burst on the scene in New York several years ago with a brash slogan: "Professional Problems. Amateur Solutions."[145] Echoing their defiant reclamation of the term, I want to argue in this book that amateurs can lead us outside a straitened approach to problems, beyond a rigid dynamic of one problem/one solution, one object/one subject. Modernist temporal regimes are based on a boundary between past and present, which in turn supports the boundary between subject and object, inside and outside; amateurs can lead us beyond such boundary marking. As I shall suggest in chapter 1 and pursue in chapter 4, even the material text and the reader are not fully distinct entities; they are not solid and unitary, founded in a self-identical present, but are rather part of a heterogeneous *now* in which the divide between living and dead, material and immaterial, reality and fiction, text and spirit, present and past is unsettled, where traces of signs, on the one hand, and tracks of the living, on the other, function differentially in displacing final meaning or a transcendent guarantee of meaning. Deconstruction, which I am echoing here, might once have seemed the most arid game of the hyper-professionalized literary critic, but I want to gesture toward its world of play amidst permeable boundaries because I think it suggests something of the radicality of the interconnectedness, the web, the mesh that describes the ideal associational world I am aiming for here. Such a world is also more just, as I suggest, following Derrida, in chapter 4.[146]

Progress — along with its twin, development — though I have used it as something of a dirty word throughout this introduction, is not necessarily only modernist and therefore only a villain thwarting my nonmodern hopes and dreams. Bruno Latour points out in his *Politics of Nature* that "progress" is problematically modernist when it refers to movement in only one direction, toward professional, polemically "scientific," Enlightenment detachment of subject from object.

> Whereas the moderns always went from the confused to the clear, from the mixed to the simple, from the archaic to the objective, and since they were thus always climbing the stairway of progress, we too are going to progress, but by always descending along a path that is, however, not the path of decadence: we shall always go from the mixed to the still more mixed, from the complicated to the still more complicated, from the explicit to the implicit. We no longer expect from the future that it will emancipate us from all our attachments; on the contrary, we expect that it will attach us with tighter bonds to more numerous crowds of *aliens* who have become full-fledged members of the collective that is in the process of being formed. "Tomorrow," the moderns cry, "we shall be more detached." "Tomorrow," murmur those who have to be called nonmoderns, "we shall be more attached."[147]

What I want to imagine via *How Soon Is Now?* is inspired by Latour here: a collective bound by ever-denser attachments on the basis of each member's singular knowledge, aspirations, desires, and capacities.[148] And in this book it is amateurs' "affirmation," as John Cochran calls it, that can point the way forward.[149] In *How Soon Is Now?* I acknowledge that there are different knowledge cultures, different ways of knowing and sources of knowledge, and different purposes and goals, and I join in the critique, therefore, of expert knowledge production.[150] I bring amateur and professional reading together in this book *not* to suggest that there is no difference between, say, the invocation of the Canterbury pilgrims by Thomas Colpeper in *A Canterbury Tale*, on the one hand, and my own apprehension of the Chaucerian text and its contexts, on the other; my specific knowledge contributes its own precision to a temporally complex sense of the past. But I do want to help create conditions in which further attachments can be made, between and among people, times, and worlds. To focus on amateurs, to find shared desire in both amateurs and professionals, indeed to find the amateur in the professional (such as myself), is to encourage real interaction and dialogue between these two estranged groups; it is to resist the soulless professionalization of the university and to help create a public space for activities that are not now recognized as intellectually consequential. It is to cheer on recent experiments in crowd sourcing in the scholarly world and to applaud new and generative forms of open review.[151] It is to remind professionals of the amateur beginnings of cherished fields of study — say, queer studies (begun in a complex interplay of nonacademic and academic agents, the latter stepping out of their trained specialties),[152] or even medieval studies (as we've seen with Furnivall) — as well as to encourage everyone to recognize the beautiful amateurism of learning new things. I want to glimpse the possibilities, most broadly, of a more just and more attached nonmodernity. "Stay on my arm, you little charmer," croons Morrissey: that is, find this *now*, this moment that is not detached and not disenchanted. I want more life.

ONE

Asynchrony Stories

Monks, Kings, Sleepers, and Other Time Travelers

A monk wanders out of the cloister very early one day only to return mid-morning — centuries later. Seven men remain somnolent as, around them, paganism is defeated and Christianity triumphs. A youngster sets out to bring a sheep from a farm back to town, turns off the road to nap in a cave, and wakes decades later; only when told of his wondrous sleep does he then age, marvelously rapidly, but he also goes on to live almost another century. A deadbeat husband drinks a potion and wakes up after the Revolution, twenty years in the future a happy bachelor. In such narratives the problem of the present is encountered head-on: the *now* of the distracted monk, the dreamless sleeper, the dutiful son, the indifferent husband — all of whom have been swept into other times altogether — is out of joint when each eventually returns to the time unwittingly left. When he confronts others around him, two different temporalities are manifest simultaneously; the present moment is multiple, the fact of temporal hetero-geneity revealed. This revelation is always wondrous and sometimes scary, prompting a temporal vertigo that can permanently disrupt one's sense of self, society, indeed ordinary expectations of reality itself.

Asynchrony stories are ubiquitous. We've already seen in the introduc-tion that Aristotle uses one; indeed, references occur in a wide range of contexts ancient, medieval, and beyond: in natural histories, in sermons, in hagiographies, historical writings, folktales, fables.[1] Time travel tales, of course, make up a large part of modern and contemporary science fic-tion and fantasy fiction.[2] Such Rip van Winkle narratives, stories of people shifted into another temporality, reveal with unusual clarity the constant pressure of other kinds of time on our ordinary, everyday expectations of one-way, smoothly progressive temporality. Sometimes, in the medieval tales that are my topic here, this pressure can be accounted for by Christian belief: because "two temporal planes" are operant in Christian doctrine — "the plane of local transient life," as Aron Gurevich puts it, and "the plane of those universal-historical events which are of decisive importance for the destinies of the world — the Creation, the birth, and the Passion of Christ" — temporal multiplicity is a structured phenomenon both general and intimate for, potentially, every Christian.[3] While being a possibility inherent in doctrine, it was not necessarily an *easy* condition to live; and when the two temporal planes were seen to collide, what was that asyn-chrony like? Moreover, sometimes temporal clashes are not accounted for or accommodated to a Christian framework, engaging other temporali-ties that are not salvific at all. What, then, is to be made of the opening of alternate temporalities? Our everyday experience tells us, as we saw in the introduction, that time is not the same always and for everyone, but what are the conditions when clashes occur, and what then?

I focus in this chapter on tales in which temporal warps occur in the mundane world. My protagonists may wander beyond their usual paths, and they may have contact with alien agents from another temporal world, but their adventures occur in the here and now. Of course, tales of the mar-velous passage of time in otherworlds that are parallel to our own abound, too, particularly in the Celtic tradition: A king enters a cave and finds, on his exit, that the entire linguistic and political landscape has shifted in the hundreds of years that have elapsed. A knight steps into a forest where the sun rises and sets at an alarmingly quick rate; his exhausted body lags behind the dawn. A woman is able to spend time with a lover without consequences to her marriage — her husband hasn't noticed she was gone, since time passes so much more quickly in that otherworld.[4] Yet because I want to emphasize the simple fact of temporal heterogeneity that inheres in the here and now, I focus in this chapter on tales in which temporal shifts occur in "our" world rather than in another world. (I do take up one medieval tale of otherworldly travel, precisely because it features a transfer of an otherworldly temporality into the here and now.) These disruptions occur in various states of (un)consciousness: not only during sleep but also in rapture or trance. And my medieval examples come from a variety of sources and from a range of years; their importance to my argument lies less in the particular circumstances of their production and reception, and more in their deployment of asynchrony as a motif that demonstrates the constant presence of other kinds of time in the *now*.

Sometimes in these narratives, as we shall see, engagement with an alternate temporality distances or removes the protagonist from the realm of usual, expected, or acceptable social or sexual reproduction — temporal experience renders the protagonist queer, that is — and sometimes it does not. Medieval Christian doctrine and belief are built on temporal heterogeneity, as I have pointed out above, but narratives in which a temporal experience is not entirely accommodated by doctrine or belief are of even greater interest here. One of my protagonists is isolated by his desire for and experience of eternity — he is separated from his monastic companions and the cycles of nature; he is unable to sustain life on two temporal planes as a good Christian should. He is marooned, too, in relation to the reproduction of patriarchal power, but his queer experience is finally used as an example for Christian doctrinal purposes. Yet another protagonist, having passed through a temporally asynchronous realm, is barely able when back in his own world to understand his interlocutors, has permanently lost his wife, and has been claimed as kin by a strange, unnerving creature. His experience of time has made him queer, too, but that queerness, rather than remaining solely his own fate, spreads beyond the narrative to infect the present-day world, frantic and unfruitful, of the writer of this legend. Moreover, I argue that one modern reader of these medieval tales, nineteenth-century American Henry Wadsworth Longfellow, finds in them the opportunity to explore a fuller temporal *now*: this amateur medievalist — precisely *as* amateur, nonscientifically refusing the putatively objective — both studies and inhabits asynchrony, a queer temporal condition that opens up other worlds of desire.

A strong thematic cluster emerges in these narratives: marriage, gestation, and procreation. Dedicated to continuing a "line," in the first of my medieval examples patriarchal reproduction is revealed as resolutely linear in not only the genealogical but also, and therefore, the temporal domain; if, as I have suggested in my introduction, queerness is experienced, at least in part, in and *as* time, patriarchal reproduction is, too. Narratives in this chapter that explicitly problematize time also explicitly engage sexual and social reproduction: beyond that first example, as I shall show, queer potentials threaten to destroy ordinary reproduction or to transform our understanding of it utterly. When time is at issue, sexual and social reproduction are on the line — or turn out to be *not* on a line.

In this chapter I take up in detail one very popular medieval tale of asynchrony, a sermon exemplum known as "The Monk and the Bird," and surround it with two other narratives: the hagiographic legend of the Seven Sleepers of Ephesus, the most popular asynchrony tale in the Western Middle Ages, and the legend of King Herla and the Herlething, less well known but more disturbing. Of these three narratives two are firmly and safely embedded within Christian frameworks — "The Monk and the Bird" in a late-fourteenth-century sermon (with roots in the twelfth century), the Seven Sleepers in a compilation of saints' lives (a fifteenth-century recension of this story whose origins date back to the sixth century) — and the unfolding of alternate temporalities is part of their Christian mission. But Christian belief does not assuage the more unsettling effects of temporal slippage in King Herla's life and afterlife, which stretched into the twelfth-century court of this tale's writer. After exploring these thematic asynchronies, their uses and their implications, I shall turn to Henry Wadsworth Longfellow's mid-nineteenth-century retelling of "The Monk and the Bird" in order to detail one modern engagement of — and, because it is amateur, in — medieval temporalities.

OUT OF TIME: THE MONK AND THE BIRD

In one of the sermons well into the *Northern Homily Cycle*, a group of fourteenth-century sermons in English based on the Gospels, the preacher gives his lay audience what amounts to a tutorial on time, engaging concepts such as linearity and cycles; change and permanence; terrestrial time and heavenly time; the human body as temporal measure; the different temporalities of labor and play; written history and the phenomenology of time.[5] This popular homily collection (appearing in the massive Vernon manuscript as well as in Harley 4196 and in numerous other manuscripts) presents sermons probably read in church, to congregations who didn't know Latin or French, and it was passionately intended to teach these lay folk what they needed to know in order to live properly and attain heaven.[6] It proceeds week by week, one Sunday after another in the ever-unfolding and ever-repeating liturgical cycle of the year. This cycle correlates the events of scriptural history with the weeks of the year: the year begins four weeks before Christmas with Advent, the anticipation of the coming of Christ; it then moves through Epiphany, Lent, Easter, and then Pentecost (when the Holy Spirit descended to Christ's disciples); finally ending twenty-four weeks after Trinity Sunday, which is one week after Pentecost.[7] There is a text for each of the fifty-two weeks in the *Northern Homily Cycle*, and I shall take up the one for the third Sunday after Easter.

A sermon in such a cycle turns out to be a likely place to address the complexities of time. It is part of a textual sequence that gains its meaning in relation to the liturgical year, which is itself a temporally heterogeneous structure wherein week-by-week progress is experienced simultaneously with the repeated recognition of the events of Christ's life.[8] Thus this homily's treatment of time begins with its very location within this sequence. Oriented around Christ's life and the restaging of it year after year, the liturgical calendar draws, moreover, on the particularly compressed Christian understanding of temporality in which both past and future inhere in the present of the incarnate Christ; this vision of scriptural history — also referred to as allegory or typology — structures this and every sermon in the cycle: each sermon takes as its theme a text from the Gospels (a text concerning Christ's life) and paraphrases it, then explains it using allegorical or typological analysis, and finally provides a narrative for exemplification, an *exemplum*. Christian scriptural history, which I touched on with regard to Augustine in the introduction, is a temporal construct of anticipation and fulfillment in which an event in the Old Testament is a figure or type for an event in the New Testament (in the life of Christ and his apostles). That New event is thus the fulfillment of the Old and, continuing the figural relationship, is itself not only a figure of embodied human lives on earth between Christ's incarnation and second coming, but also a figure of the events of the second coming and the end of time.[9] Scriptural history understands the world as God's "discourse," as Michel de Certeau puts it: God is an allegorist, a rhetorician, and God — "in a single gesture," eternally—creates and disposes all things in sequences of before and after. Such allegory therefore depends on both chronology and "a time out of time" in which the text becomes legible in its completeness. In order for allegorical correspondences to obtain, God inscribes "homologies *in re*, in the things themselves"; if Abraham's wife Sarah is to be understood as the Church, there must be real resemblance between them.[10] This is the way God deploys the rhetoric of temporality; this is the way God writes history (thus "*scriptural* history")—God to whom past, present, and future exist simultaneously. A generally figural outlook—construing the present in relation to scriptural events, past and future—is fundamental to Christian theology and thus is potential in every Christian's everyday life: this is what I take from Gurevich's formulation above. But this also means that a more drastic temporal break or rapture—moving from one plane into another, or even out of time into eternity altogether—is always a potentiality for the believer, if not ordinary in the course of everyday life, precisely because of the multiple temporalities of this Christian doctrinal world.

Our homily from the *Northern Homily Cycle* draws on this framework and its ecstatic potential even as it treats time explicitly and topically. For the third Sunday after Easter, the preacher takes as his theme a verse from the Gospel of John: "Modicum & non videbitis me" [*A little while, and you will not see me*]. The full text of John 16:16 adds, "et iterum modicum, et videbitis me, quia vado ad Patrem" [*and a little while, and you will see me, for I am going to the Father*].[11] As the preacher paraphrases it:

"A litell while," he [i.e., "Crist"] said, "sall be
  In the whilk ye sal noght me se,
  And efter a litell while ful right
  Of me ogaine ye sal haue sight,
  For to my Fader sal I wende." (12381–85)

"There will be a little while," he [Christ] said,
"In which you will not see me,
  And after a little while indeed
  You will again have sight of me,
  For to my Father must I go."

Christ's disciples, those earth-bound followers, don't understand these words at all. They particularly wonder what *modicum*, "a litell while," means, and the rest of the sermon undertakes to explain this strange, vague phrase.[12] It's like the "now" in "How Soon Is Now?," and it's just as unsat-isfying: his disciples hear that he will be gone and then — sometime, but when? — he will reappear. Christ knows what is bothering his disciples ("Crist wist ful wele what thai wald mene" [*Christ knew fully what they were getting at*], 12389), because he knows all, and he goes on to explain:

> Of my wordes yow think ferly,
> And suthly vnto yow say I:
> Ye sall grete and haue sorows sad,
> When werldly men sal be ful glad.
> Kare sal fulfill yowre hertes, iwis,
> Bot sethin it sall be turned to blis. (12391–96)

> You wonder at my words,
> And truly I say unto you:
> You will weep and experience lamentable sorrows
> When worldly men will be very happy.
> Care will fill your hearts, indeed,
> But afterwards it will be turned into bliss.

The little while in question, Christ spells out, will be marked by your sad-ness while others feel happy, but after that little while your grief will be turned to bliss. Christ knows the future, and everything else, because he is not constrained by earthly time. But he is able nonetheless to address what an earthly "litell while" is because not only is he beyond time's limitations but also he lives in an earthly body, in time.

"A litell while," an interval of time, Christ suggests, is perceptible through some kind of change: a *modicum* is a passage of time that can be perceived because a change occurs between one *now* and another. This sounds very much like Aristotle: as we saw in the introduction, in his own theorizing in the *Physics* Aristotle determines that time is intimately re-lated to change — it is not itself change but is "something of change," as Ursula Coope puts it.[13] Here, Christ indicates the passage of time by a (future prediction of) change in his disciples from grief to joy: while he is away, they will feel sorrow; but after, while he is visible to them again, they will celebrate. And for further clarification Christ goes on to provide his disciples with an everyday example of this very change and the passage of time: he explains this principle via a woman's experience of childbirth. There will be pain, but then when a son is born, sorrow ends and comfort begins:

Ane ensaumple he set sertayne
And said, "A woman suffers paine
When that the tyme neghes nere
That scho sall trauail of child here.
And sune when that scho has a sun
Than es hir dole nere-hand done.
Scho thinkes noght on the paine biforn,
For a man in the werld es born.
Scho has slike comfort of hir childe
That all the wa fra hir es wilde." (12399–408)

An example he proposed, indeed,
And said, "A woman suffers pain
When the time draws near
In which she must go into the labor of childbirth.
And immediately, when she has a son,
Then her recent sorrow is done.
She doesn't think of the pain before,
Because a man is born into the world.
She has such comfort of her child
That all the woe is gone away from her."

It's a slightly strange example to choose right at that moment because, of course, none of his disciples, all male, could have had this experience themselves. Moreover, its very point depends on an unspoken gender hierarchy: would there be such a dramatic cessation of woe if a daughter had been born? The woman's pleasure is specifically a pleasure in sons: "For a man in the world es born." Christ in his example explicitly correlates change, with its before and after, with patriarchal reproduction; the woman's body is time's instrument and her pleasure is but an indicator of the successful operation of the system. As the provocative rhymes "biforn/born" and "sun/done" suggest, the birth of sons is the proper measure of time's passing. Patriarchal reproduction enacts temporal progress: in the terminology of José Esteban Muñoz, this is straight time.[14]

This is but one way among many in which to construe a "litell while." In the next section of the sermon — its allegorical exposition (*exposicio*) following the paraphrase of Christ's words — the preacher of the *Northern Homily Cycle* explains the significance of the Gospel passage in terms of Christ's life, invoking the multiplicities of scriptural history. The first "litell while" means the interval after Judas's betrayal, the preacher notes, during which Christ was hidden in the tomb, before the disciples knew of his resurrection. Once Christ did rise, the disciples saw him on earth for forty days in the second "litell while," whereupon he at last ascended to heaven to join the Father. But in a final shift in the preacher's typological reading those forty days are not merely your ordinary, count them, forty days; the temporality turns out to be even more complex. Forty days are finally not a little while at all; they betoken eternity, the time after time, as it were, not a measurable *modicum* marked by change but the changelessness of heavenly bliss.

His disciples can understand patriarchal reproduction, they get straight time, but how can they—or any humans, stuck in the sublunar—begin to apprehend such changelessness, this timelessness, this bliss? The atemporality of heaven challenges rational understanding. The typological exposition here begins to address not only the nature of eternity but also what it feels like: in heaven, paraphrasing 2 Peter 3:8, a thousand winters seem but a part of one day. But for elaboration of the experiential the preacher here turns to "a tale" (12456), an *exemplum*.[15] And it is in this narrative that the extraordinary temporal experience potential in Christian doctrine is seen to come to pass.

The preacher tells the story of a holy monk who wanted in his life on earth to see the least token—to get just a little taste—of this unfailing heavenly joy. In this enormously popular narrative—"one of the most popular of the *exempla*," existing in countless versions, as J.-A. Herbert attests—the aged monk has a great longing to see some "takining" (12458), some sign or event by which he might know the celestial *now*.[16]

And when he was man of grete elde,
And wex waike and ful vnwelde,
Of couent werke he was made fre,
And all at his awin will was he,
Als yong man that trauailes trewly
To haue ese in eld es worthi. (12463–68)

And when he had become a man of great age
And grew weak and very unsteady,
He was released from convent work
And followed his own will,
As a young man who works dutifully
Is worthy to be at ease in old age.

"Grete elde / ful vnwelde": he has had enough of earthly time and its enfee-bling corporeal effects. The canonical hours have calibrated his life *modi-cum* by *modicum* and have imposed their attendant labors,[17] but after a lifetime of duty this monk has been released from "couent werke" into the time of "ese," of leisure. One day, when the whole convent goes "To kirk" [*church*] (or "To heore werk" [*their work*], the Vernon manuscript has it, contrasting with the monk's free time) after "prime," the monk remains alone in the cloister, praying "To se sum point of heuyn blis / Out of this life or he ferd" [*To see some little bit of heaven's bliss before he passed out of this life*] (12476–77). And lo, God hears his prayer:

> A foule he saw bifor him sit,
> And wele him thoght he suld tak it.
> So faire a foule had he neuer sene,
> His hert tharto was casten clene. (12479–82)

> He saw a bird sitting in front of him
> And certainly it seemed to him that he should capture it.
> So lovely a bird he had never seen,
> His heart was entirely dedicated to it.

But the bird eludes his grasp, hopping before him and leading him onward, beyond the abbey gate and into a wood. Perching on a bough, the bird be-gins to sing, and the monk, delighted and at ease in the forest, listens to the lovely avian song with no thought of leaving.

> Bot when the sang was broght to ende,
> Than he thoght wele for to wende
> Hame ogaine, als he was won,
> Vnto the howre of vnderon. (12497–500)

> But when the song had ended
> Then he thought it best to get going
> Home again, as was his wont,
> Unto the mid-morning service.

The bird flies away, and the monk returns to the abbey, home again as usual for the service at the third canonical hour. (In the Vernon manuscript, he seems to sense, through his own time consciousness, that it's time for the bells to ring at the abbey.)

But "the howre of vnderon" is a legendarily strange time: the *Middle*

English Dictionary quotes this line (in the Vernon version) in its definition of "undern" as the service at the third canonical hour, *tierce* — about nine A.M. — but the word has a broader temporal range, from nine A.M. to noon to three P.M., and it presents a moment of instability or vulnerability in both secular and biblical traditions. The king of the faeries visits Heurodis then in *Sir Orfeo*, the psalmist warns of the dangers at noon, darkness descends on the earth at "vndurne" when Christ was crucified.[18] Strangely, indeed, as the monk approaches the abbey gate, "A mose-bigrouen [*moss covered*] wall he fand," though he is sure he passed through this very gate on his way out earlier this morning. He thinks this is odd ("ferly") and goes on, finding yet other gates that he hasn't ever seen. The porter does not know him, at which the monk marvels:

> He said, "I am of this abbay,
> I went right now out me to play."
> The porter said, "Thou has gane wrang,
> Thou was neuer monk here vs omang.
> Here wond thou neuer, that wele wate I." (12515–19)

> He said, "I am from this abbey,
> I went out just now to play."
> The porter said, "You've gone wrong,
> You were never a monk among us here.
> You never lived here — that I know well."

Now the monk is truly wonderstruck — "And than the monk thoght grete ferly" — and the evidence of his weird temporal displacement only mounts:

> Howses and werk he saw all new
> And menye that he neuer knew.
> Vnto the kirk he wald haue gane,
> Bot thederward way wist he nane.
> The porter him vnto the kyrk lad
> Als man that was mased and mad. (12521–26)

> Houses and construction he saw, all new,
> And people that he never knew.
> He would have gone to the church,
> But he didn't know the way.
> The porter led him to the church
> As if he were a crazy nut case.

The prior summons him, and the monk tells how he followed a bird out of the abbey that very day. "Grete ferly thinkes me / That I this hows thus changed se" [*It's a wonder to me, how changed I see this house to be*]; he wonders how he can account for himself if everything around him has changed so quickly and completely. Like the sleepers in the cave of the heroes of Sardinia the monk joined the *now* at the beginning of his experience in the forest to the *now* at the end, making them one, because he was unconscious of change between the two; but back in the monastery, he sees such a huge change that he can't comprehend how just a little time — the time of his trip out to the forest and back — can account for it.[19]

Finally the prior, sensing that this monk is of another era, asks who was abbot "in that time," and the monk "neuynd than the mans name / That was thare when he went fra hame" [*named then the man's name / who was there when he left home*] (12540, 12543–44). Many monks having been consulted, in old "cronicles" they finally find that that particular abbot died three hundred years earlier! And they find, too, that that same year "ane olde monk went him to play" (12550), never to be heard of again. They all thank God that the monk now before them is in fact he; and once the monk hears that he's been gone from home for three hundred years, he opens up to tell his tale of "What made him so lang [*long*] to dwell" (12558). Quickly asking for Holy Communion, he then gives up the ghost. The measurable and measured times of the monastic hours, of labor and even of play, of chronicles, of the pain and weariness of the body, and of the decay of the natural world yield to the experience of changeless pleasure with which mundane temporalities are incommensurable.

There's something both reassuring and unsettling about this tale, and that very combination, I hypothesize, contributed to its extraordinary popularity. For a sermon audience that believes in the eternal divine presence and looks forward to everlasting life, the monk's experience fulfills expectations and desires, and promises ever more. Continuous, forward-moving time is a good (because created by God), but is radically limited in comparison to the overarching temporal abundance of eternity; eternity is in fact the reality of which earthly time is but a shadow. Thus the clues throughout the narrative as to the nature of the monk's marvelous temporal experience are intriguing and pleasurable to track: the audience can follow the traces (the moss-covered stones, the unfamiliar porter) and try to make sense of the monk's experience. Various versions in fact exaggerate the clues: one emphasizes the monk's own increasing puzzlement in vibrant, extensive dialogue.[20] In other versions biblical intertexts make manifest the meaning of the bird's song or the monk's experience: in one the bird right away spills the beans by explicitly entuning Psalm 88:2, "Misericordias Domini in eternum cantabo" [*I shall sing eternally of the mercies of God*]; in another the monk walks out of the abbey meditating on the text of 2 Peter 3:8, and the lyrics of the birdsong he hears are even more obvious cues: "Bien face li home qui est vix, / Quar grant est li joyos de Paradis."[21] The bird is specifically identified in many sources and analogues of the text here as an angel in avian disguise.

The sermon audience pleasurably contemplates the narrative unfolding of eternity but it also witnesses its unsustainable intensity. The preacher lingers on the monk's own confusion and fear:

> Me think I wate noght what I may
> In this case of myself say,
> That it es in so litell tyme
> Changed sen this day at prime,
> For now I se here na felaw,
> Ne no man that I can knaw. (12531–38)

> I don't know what I may
> Say of myself in this situation,
> That is in so little time
> Changed — since today at prime;
> For now I see here no one
> Nor any man that I can possibly recognize.

The tale displays a deep fascination with the person of the monk, with his having lived through such a great period of time, with what he is or becomes through the experience. A late-twelfth-century version (deriving from the same source as this text) has the abbot and prior marvel that in three hundred years the monk has not become wizened, neither his clothes worn nor his shoes pierced with holes.[22] The ultra-aged monk is a figure of temporal incongruity, an awesome figure opening onto "the more," as Eileen Joy puts it.[23] His body powerfully contrasts with the body of the woman in Christ's example; her experience is a happy progression: comfort comes after pain; she gives birth in a before-and-after sequence that is so predictable it can be used as an example. But his experience is not so straight. No wonder he almost immediately must die: that kind of experience isn't for the sublunar, for humans caught up in the process of patriarchal reproduction, stuck in linear time. But unlike Rip van Winkle, too, another character who ventures beyond the known schemes of kin, community, and reproduction, the monk cannot simply live on with a temporal gap inside. He has been invaded by the incommensurable.

So there are elements here of unease as well as sheer pleasure in this representation of the rupture of mundane time by eternity. This tale of the monk and bird is, of course, intended to reinforce basic Christian doctrine and spiritual practice, and the peroration of the sermon emphasizes this fact: the auditors are admonished to do good works and accept sorrows for Christ's sake, and to believe — returning to the motif of the sermon — that their momentary cares will be turned into everlasting joy. In one strand of the long history of this narrative, in fact, the monk initially doubts God's eternal nature, and his extraordinary extratemporal experience is given to him precisely to dispel those thoughts, clearly tending toward the heretical.[24] Time is not only God's, as Augustine indeed maintained, but it is also administered by an ecclesiastical structure whose bells continue to ring and which can absorb even the suggestion that its own monastic records are inadequate to the task of representing the true complexity of time. The sermon introduces temporal varieties indeed: the schematic multiple temporalities of the liturgical calendar and scriptural history, on the one hand, and the individual experiences of mundane time and changeless eternity, on the other; the straight time of patriarchal reproduction; the extraordinary experience of contact between two disparate temporalities. Such complexities are deployable in any number of ways, for any number of purposes. Here the monk's queer voice on earth, desiring another kind of time and indeed experiencing it blissfully, is contrasted to that of his monastic brothers, who work and pray and write in a regulated temporality; it is contrasted to the doctrinally predictable Christian experience of contentedly living on two temporal planes at once; it is contrasted, too, to straight time and a woman's satisfaction and pleasure in it. But if the monk's experience is far from ordinary, it is nonetheless potential in the Christian temporal scheme of scriptural history and the liturgical year that draws on it. Queer in the mundane world, the monk's temporal desire and enjoyment are finally not disruptive of the orthodox Christian temporal scheme or its institutions. Though such bliss rarely occurs on the level of the individual worshipper, it is accounted for within the doctrinal framework of temporal multiplicity and its promise of eternity.

TIME WILL TELL: THE SEVEN SLEEPERS

The enduring tale of the Seven Sleepers of Ephesus was fantastically popular: recent scholarship clocks a manuscript tradition spanning fifteen centuries in genres ranging from saint's life to charms.[25] In contrast to the exemplum of the monk and the bird and its cloistered little world, this tale is very much about world-historical change: in its Christian renditions it is about the historical spread of the faith across the Roman Empire. While our monk wanted to taste eternity and thus was granted his (solitary) experience, these seven Ephesians refuse to sacrifice to idols, and God grants them a wondrous sleep that takes them through the time of persecution by the emperor Decius up to a meeting with the Christian emperor Theodosius himself. The shared, group character of the experience — there are *seven* sleepers, brothers in some versions — contributes to the sense of the narrative's historical purchase. History here, as it turns out, is not what hurts; sometimes history is merely what you sleep through.

The atmosphere of asynchrony is indeed thick in this tale. The narrative was used polemically early in Western Latin tradition to demonstrate the truth of the doctrine of the resurrection of the body. (Its reach was so great that it was even adapted in the Qur'an for the same eschatological purpose.)[26] The topic of the resurrection of the material body proved enduring in medieval Christian thought; precisely because change is at stake, time is an element of the fundamental quandary posed by the issue, and asynchrony is an implicit part of the whole problem: In what way could the material body (on earth subject to time and change) continue in the eternal *now*? If we rise from death into heaven the same, but changed, as Pauline writings promise, what does that really mean about the matter of our flesh? Intricate theological analyses from the patristic period onward debated the problem of the continuity of personhood between life on earth and life in heaven, at points articulating solutions to this "problem of what accounts for personal identity" by obviating the "need for body's material continuity." But as Caroline Walker Bynum explains, an "insistence on bodily resurrection" persisted: "From the second to the fourteenth centuries, doctrinal pronouncements, miracle stories, and popular preaching continued to insist on the resurrection of exactly the material bits that were laid in the tomb."[27] This doctrinal matter and its implied temporal dilemma provide context for vivid narrative representations of the corporeal struggles and triumphs of the Seven Sleepers, their faces finally shining like the sun, still materially in their cave but appearing as if already in heaven.

The hagiographical nature of the narrative as well is temporally very provocative. Canonization was an acutely political process, deeply entrenched in lives and stratagems in the here and now; but the *theory* of sainthood suggests that saints are a peculiarly temporalized bunch existing beyond everyday politics. They share a common temporality that is synced up with the life of Christ. Thus do their feast days align with the liturgical calendar (the Seven Sleepers' feast day in the Western church is July 27). And thus does Gregory of Tours (who wrote the earliest Christian Latin versions of "The Seven Sleepers") claim that, "it is better to talk about the life of the fathers than the lives, because, though there may be some differences in their merits and virtues, yet the life of one body nourished them all in the world."[28] Again here, as in other Christian temporal schemata I have discussed, the life of Christ is the capacious *now* in which what we know as past and future time is contained; in some saints' lives the conformity to the events and sufferings of Christ's life is quite marvelous. This hagiographical theory with its gratifyingly multiple *now* is further context for the representation of temporal heterogeneity we see in narrative renditions of "The Seven Sleepers."

Among the later versions the tale was rendered in Latin by Jacobus de Voragine in his enormously popular late-thirteenth-century compilation of saints' lives, the *Legenda aurea* (*Golden Legend*) — "almost a cultural institution" in the Western Middle Ages, as Sherry L. Reames describes it[29] — which was in turn translated into English by the printer William Caxton about a hundred years after the *Northern Homily Cycle*. It is this English version of "The Seven Sleepers," in Caxton's 1483 *Golden Legend*, that I shall discuss here: Caxton enthusiastically promoted Jacobus's *Legenda*, this "most noble ... Legend," despite its biases and limitations, in his efforts to fashion a lay reading public in England.[30] The theme of the resurrection of the body and the theory of saints' lives frame our understanding of the temporal manipulations in his "Seven Sleepers"; I want to focus my brief analysis here, however, on a simple image at the tale's end. What strikes me in particular is a homely image that reveals, in the face of the spectacular asynchrony interposed by the divine onto the lives of these men, the utter commonness of temporal heterogeneity. It is an image of a pregnant woman.

Let me narrate, briefly, the legend and then turn to this final moment.[31]

In the reign of Decius Christians were persecuted and forced to sacrifice to pagan gods. But seven Christian men, though beloved of the emperor, refused to do so; as a consequence they were brought before Decius, then freed and given more time to change their minds, because they were so valued by the emperor. Terrified by this predicament, they gave away their possessions and, taking just a little money, fled to a cave. Malchus, one of their number, was appointed to go into town—dressed as a beggar—to buy necessities for their sepulchral stay; when he heard in town that the emperor had in fury commanded that they all be brought in, he returned to tell the others, who in fear and trembling sat and wept. "Suddenly, as God would, they slept," and those who went in search could not find them. Decius ordered that the mouth of the cave be blocked so that they would starve and die—but not before two Christians among the pagans wrote out their martyrdom and subtly placed it among the stones blocking the entrance.

In a precise temporal calculation—critics remark on the use of exact times to convey "an air of precision and truth to the wondrous event"—the narrative then states that three hundred sixty-two years pass; Decius dies and all of that generation, and the thirtieth year of the reign of Theodosius is reached.[32] A certain man in Ephesus opened the cave as he was making a stable for his workers. The noise of the builders awakened the seven, who—as did the sleepers in the legend of the heroes of Sardinia before them—thought they had slept for only one night. The narrative is minute in its observation of the men as they awaken, and it plays up the supposedly regular progression of day after day: they "awoke and were raised and intersalued each other, and had supposed verily that they had slept but one night only, and remembered of the heaviness that they had the day tofore." Equally exaggeratedly, Malchus reminds everyone of their predicament: "like as I said to you yesterday, the emperor is searching for us in order that we should sacrifice to idols."

Malchus is sent to get provisions—another of the seven, Maximian, instructs him to bring "more than he did yesterday"—and when he leaves he sees amazing things, among them, the sign of the cross over the gates of the city. The narrative is full of vivid details of Malchus's growing confusion, similar to what we've seen of the monk. Muttering to himself, he doubts whether he is in fact in Ephesus at all, since no one yesterday would have professed Jesus Christ but today everyone confesses to be a Christian. Using his now-antique money to try to buy bread, Malchus is thought to have robbed some ancient hoard; intensely confused and frightened, he is dragged through the city, seeing no one of "his kindred ne lineage." Brought before the bishop and consul, he is interrogated. They determine from the inscription on the money that it is more than three hundred seventy-two years old. Malchus asks where Decius, the emperor, is; all are amazed at this since Decius is long since dead ("he was emperor many years since"). Malchus claims to have seen him yesterday.

The officials and a great multitude of people are led by Malchus back to the cave to meet the others and prove his story. The bishop finds the martyrology among the stones and reads it, then sees the seven themselves sitting in the cave, "their visages like unto roses flowering." They haven't aged a bit. And when the emperor Theodosius arrives, he exclaims typologically, "I see you now like as I should see our Lord raising Lazarus." Theodosius resolves the apparent temporal impossibility by invoking a Christian understanding of temporal multiplicity, and as it turns out God in fact has provided the extraordinary temporal episode of the sleepers for the emperor's benefit: Theodosius, a Christian emperor, is battling the heresy of those who deny the resurrection of the dead, and God intervenes in time in order to demonstrate this doctrinal truth. Maximian explicitly clarifies the relationship between the experience of the Seven Sleepers and the doctrine of resurrection: "Believe us, for forsooth our Lord hath raised us tofore the day of the great resurrection. And to the end that thou believe firmly the resurrection of the dead people, verily we be raised as ye here see, and live." The seven have not died, though; they have been but sleeping. Maximian uses a striking image to explain what exactly their physical state has been: "And in like wise as the child is in the womb of his mother without feeling harm or hurt, in the same wise we have been living and sleeping in Iying [*sic*] here without feeling of anything." This returns us to the imagery of reproduction that we saw earlier in the *Northern Homily Cycle*. In that sermon the labor of childbirth is set into a temporal scheme of before and after, wherein the painful time before will be forgotten in the comforting time after a son is born: patriarchal reproduction, working through the woman's body, advances moment by moment in a smooth progression. Eternity in contrast in that sermon suspends all pains of labor and even all comforts of play, removing the monk's body from any punctual chronology and asynchronously rendering him queer.

Here in the Seven Sleepers legend, though, the perspective shifts. The experience in the cave is likened to the child's experience in the womb: the sleepers have been alive, completely insensible and invulnerable, protected like a baby in the mother's body. And in a remarkable twist, the physiological experience is not plotted on the patriarchal temporal line but is, rather, understood as profoundly asynchronous. Unconscious of ordinary time, the baby rests, comfortably and safely. The mother presumably continues on her everyday path while providing protection from harm, from even the harms of time. In a moving reversal of the monk's fate — with a touch of the atemporal in him, he cannot live, he must die — the mother with the atemporal in her gives life, and is associated with even more life: resurrection.

Saints' lives can be extreme spectacles of asynchrony: this is what Margery Kempe knew and performed, and such a spectacle blazes forth when the Seven Sleepers' den is pried open to view. Yet this particular womb analogy brings asynchrony firmly into the realm of the everyday and of everyone as well. The womb experience of atemporality, of asynchrony with smoothly continuous forward-moving time, may be surprising conceptually, but it is experientially comforting, and is shared by all humans. While offering a most vivid example of extraordinary temporal multiplicity, this saint's life also suggests that *everyone* began life in a nine months' sleep. This doesn't mean that everyone is rendered queer by this asynchronous temporal condition. But the potential is there; what it does mean is that asynchrony is in our bones, providing the ground for that constant sense that other times press upon merely sequential chronology. Augustine, as we saw in the introduction, analyzed human life as essentially asynchronous, and tragically so, contrasting it with the perfect simultaneity of eternity from which we as fallen humans are ever exiled; but this brief moment at the end of the tale of the Seven Sleepers gives us a glimpse of another image of human life, life as unfolding noncontinuously and yet purposively, meaningfully, and productively in the world. Asynchrony is not destructive or painful here; the temporality of ordinary, everyday life does not necessarily differ from or contrast with other temporal planes (as, say, Gurevich's model of temporal multiplicity, the simultaneity of "two temporal planes," implies) but potentially incorporates them by drawing from the multiplicities of Christian scriptural history or other supernatural temporalities. Hinting at a more capacious and positive sense of quotidian human life, this is indeed the mother of all asynchrony stories.

TIME WON'T TELL: KING HERLA

When the Welshman Walter Map tells the tale of King Herla, another
sepulchral story of asynchrony, the passage of time is paradoxical and mysterious, and the reproductive institution of marriage bears a large part of
the trouble. Walter, a university-trained courtier in Henry II's court, wrote
De nugis curialium in 1181–93; this is a big, ambitious volume combining
historical writing, fabulous tales, satire, and saints' lives into a "kind of
secular *summa*" of the world from an English "school-trained courtier's
point of view."[33] It is an attempt to convey a sense of the variety and heterogeneity of the world. Walter is especially concerned to express the temporal "jumble" that is the present—our now (*modernitas*) that, he sees, will
eventually be someone else's authoritative past (*auctoritas*), our past which
was someone else's *modernitas*.[34]

Walter begins with a very familiar quotation from Augustine—not only
familiar to us now, quoted with stunning frequency even today, but also
a touchstone in Walter's day, the late twelfth century. Walter is clearly angling to claim legitimacy for his own work through Augustine's established
authority and eloquence:

> "In tempore sum et de tempore loquor," ait Augustinus, et adiecit: "nescio
> quid sit tempus." Ego simili possum admiracione dicere quod in curia sum,
> et de curia loquor, et nescio, Deus scit, quid sit curia. Scio tamen quod curia
> non est tempus; temporalis quidem est, mutabilis et uaria, localis et erratica,
> nunquam in eodem statu permanens.

> "In time I exist, and of time I speak," said Augustine: and added, "What
> time is I know not." In a like spirit of perplexity I may say that in the court I
> exist and of the court I speak, and what the court is, God knows, I know not.
> I do know however that the court is not time; but temporal it is, changeable
> and various, space-bound and wandering, never continuing in one state.[35]

Yet the basic Augustinian paradox enunciated here—I am in time yet I
don't know what time is—is powerful and complex enough to govern
Walter's whole intellectual style in *De nugis curialium*, as Monika Otter
has demonstrated.[36] I want to argue, more narrowly, that the ambivalent
view of time we saw in Augustine's *Confessions* is conveyed in at least one
of Walter's many narratives as well: Augustine's sense of time as painful
carries into Walter's story of King Herla, a marvelous narrative that offers
a representation of a strange infiltration of and threat to the institution of

marriage and an explicit origin of the distressing problems in the court of
Walter's own day.

Soon after his introductory Augustinian section, and after a series of
short chapters comparing the court to hell, Walter turns to a wondrous
story (the first marvel of many in the work), a tale of asynchrony. Walter
uses this tale to trace the genealogy of what he views as the painfully "errant
ways" of the court in his day. Old stories tell us that long ago King Herla,
of the ancient Britons, was visited by another king — "a pygmy in respect of
his low stature" [*pigmeus uidebatur modicitate stature*] — who led him into
making a contract with him. The small king, who claimed Herla as kin, re-
spectfully asked that Herla allow him to attend at Herla's wedding — a wedding Herla himself had not even heard of — if Herla would return the favor
when requested to do so a year later. Herla agreed, and his wedding indeed
took place; the "pygmy" king brought his retinue and catered the wedding
with every beautiful accoutrement imaginable. Vanishing around cockcrow
the "pygmy" reappeared a year later and called on Herla to repay his debt;
dutifully Herla discharged his obligation. The second wedding was in the
little king's own country, in a deep cavern, gloriously lit. Herla afterward
withdrew into the darkness to head home. In parting the "pygmy" gave
him a small dog to be carried, forbidding anyone in Herla's company to
dismount until the dog leapt forth from his bearer. The "pygmy" returned
to his people; Herla proceeded into the sunlight and his own kingdom.

But of course, once in the light he learns from an old shepherd that he
has been gone rather longer than the three days that he feels to have passed.
The shepherd is amazed when King Herla asks for his queen:

> Domine, linguam tuam uix intelligo, cum sim Saxo, tu Brito; nomen autem
> illius non audiui regine, nisi quod aiunt hoc nomine dudum dictam regi-
> nam antiquissimorum Britonum que fuit uxor Herle Regis, qui fabulose
> dicitur cum pigmeo quodam ad hanc rupem disparuisse, nusquam autem
> postea super terram apparuisse. Saxones uero iam ducentis annis hoc reg-
> num possederunt, expulsis incolis. (28–29)

> Sir, I can hardly understand your speech, for you are a Briton and I a Saxon;
> but the name of that Queen I have never heard, save that they say that long
> ago there was a Queen of that name over the very ancient Britons, who was
> the wife of King Herla; and he, the old story says, disappeared in company
> with a pygmy at this very cliff, and was never seen on earth again, and it is
> now two hundred years since the Saxons took possession of this kingdom,
> and drove out the old inhabitants.

The king almost falls off his horse in amazement; some of his men do indeed get off their horses, heedless of the "pygmy"'s warnings about the dog, and are immediately turned to dust. The king orders no one to dismount before the dog descends, but the dog never does. Thereupon the king and his army wander endlessly. Only recently, adds Walter, did the mad army cease its wanderings, having sunk into the river Wye at Hereford, and he suggests that they have transfered their desperate, perpetual motion to Henry II's court: "From that hour the phantom journeying has ceased, as if they had transmitted their wanderings to us, and betaken themselves to repose" [*Quieuit autem ab illa hora fantasticus ille circuitus, tanquam nobis suos tradiderint errores, ad quietem sibi*] (30–31). The army's crazed restlessness lives on in the current court, errant and fractious: "They seem to have handed over their wanderings to us poor fools, those wanderings in which we wear out our clothes, waste whole kingdoms, break down our own bodies and those of our beasts, and have no time to seek medicine for our sick souls" [*nobis insipientibus illi suos tradiderint errores, quibus uestes atterimus, regna uastamus, corpora nostra et iumentorum frangimus, egris animabus querere medelam non uacamus*] (370–373).[37]

So much differs here from the narratives of the monk and the bird and the Seven Sleepers. The magical time of the King Herla episode is not the Christian eternity. Granted, its representation of a passage from a mundane temporal zone into a supernatural one, as in those other fables, is amenable to Christian interpretation or assimilated into a Christian framework, as C. S. Lewis suggested of some fairy worlds; the supernatural temporality of the fable draws on a long tradition of marvelous time lapses in romance, lapses that convey the impression of other kinds of time pervasively pressing on the measured chronology and that can be understood in some relation to Christian time frames.[38] *Oisin in Tirnanoge* is one striking example among many. It is a Gaelic romance sharing numerous narrative elements with Walter's story, including a trip to a beautiful and sumptuous otherworld, seeming to last three days that are really three hundred years; the insistent taboo on dismounting; and the association of the other place with death.[39] Tirnanoge, the otherworldy Land of Youth, is in the Gaelic tradition sometimes far across the ocean, as in *Oisin in Tirnanoge*, but sometimes it is in the interior of a hill, as is the otherworld in Walter's tale of Herla.[40] And in *Oisin in Tirnanoge* the curious passage of time is explained in contrast to a Christian time frame. But in *De nugis curialium* the warped passage of time remains entirely unexplained; instead, asynchrony caused by immersion in the temporality of the otherworld is used to diagnose Walter's own unbearably out-of-joint present.

The time lapse certainly means trouble in the narrative itself. As we see in Walter's tale, representatives of different historical periods — Briton, Saxon — talk distractedly with one another, barely understanding, and the legacy of the historical violence they represent (the Saxons conquered the natives) remains unresolved. The ritual of marriage, an element of the patriarchal reproductive structure we've seen in the pregnancy and child-birth imagery in the tales of the monk and the bird and the Seven Sleepers, is strangely implicated in the temporal distortion of Herla's experience. The queen has clearly lost her king to supernatural temporality, and the odd figure of the pigmy claims Herla as kin: Herla is queered by time, taken out of the arena of ordinary patriarchal reproduction.[41] Moreover, the displacement, loss, and sadness of him and his wandering men — their removal from productivity or reproductivity, their queerness — are directly handed down to the present as a temporal disease; as Walter says, Herla's ragged band prefigures the men of Henry II's court in their frantic and heedless activity: "We rush on at a furious pace; the present we treat with negligence and folly, the future we entrust to chance, and since we are knowingly and with open eyes always wending to our destruction, wandering timid waifs, we are more than any man lost and depressed" [*Furia inuehimur et impetu; presencia necligenter et insulse curamus, futura casui committimus; et quia scienter et prudenter in nostrum semper tendimus interitum, uagi et palantes, pauidi pre ceteris hominum exterminati sumus et tristes*] (372–73).

Asynchronous experience can be individually traumatic and socially disruptive; this is the burden of Walter's tale. Such experience spoils any possibility of a clearly purposive present, producing the agonies of that desperate, sterile, "pitiable and care-ridden court" of his day in which he languishes (*in hac ego miserabili et curiosa languesco curia* [372–73]). Walter's tale conveys something of the feeling Augustine conveys in the *Confessions*, that life in the present is an excruciating temporal exercise, an agonizing push and pull; but here in Walter's world there is no horizon of eternity, nothing to provide relief or even to remind one of its lack. Walter is not merely using a parallel temporality to critique present-day social ills; in his version asynchrony interrupts and perturbs the hoped-for wholeness of the present day, splits, upsets, queers the *now*.

THE MONK AND THE BIRD, REDIVIVUS

For Henry Wadsworth Longfellow, nineteenth-century American writer and dedicated medievalist, the asynchrony of the exemplum of the monk and the bird opens up a positively reorganized sense of *now*: eternity, the everyday, change, hope, intimacy are all present, as is an expanded sensory perspective on the mundane. When he plucked it from its sermon context and grafted it onto a romance in his *Golden Legend* (1851) the anecdote stood for all that Longfellow, much of whose oeuvre is animated by medievalism, found attractive and ideal in the Middle Ages.[42] His medievalism is nostalgic, of course, but as I argue in my introduction, nostalgia can be complex. Here it is not merely a desire to return to a simpler time, though that is a large part of it; more fully understood, it is an enactment of a kind of double vision, a temporal copresence. It is, to invoke for a moment the terms of T. J. Jackson Lears's influential study, both antimodernist (an absorption in the medieval past) and modernist (a way of being in and accommodating to the present day) at once.[43] Ruskin in *Modern Painters* associates him with an approach to the "resuscitation of the past" that proceeds "by habitually dwelling in all [his] thoughts among vanished generations"; Longfellow himself, to put it in my terms, was asynchronous.[44]

Though it is not much read today, *Christus: A Mystery*, a trilogy consisting of the *Golden Legend* and two other verse dramas, was intended by Longfellow himself to be his great work.[45] Virtually ignored now—for reasons that may start with the archaism of the verse drama form itself—the *Golden Legend* nonetheless suggests an attitude toward time shared by his much more enduringly popular works, particularly *Evangeline* and *Hiawatha*.[46] The *Golden Legend* is Longfellow's dramatic retelling of Hartmann von Aue's *Der arme Heinrich*, a Middle High German romance from the late twelfth century. (Longfellow's title is somewhat confusing, since his drama has nothing to do with Jacobus de Voragine's *Legenda aurea*, which he encountered after the *Golden Legend* appeared in print.) The monk and bird exemplum does not appear in Hartmann's poem and is completely extrinsic to the plot of the *Golden Legend*; clearly drawn to it and determined to make it fit, Longfellow added it when the *Golden Legend* was nearly finished.[47] The patently superfluous exemplum is important, as we shall see, in ways that exceed the plot: it points to the possibility, on earth, of a temporally multiple consciousness, something that the poet can be said to share with the monk.

The narrative of the *Golden Legend* concerns the mortal sickness, moral triumph, and miraculous cure of Prince Henry, a simple plot arc elaborated with many scenes of medieval life. In the drama's tumultuous prologue Lucifer and the evil Powers of the Air try to topple the cross atop Strasburg Cathedral; this portentous entrée is followed by the opening scene, in the tower of the Castle of Vautsberg on the Rhine, where ailing Prince Henry is visited by Lucifer in the guise of a physician. We learn that the prince's disease is a total mystery — in Hartmann it is identified as grossly disfiguring leprosy but here more vaguely "a kind of leprosy drinks and drains" the prince's heart — and he has "bleared his eyes with books" (145, 155) trying to find a cure. Lucifer disguised in doctor's garb contemptuously dismisses old dead medical authorities and their mute writings:

LUCIFER.
And has Gordonius the Divine,
In his famous Lily of Medicine, —
I see the book lies open before you, —
No remedy potent enough to restore you?
PRINCE HENRY.
None whatever!
LUCIFER.
           The dead are dead,
And their oracles dumb, when questioned
Of the new diseases that human life
Evolves in its progress, rank and rife.
Consult the dead upon things that were,
But the living only on things that are. (145–46)

According to this diabolical visitor human progress is but a festering forward march of disease. The prince in his own version of hopelessness goes on to explain that the living doctors at Salerno can't save him either because they have prescribed a remedy that is impossible actually to attain: the blood of a maiden who will give her life for his. Lucifer himself admits that the prince might find such a girl — "who knows?" (147) — but goes on to administer "the Elixir of Perpetual Youth" that temporarily and deceptively lifts the Prince's spirits. The scene then turns to the castle courtyard, where Walter of the Vogelweid, a minnesinger (modeled on the medieval Walter von der Vogelweide) and old friend of the prince, returns after a long absence.[48] We learn from his conversation with the aged seneschal that the prince has been banished like a plague victim because of his illness. The prince is taking shelter with a faithful family in the Odenwald, where the scene then shifts. Daughter Elsie will soon determine against her family's wishes that she will be the maiden who will sacrifice herself to save the prince's life.

As the next scene opens, the prince, in the farm garden with Elsie, reads of the monk and the bird. Longfellow's version of the legend is notable for its condensation and simplicity. The narrative is spare, eliding any introduction or description of the monk and beginning abruptly in medias res: "One morning, all alone, / Out of his convent of gray stone, / Into the forest older, darker, grayer, / His lips moving as if in prayer, / ... / Walked the Monk Felix" (158–59).[49] (Felix is the name of the monk in several medieval versions.) Details are few: the monk is meditating on a verse in the Psalms (the lines paraphrase Psalm 90:4: "A thousand years in thy sight / Are but as yesterday when it is past, / And as a watch in the night!"), noticing nothing of the summer sunshine. He is suddenly surprised and soon enraptured by the singing of a "snow-white bird." He listens long,

> Until he saw, as in a vision,
> The land Elysian,
> And in the heavenly city heard
> Angelic feet
> Fall on the golden flagging of the street. (160)

When Felix tries to catch the bird, it flies away, and he then hears the convent bell ringing for the noon service. Longfellow's version, following his source which differs from the *Northern Homily Cycle* version in this, does not emphasize the gradual process of recognition or the various material clues to the nature of Felix's extended time away, focusing only on a difference in the people he encounters: "the faces were new and strange" while "the place was the same place." The energy of the narrative instead is concentrated on "an aged monk" who actually recognizes Felix from the old days.

> "One hundred years ago,
>   When I was a novice in this place,
>   There was here a monk, full of God's grace,
>   Who bore the name
>   Of Felix, and this man must be the same." (162)

This superannuated monk's life is itself a wonder: he has lived for well over a century. The past is in fact alive and present here in the person of this ancient monk, and he confirms what is recorded in the martyrology of the convent:

> That on a certain day and date,
> One hundred years before,
> Had gone forth from the convent gate
> The Monk Felix, and never more
> Had entered that sacred door.
> He had been counted among the dead! (162–63)

Like the Seven Sleepers, Felix is associated with resurrection of a sort here; moreover, he has seen both the future of his convent and heavenly bliss. There is no hint (either here or in Longfellow's source) that he will or must now die: he may just continue to live in the convent (his appearance is unchanged) with that miraculously, phenomenologically compressed excess of time—with a touch of eternity—in him. He joins the superannuated monk in creating there a temporally extended community, a brotherhood that marvelously spans centuries.

The exemplum in fact breaks down distinctions between the living and the dead, the present and the past. And it does this in a scene of reading, an activity in which boundaries are radically breached. Indeed, the distinction between people and texts is consistently perforated in the *Golden Legend*: already in the prologue the distinction is associated with the devil when Lucifer dismisses the past, the dead, and books in one fell swoop, rigidly cordoning them off from a putatively more progressive, if diseased, present. Further on, after Prince Henry reads the monk and bird anecdote, he immediately likens Elsie to the angel of saintly legend who brought roses to Saint Cecilia's bridal chamber, then to Saint Dorothea, and then to yet another maiden of Christian lore, the sultan's daughter (163–65). And as we've just seen, the ancient monk and the monastery's martyrology speak in one voice. In the dramatic finale, life blends with legend definitively: on their wedding night at the Castle of Vautsberg on the Rhine—finally, Henry's "nobler self prevailed" (284), and he not only saves Elsie from the necessity of death but also weds her—Prince Henry listens to the distant bells of Geisenheim and recalls the legend that the same bells rang as Charlemagne sat at the side of his wife Fastrada. A few more lines and the verse drama ends, a reworked medieval text that has come to dramatic life; in the characters' own voices other written medieval legends come to life in the process as well.[50]

Reading — textuality, bookishness — is so central to Longfellow's poetics here that it is hard not to see the poet himself in the figure of the protagonist of the *Golden Legend*, when Prince Henry is depicted reading of the monk and the bird one morning. In his journal entry for March 6, 1851, Longfellow wrote, "A soft brown mist fills the air. I have a leisure day, and shall give the first hours of it to the Monk Felix."[51] But more essential is his identification with the Monk Felix himself: for Longfellow, reading and recounting medieval texts foster a productive asynchrony, bringing the past into the present. In this he shares an asynchronous disposition, too, with his colleague at Harvard, James Russell Lowell, whose essays (particularly an early one in 1845) situate another medieval writer — Chaucer — in a past that is, however distant, at the same time also present.[52] Language, Longfellow wrote in 1832, discussing the importance of knowing the history of a language, functions like "armor and weapons of the Middle Ages," demonstrating "very clearly and forcibly not only the character of the times, but also the stature and physical strength of those who wore and wielded them." In this way language delineates "the strength and stature of the intellect, by which its various parts were worn and wielded"; this analogy draws its power from the sense that words in a way bring to life people from the past.[53] This is not philology in the Germanic university tradition; in fact in the classroom at Harvard Longfellow's impassioned approach was disparaged by an undergraduate as well as by "elders" as "too flowery" and "very much out of taste."[54] It instead might be seen to resemble Frederick James Furnivall's amateurism, as we saw it in the introduction, which served his interest in connecting people, past and present, Old World and New. Longfellow enters into a temporally complex *now* through medieval poetry and prose, connecting him to other people across time and space.[55]

The *Golden Legend* features a full range of stock medieval characters, including a vituperative preacher, pedantic scholastic theologians, university medical students, a manuscript illuminator, players in a miracle play, and plenty of clerical figures, saintly and wanton. But Longfellow's medieval reading far predated his *Golden Legend*. His first major book was *Outre-Mer: A Pilgrimage Beyond the Sea* (1835), a collection of travel writings and essays based on his years in Europe from 1826–29:[56] that title, as he explains, refers to the language of medieval pilgrims and crusaders as they spoke of the Holy Land, *le Pays d'Outre-Mer*, "the Land beyond the Sea." The epigraph to *Outre-Mer* is in fact from the *Book of John Mandeville* itself, the famous fourteenth-century travel narrative, and in *Outre-Mer* Longfellow assumes the voice of a medieval pilgrim: "Lystenyth, ye godely gentylmen, and all that ben hereyn!"[57] The book is written in the style of Washington Irving's Geoffrey Crayon, the dilettante medievalist and tourist in the Old World whom we will encounter directly in chapter 4; here, too, we hear that voice, the deliberately amateur antiquarian, speaking.

In this medievalizing narrative Longfellow equates the European "Old World" with the Holy Land itself: travel eastward, across the Atlantic, is travel back in time. The Old World is the seat of reverence for this American, his spiritual source and ultimate origin, the place that has not developed or progressed. This spatiotemporal formula, travel east equals travel back in time, is always ideologically fraught: in the *Book of John Mandeville* we feel its Christianizing force over the globe, as we shall see in chapter 2; here, a certain colonial ambivalence about Catholicism is expressed in the tension between the imputation of backwardness and exhaustion of the old country, on the one hand, and desirous idealizing of the ancient origin, on the other. Longfellow condemns "the corruptions of the Middle Ages," as he puts it in the notes to the *Golden Legend*, including the dissolute monks, lecherous and fatuous friars, and strenuous but sterile scholasticism in his verse drama, and maintains that the New World has left behind the mystifications and superstitions of the Old. But Longfellow had an "attraction of repulsion," to use a contemporary commentator's phrase, to Roman Catholicism, that repository of tradition and ritual that fascinated him and that, moreover, provided a much-desired link between ancient origin and the present.[58] Catholicism was found not only in the Old World to the east, moreover, but also in the New World, Latin America, to the south (as well as in North American Spanish-speaking cultures to the west), with whose very present-day living "traditions" he had a complex relationship.[59] Thus Longfellow's literary endeavors took place in complex asynchronous relationship to the Old and, as Kirsten Silva Gruesz has shown, to the New World, to the past and to the present.[60]

The fable of the monk and the bird, to mention that exemplum of temporal asynchrony one last time, signals that for Longfellow reading the medieval text offers not merely a return to a time past or a reversal of the "wheels of activity" of present-day America.[61] Resembling the monk Felix, who lives a double temporality, having experienced the eternal while continuing to exist in the here and now, Longfellow evinces another kind of time altogether, a temporal simultaneity in which past and present appear in the *now* simultaneously. Ruskin in *Modern Painters* claimed that in the *Golden Legend* Longfellow "has entered more closely into the temper of the Monk, for good and for evil, than ever yet theological writer or historian, though they may have given their life's labour to the analysis." Longfellow can do this — and this is a key to his modernity, as Ruskin would have it — because he has steeped himself in the medieval while he remains "in another element," that is, while he is in the present day and thus has "*seen other things*" beyond what the medieval man has seen.[62] In Ruskin's view, Longfellow's is a complex form of time-consciousness in which perceptual attention in the present day allows for a sharper perception of another time.[63] Ruskin's comment can be taken to suggest that the modern poet *in his very modernity* can distinguish and apprehend what is in fact medieval — thus the asynchrony of the modern poet himself, even (or especially) one on the way to becoming outdated. Reading and retelling medieval tales produce other temporal possibilities not only because the tales represent different temporalities, but also because the act of reading itself is asynchronous, as I take Ruskin's description to suggest; and that asynchrony echoes the multiple temporality of the medieval texts with which Longfellow is dealing. It is exactly this asynchrony that Ruskin contrasts to the "life's labor" of theologians and historians — professionals, that is. Longfellow's reading is, in my terms and again like Furnivall, amateur reading.

Powerful evidence of this asynchronous temporality appears in the final moments of the dramatic action, when the queerness of asynchrony gets played out. Eric L. Haralson has pointed to the "cross-gendered sensibility" and "sentimental" masculinity of Longfellow's poetry, arguing that Longfellow's poetry of the 1840s and 1850s "enacted and encouraged" what was already an ongoing feminization of the American public arena and civic virtues (which was, however, soon to wane). In this light Elsie's passivity, waiting, and self-sacrifice are models for a redefined masculinity, as is Henry's weakness and "somewhat epicene" quality, as Newton Arvin sees; and the friendship between Henry and Walter, the minnesinger, points toward the possibility of affective homosocial bonds.[64] Indeed, in the last scene, on their wedding night, as Elsie joins softly with her new husband on the castle terrace, we see such cross-gendering and homosociality in a startlingly explicit way: Prince Henry recalls that in earlier days he used to stand on that same terrace with Walter, who is now fighting in the Crusades. On his way to Salerno Henry had encountered Walter, who was journeying to the Holy Land, but Henry felt unable to travel with him through Italy as the latter had suggested; now, in the final words of the play, Henry muses to his new wife — strangely, it may seem to the twenty-first century reader, because of the intimacy of the occasion, but even more poignantly, to the play's first readers, precisely because of the abruptness: [65]

> Oft on this terrace, when the day
> Was closing, have I stood and gazed, . . .
> But then another hand than thine
> Was gently held and clasped in mine;
> Another head upon my breast
> Was laid, as thine is now, at rest.
> Why dost thou lift those tender eyes
> With so much sorrow and surprise?
> A minstrel's, not a maiden's hand,
> Was that which in my own was pressed.
> A manly form usurped thy place,
> A beautiful, but bearded face,
> That now is in the Holy Land,
> Yet in my memory from afar
> Is shining on us like a star. (289)

Marriage — infected, even destroyed, by asynchrony, as we've seen in the King Herla tale — is here surprisingly expanded into a sort of mystical love triangle in which constraints on object-choice collapse as temporal boundaries are abolished: we had earlier learned of the minnesinger's role as lover of the now-cloistered Lady Irmingard, but at this climactic wedding-night moment of the play the man's form and face are superimposed imaginatively on the bride's and the love between the two men, which is effected across time and space, illuminates the wedded couple. This manly figure had "usurped" the (future) wife's place in the past, as if he had always been the bride. The language of homosociality would soon become culturally unacceptable in Longfellow's America, as Haralson observes, but here in his Middle Ages Longfellow uses it to express attachments and ways of being that were obsolescent in his present world: the dissolution of temporal boundaries serves as imaginative and affective — serves, that is, as queer — resource. I have claimed in the introduction that desire for another time, or another kind of time, is a queer desire; here, queer desire is expressed not only in a different era but also in a different kind of time that crosses boundaries of present and past, here and there.

So the medieval here prolongs a waning trend in Longfellow's day, but it is threatened by the suggestion of a destructive modernity in Prince Henry's last words. The ravages of time and especially death are suspended in Longfellow's version of "The Monk Felix," but they return with a vengeance at the play's end and dispel this mystical scene on the terrace. Death, no longer freely chosen by Elsie, now menaces the actual marriage: Prince Henry's next lines, the final lines of the main dramatic action, follow: "But linger not. For while I speak, / A sheeted spectre white and tall, / The cold mist climbs the castle wall, / And lays his hand upon thy cheek!" (289). This does not portend the blissful eternity here that Felix experiences: these lines terminate the action, with only a brief Epilogue (spoken between two angels) remaining. The disturbing incommensurability in that legend becomes the chilling and unavoidable touch of death on Elsie's face. This final scene leaves us with a complicated play of potentialities: earlier the superannuated monk and Felix have expanded life's possible chronologies together in the monastery, but at the last the prince, his wife, and Walter live on in a new sort of relationship that proceeds across space and time yet is finally subject to time and mortality. The eternity of the exemplum — perhaps even the medieval era in toto — is counterpoised against an insidiously creeping modernity, its ghostly hand with grim finger pointing ineluctably forward, endward.

But queerness is potential even in that deathly progression. Old and infirm, months away from his own death, Longfellow hosted the young dandy Oscar Wilde for breakfast as the latter was making his infamous trip to Boston in 1882. This breakfast can be read as the final in my series of asynchrony stories, the dying poet of sentimentality (who had been something of a dandy in his day) meeting the ironic, up-and-coming aesthete, men of two eras meeting in a temporally complex encounter.[66] This meeting with Wilde brings out the queerness that I suggest is inherent in Longfellow's temporality (his desire for past worlds, his asynchronous reading, his amateurism) even as it brings out the temporality of Wilde's queerness. Wilde experienced the meeting as, in fact, reading: he commented later, "Longfellow was himself a beautiful poem, more beautiful than anything he ever wrote."[67] Longfellow is an old poem, maybe even a medieval poem, that Wilde reads, and we may hear in Wilde's wittily ambivalent comment, at once appreciative and scornful, something of a desire for another kind of time that all asynchrony stories express.

Only the amateur's superficial interest in the Middle Ages
can find pleasure in it.

—**PAUL HAMELIUS**, "The Travels of Sir John Mandeville"

Temporally Oriented

The Book of John Mandeville, *British India,*
Philology, and the Postcolonial Medievalist

Far into India, toward the easternmost end of his
travels, Sir John, the fictional narrator of the *Book*
of John Mandeville, comes upon a well at the foot
of a mountain. He has already passed through the
Holy Land and has now moved significantly beyond
it, through countries of one-legged people, Ama-
zons, diamonds that beget little baby diamonds, and
other marvels animal, vegetable, and mineral. "Ynde"
(India) in Mandeville's *Book*, as in the Western European Middle Ages in general — for the *Book* is a long
compendium of Western European travel literature
and lore written in the eyewitness first person but
actually compiled of many sources — was a huge and
vague geographical designation encompassing much
from the border of Ethiopia to China and usually
divided into three parts: "Greater," "Lesser," and
northern. "As a result of this geographical sprawl,"
writes Michael Uebel, "'India' represented for medieval Europeans an immense *terra incognita* that

became synonymous with the alien, the remote, and . . . the marvelous."[1] And accordingly, in India Sir John finds more than five thousand islands, the book claims, lands filled with "gret plentee of cytees [*cities*] & of townes & of folk with outen nombre" and many, many wonders: a magnetic sea, sun worshippers, dog-sized rats, exotic peppers, snakes.[2]

Another marvel arrests Sir John's attention:

> Also toward the heed [*head*] of that forest is the cytee [*city*] of POLOMBE, And aboue the cytee is a grete mountayne that also is clept [*called*] PO-LOMBE And of that mount the cytee hath his name, And at the foot of that mount is a fair welle & a gret that hath odour & sauour [*savor*] of alle spices, And at euery hour of the day he [*it*] chaungeth his odour & his sauour dyuersely[.] (ch. 19, p. 112, l. 35–p. 113, l. 5)

Its changeable spicy smell and taste are the least of its supernatural properties, though: "And whoso drynketh .iij. tymes fasting [*whoever drinks three times while fasting*] of that water of that welle he is hool [*whole*] of all maner sykeness that he hath" (ch. 19, p. 113, ll. 5–7). In fact, says Sir John, regular indulgence in the waters of the fountain keeps you not only ever healthy but also always young looking: "And thei that [*those who*] duellen there & drynken often of that well thei neuere han [*never have*] sekeness & thei semen all weys yonge [*they seem always young*]" (ch. 19, p. 113, ll. 7–9).

At this fountain in Polombe (present-day Kollam, on the Kerola coast in the land now known as India) Sir John drinks: "I haue dronken there of .iij. or .iiij. sithes & yit me thinketh I fare the better" [*I have drunk thereof three or four times and still it seems to me that I am better off*]. The use of the present perfect tense here emphasizes the continuity of his present with that past action; his imbibing has had a lasting effect into the present: still "I fare the better." Or at least it seems to him that he does ("me thinketh"). Anyway, he's chipper, hopeful, optimistic. "Sum men clepen it the well of youthe [*call it the well of youth*] for thei that often drynken there of semen allweys yongly [*seem always youthful*] & lyuen with outen sykeness [*without sickness*], And men seyn [*say*] that that welle cometh out of paradys & therfore it is so vertuous [*has such powers*]" (ch. 19, p. 113, ll. 11–14). So this is the legendary Fountain of Youth! Sir John has found and sipped from it. This puts him in the august company of—among others—ancient Ethiopians, Alexander the Great, and the mighty heroes of Charlemagne romances.

Of course Sir John doesn't believe in the reputed effects of this well, not exactly: at the end of his *Book* he admits that he had to cease his travels because he is gouty and arthritic, stricken by the infirmities of old age. He doesn't even refer to the Fountain of Youth at that point; of course it didn't work. His earlier claim to feel the better for having partaken of it seems to have functioned as little more than an offhand gesture toward the fountain's reputation. And of course this is just a tiny slice of the vast over-ripe fruit that is the *Book*, which is full of the outlandish sights this narrator supposedly sees. Yet Sir John does have a reason to believe in this marvel, a condition that distinguishes his reaction here from his reactions to the many other weird phenomena he reports in his *Book*: because the fountain is said to issue from Paradise there is a framework for the Christian traveler to entertain the possibility that it could be real and could alter one's earthly temporality—that it could transform one's life course into one of perpetual youth featuring a hale and hearty body that is not subject to the sublunar processes of decrepitude. In this little episode that is certainly "tongue-in-cheek," as Rosemary Tzanaki calls it, but also momentarily wistful, Sir John indulges in a wish—a realizable wish—to stop or even turn back the time that is meted out on the body every day as progressive aging.[3]

The *Book of John Mandeville* is in fact dense with different kinds of time, different experiences of time, and desires for different temporal experiences, all of which unfold as the narrative moves east. The book of Sir John's travels is of course about space, but space is correlated with time in significant ways here (as everywhere), and time, as we shall eventually see, exerts its own particular, intense attractions. To travel east in this book is an asynchronous activity: it is to travel back in time. But eastward travel is more than that; even as the East is associated with the past in Sir John's view, time and its correlation with space are more complex than that equation suggests.[4] In this chapter I want to open up temporal multiplicity and desire in this very heterogeneous book and see their refractions in later engagements with the book.

So this chapter, in three diverse parts, will explore some of the complex and paradoxical experiences of time associated with the East in this Middle English text and in readings of this text. In the first part, on the *Book of John Mandeville*, I lay out the broad narrative framework of travel eastward—a framework that is based on a Christian asynchronous space-time scheme—but turn then to ways in which Sir John moves beyond, or tries to move beyond, that scheme. To be sure, the book takes its place in

Western post-Crusades longing for worldwide Christianization, and any relation of otherness ends up contributing to a total vision of eventual Christian triumph. But in this multifarious book there remains curiosity and longing to experience another kind of time. The Fountain of Youth reflects such desire. That fountain must in turn be understood in relation to its source in Eden, which has a beautiful but inaccessible temporality all its own: Eden is still on the map but is nonetheless forever lost to humans. At the end of the book temporal desire still lingers.

Victorian readers with their own investments in the East — as members of the British Empire — read the geographical-temporal mapping of the world of the book as proto-imperialist: they relied on an Orientalist valuation of movement east, maintaining that the West had progressed while the East had not. Such Orientalism correlated the book's eastward progress with the expansion of the British Empire: asynchrony in this colonialist context had thus a particular political and affective value. I turn in the second part of this chapter to two short but intriguing nineteenth-century English engagements with Mandeville's *Book* that implicate Orientalist temporality in medieval reading. The first of these pieces, Andrew Lang's 1886 "Letter" to "Sir John Manndeville [*sic*], Kt.," one of Lang's *Letters to Dead Authors*, addresses "Sir John" himself in made-up Middle English, castigating him as a liar and comparing him unfavorably to none other than Colonel Henry Yule, the celebrated editor of the *Book of Ser Marco Polo* and colonial administrator in India; Yule was author of a widely influential *Encyclopaedia Britannica* article that confirmed Mandeville's supposedly eyewitness account as a tissue of many earlier texts. In the second piece, M. R. James not only parodies Sir John's voice but also mocks the voice of a philologist himself; by reading this very short 1887 parody by James, I open up questions about the relationship of philology, that systematic analysis of historical forms and structures of language, to the colonialism that equates India with the medieval. In both of these short pieces I find a complicated play of affects in the depiction of English colonialism and English philology. The loss of Eden that lingers at the end of the *Book of John Mandeville* recurs here as melancholy for the already lost glories of empire and medieval past. Lingering desire is converted into horror, though, in M. R. James's ghost stories, his famous amateur productions that depict the past as a restless and malevolent sexual realm. The blatantly queer implications of the protagonists' desires for the past bring out what will have been merely implicit theretofore in my argument: the queer potential of the affective ambivalence of the imperial philologist and amateur medievalists and, indeed, the queerness of Sir John's desire for another kind of time.

Dependent upon the work of such philologists for the very texts I read, in the third and final part of this chapter I turn my attention to my own practice as a medievalist. That Orientalist equation of the East with backwardness resonates with my personal history: excavating the East in my own postcolonial past but reclaiming its asynchrony, as it were, for another purpose, I argue for an approach to this and other medieval texts that acknowledges the heterogeneity of times in the present, recognizing the generative possibilities of the sense of longing, incompleteness, and loss that characterizes the voices of the medieval traveler, the colonialist, the philologist, and the amateur medievalist.

Animating the chapter, indeed, is the spirit of the amateur, identified by Paul Hamelius in my epigraph here as the only kind of reader who will be satisfied by the *Book of John Mandeville*. Hamelius would seem to have a point: Andrew Lang and M. R. James were both amateurs when they wrote their parodies (Lang a belletrist, James a student), and Henry Yule was a leisure-time philologist (though, contra Hamelius's point, it seems he was not satisfied by the text). Moreover, James invents a fictional amateur, to boot. But I of course reject the two-edged value judgment Hamelius makes, that amateurs represent a debased reading practice and that the *Book of John Mandeville*'s appeal to them evidences its own second-rate nature.[5] Hamelius implies that superficial reading lacks revelatory power, but our amateurs create brilliant imitations of the surface of the text, lovingly replicating Sir John's voice with their own, and thus open up the desire that lingers in Sir John's text. Out of such longing we in turn can read suggestions for apprehending a vibrantly asynchronous *now*.

THE *BOOK OF JOHN MANDEVILLE*

EASTWARD INTO MORE TIMES

To travel east in the *Book of John Mandeville* is to travel temporally in reverse. Pilgrimage to Jerusalem from the West is a "journey backward in time," Donald Howard demonstrates, for Mandeville as well as for the pilgrimage narratives that inform the context for his work. Mandeville coordinated the chronology of pilgrimage with the Gospels, Howard argues.[6] The Holy Land is hallowed by the touch of Christ's foot; his actual footstep is visible there still, Sir John observes, on the Mount of Olives ("And yit there scheweth the schapp of his left foot in the ston" [*And still the shape of his left foot in the stone can be seen*], ch. 12, p. 64, ll. 10–11), as are the hoof marks of the ass on which Christ entered Jerusalem on Palm Sunday (ch. 11, p. 53, ll. 7–9). The historical past is obviously the reason for the continued importance of these places; these places now are imprinted by that past, inseparable from it, imbued with it. Recent editors Tamarah Kohanski and C. David Benson speak of "geographical palimpsests" in the Holy Land.[7] And as Sir John's path takes him further east, the time of the New Testament leads even further backward into the Old, as Noah's Ark is reported to be on Mount Ararat in Armenia (ch. 17, p. 98, ll. 32–35), a lake in "Silha" (now Sri Lanka) proves to be the tears of the exiled Adam and Eve who wept for a century after their removal from the Garden (ch. 22, p. 131, ll. 19–24), and finally the edge of the terrestrial paradise, the Garden of Eden, looms before our traveler. The place of the momentous origin of human life is the furthest locus on Sir John's eastward itinerary: he actually verges on the space of the beginning of human time.

But the space-time movement of the book is not only a linear journey back in time.[8] Traveling east is better understood as traveling toward and into more explicitly heterogeneous temporalities. The Garden of Eden is certainly in a time zone of its own, as we shall see in the next sections, but the Holy Land is itself a complex temporal locus. Futurity as well as pastness inheres in it, as Suzanne Conklin Akbari has shown in this context: Jerusalem is not only the point of origin of Christian salvation history but also the point of final return, "anchoring Christian salvation history both in its past, as the place of the Crucifixion and mankind's consequent salvation, and in its future, as the site of the first signs of Apocalypse and the gathering place for the Last Judgment."[9] The structure of typological fulfillment, as I've described it in earlier chapters, is expressed here geographically, as the waters of Eden are said to flow under Jerusalem, humankind's Original Sin redeemed by Christ's incarnation and sacrifice (ch. 12, p. 58, ll. 15–16; p. 63, l. 9). One prominent strand of late medieval cartography, as Alessandro Scafi has elegantly shown, with Jerusalem in its middle, was configured by the concept of salvation history whose fulcrum was Christ's incarnate life.[10] Even as Jerusalem sees Christ's sacrifice, so travel there brings one to the very site of the beginning of the end. And further east, beyond Cathay, that futurity weighs heavily, as Sir John anxiously narrates the events of "the tyme of ANTECRIST" when "the Iewes" intend "to destroye the cristene peple" (ch. 30, p. 177, l. 34–p. 178, l. 3).[11]

But in the book some places are even denser with times. A systematic typological mapping does not explain Sir John's account of the rock of the Temple of the Lord in Jerusalem, for example (ch. 12, p. 56, l. 8–p. 57, l. 34). This rock contains a riot of historical significance: on that rock rested the Ark of the Covenant, in which were held the Ten Commandments, Aaron's rod, Moses's staff with which he parted the Red Sea, and other "relykes of Iewes" [*relics of Jews*]; on that rock, too, Jacob dreamt of the ladder to heaven; Christ preached there and drove the merchants out of the temple; David was prohibited from building the Temple by God; the Virgin Mary learned her Psalter; Christ was circumcised; numerous events from the Old and New Testaments, and some not even biblical, took place.[12] A glorious jumble of Christian times is present in that one rock.

Movement from West to East makes particularly visible such multiplicity of time in particular locales in the Holy Land and beyond, and such heterogeneities can be thrilling. There is an excitement that accrues to this heterogeneity, as in the rock of the Temple passage. Sir John can be cool and deliberative, too; indeed, that is one prominent affective mode as he passes through these lands. When it comes to consideration of the veracity of relics, his assessment is calm (that cross in Cyprus, for example, is the cross on which Dismas hung, but they say it's Christ's cross just to profit from the offerings [ch. 2, p. 6, ll. 5–12]), and he is mindful of distances between past and present (in, say, the present city of Nazareth, much diminished from its former glory [ch. 14, p. 74, ll. 32–36]), even as he reveres the Holy Land because of Christ's presence there still. But that coolness can in other circumstances be mixed with less-distanced affect.

When he gets further east and sees the marvels of timekeeping and time management in the court of the Great Khan, for example, he is fascinated by them, and this allows him to turn a critical eye on his own limited European Christian culture with its "epistemological provincialism."[13] Actual clocks fascinate Sir John when he reaches the court of the Great Khan: "Oriloges [*clocks*] of gold mad [*made*] ful nobely & richely wrought" are among the "Instrumentes after hire [*their*] sciences" used by legions of "PHILOSOFRES . . . in many dyuerse sciences, as of ASTRONOMYE, NIGROMANCYE, GEOMANCYE, PIROMANCYE, YDROMANCYE, of AUGURYE & of many other sciences" (ch. 26, p. 154, ll. 9–11, 1–4), glamorous and mystifying instruments that include golden astrolabes, spears, the brainpan of a dead man, golden vessels full of gravel or sand, burning coals, water and wine and oil.[14] The philosophers seek the most auspicious hours for activities related to the Great Khan, but what impresses Sir John is the somatic ritualization of these particular moments. When philosophers determine it is an auspicious time, they have their officers announce, "Now pees [*peace*], lysteneth"; thereupon another philosopher will order every man to do reverence and bow to the emperor, "for now is tyme"; they kowtow, all bowing their heads to the ground, then, when told to do so, all standing up again. "And at another hour seyth another Philosophre: Putteth youre litill fynger in youre eres [*ears*], And anon thei don so. And at another hour seyth another Philosophre: Putteth youre hond [*hand*] before youre mowth, And anon thei don so. And at another hour seith another Philosophre: Putteth youre hond vpon youre hede, And thei don so. And after that he byddeth hem to don here hond awey & thei don so" (ch. 26, p. 154, ll. 14–15, 17–18, 20–27). These bodies are turned into temporally regulated signifying machines: "And so from hour to hour thei commanden certeyn thinges, And thei seyn that tho [*those*] thinges han dyuerse significaciouns" (ch. 26, p. 154, ll. 27–29): bowing the head betokens loyalty, finger in the ear betokens an obligation to report all contrary utterances, and so on (ch. 26, p. 154, l. 29–p. 155, l. 6). Sir John curiously watches these weird rituals; he inquires "preuly" [*privately*] about their meaning (ch. 26, p. 154, l. 30).[15] European Christians, to be sure, have "Oriloges" and astrolabes, too, as well as their monastic hours, but this whole temporal performance, combining technology, sciences, and signifying practices — this combination differing from its source in Odoric of Pordenone — is radically unfamiliar to European frameworks, and in turn opens up a defamiliarizing gaze on Sir John's own culture.[16] As Karma Lochrie points out, Sir John acknowledges that the "science" and "craft" of the court of the Great Khan outstrip that of all other nations; in the court of the Great Khan they themselves boast that they see with two eyes while Christians see with but one ("thei seyn hem self that thei seen with ij. eyen & the cristene men see but with on [*one*] be cause that thei ben more sotyll [*subtle*] than thei" [ch. 24, p. 143, ll. 14–16]).[17]

Sir John's own culture may become other at times, but he also turns others into versions of his own culture in his eastward travels. Sir John encounters figures whom he interprets with great longing as reflections of the reality of Christians at an earlier, purer stage in human history. He has already in his travels in the Holy Land met the sultan of Egypt, who in a private audience in his own chamber castigated Christians at length for their egregious spiritual faults; the sultan's lords know Sir John's land and other Christian countries as if they were native, and they all speak excellent French (the original language in which the *Book of John Mandeville* was composed, and thus the language Sir John would have been speaking: they speak his own language). These Saracens, in the Holy Land at the climactic end of the first part of the book, are objects of Sir John's identification and admiration ("I had gret meruaylle" [*I greatly marveled*] of their French, he says [ch. 16, p. 89, l. 36]) as well as shame ("Allas, that it is gret sclaundre to oure feith & to oure lawe, whan folk that ben withouten lawe schull repreuen vs & vndernemen vs of oure synnes" [*Alas, it is a great slander to our faith and our law when people without the law reprove and rebuke us for our sins*], ch. 16, p. 89, l. 37–p. 90, l. 2]).[18] Moving further east, among the thousands of islands of India, Sir John describes in great detail the Isle of the Brahmins, where people, though not Christian, live in a state of natural obedience to the Ten Commandments; they live under "kyndely lawe" [*natural law*], as if before the time of grace (ch. 33, pp. 194–97). They are an implicit rebuke to Christians of Sir John's own time who are preoccupied with cheating and deserting their neighbors rather than with winning back their rightful Holy Land heritage after the losses of the Crusades (prologue, p. 3, ll. 1–2; p. 2, ll. 24–28). In the whole realm of Prester John (wherein are located these Brahmins) there are many Christians, too, living as if in an earlier, apostolic age, the priests celebrating the mass without any newfangled additions.[19]

These Christians as well as the Brahmins and the Babylonians, too, located in the far East and associated with the distant past, offer critical but ultimately flattering and "consoling" examples for Sir John's own time. After all, turning others into versions of oneself is aggressive mastery of them even as it might also perform some self-flagellation. The book might construct an Eastern utopia as critique of the West, but the cultural criticism prompted by these others is finally absorbed into an overall Christian scheme; they function, Iain Higgins argues astutely, "not only to point up the numerous practical failings within Latin Christendom itself, but also, if paradoxically, to affirm the ultimate superiority of that community by imagining it as somehow capable of containing all others."[20] The Saracens *themselves* predict that Christians will finally return to their righteous ways and take back the Holy Land in the future: "And that knowe we wel be [*by*] oure prophecyes," says the sultan, "that cristene [*Christian*] men schull wynnen ayen [*shall win again*] this lond out of oure hondes whan thei seruen [*serve*] god more deuoutly" (ch. 16, p. 89, ll. 19–21).[21] And when they do, then an earlier stage of Christian history—when Christianity reigned widely—will in fact have returned. Sir John's narrative is animated by post-Crusades geopolitical desire in which the Christian glories of the past will be manifest again, finally and triumphantly in the future; such desire itself draws on a spatiotemporal mix of distance and hope. But even as anxiety about "the Iewes" at the end of time is registered toward the end of the book, so is there an undercurrent of unfulfillment running through the book, through fountain and rivers: on the scale of Sir John's own life course the marvelous promise of Christian temporalities proves frustrating.

FOREVER YOUNG?

Playing out proximity and distance, attraction and repulsion on an everyday scale, Sir John in the course of his travels looks and inquires, but tends to stay aside and keep aloof. He eagerly reports an enormous number of sights as he passes from one land to the next—cynocephali, magnetic waters, hippopotami, and so on and so forth—but rarely participates in or partakes of what is before him. Entering the Vale Perilous in the one encounter in which he registers deeply felt threat, he is careful not to touch the deceptive treasure or deviate from his devotion; despite being thrown and beaten down he and his companions emerge inviolate and unscathed (ch. 32, pp. 188–89). Even when he joins the army of the sultan of Egypt and dwells with him "a gret while," Sir John remains fundamentally apart, so that when the sultan offers him a great prince's daughter in marriage (so intimate is he with the sultan) Sir John declines, refusing to convert from Christianity to Islam (ch. 6, p. 21, ll. 20–24). He serves the Great Khan for fifteen months in war against the King of Mancy in order, as he says, to see if the court is as noble as he heard it was—just gathering materials, as it were, for his book.

But at that fountain in Polombe Sir John nonetheless drinks—three or four times: "I haue dronken there of .iij. or .iiij. sithes & yit me thinketh I fare the better."[22] Sir John's tone in this passage is, as usual, measured: he has come upon the mythical and sought-after Fountain of Youth and even has tasted it, but he reports his adventure in a most understated way.[23] He establishes first that drinking the water thrice heals you and then that drinking often makes you look younger; though he does seem to feel the healing properties, he himself has not drunk often enough to look younger. Moreover, he claims only that regular drinkers *look* younger ("thei semen all weys yonge") not that they necessarily *are* younger. Some people — and not necessarily he — say this is the Fountain of Youth, he diligently reports, issuing from Paradise. And though the well is said to flow from Paradise, it does not confer immortality: in the Egerton version, in fact, Sir John remarks that he supposes he will feel better until the day he dies.[24]

Magical fountains do all kinds of amazing things in ancient myth and folklore, of course. A quick look at Stith Thompson's *Motif-Index of Folk-Literature* just begins to reveal the variety of legendary materials, secular as well as religious, that form the broader context of Mandeville's work: there are fountains that render a person invisible, fountains that cause storms, fountains from which issue many other effects. Among the fountains that affect the ordinary temporality of human life there is also a range. There are fountains that endow the drinker with immortality: for these we need look no further than biblical materials, both the Hebrew, Psalm 35, on the one hand, and the Greek, Revelation 22, on the other, to find the "living water that gives everlasting life."[25] There are fountains that resuscitate: the *Gesta romanorum* recounts a tale in which a Roman emperor's son seeks out a garden with a well of life, which brings back several dead men.[26] There are wells that extend human life: Herodotus reports that long-lived Ethiopians, whose life span was one hundred twenty years, bathe in a fountain from which they emerge oil-smooth and fragrant. There are fountains that rejuvenate, metaphorically (bringing a return of manly strength, say, that enables marriage and procreation) or literally (turning back the clock so that a one-hundred-year-old man is thirty again).[27] And marvelous fountains at the sites of Christian martyrdoms in England may have grounded the fictive Sir John's imagination of miraculous wellsprings.[28]

All these transformative possibilities bubble in Sir John's fountain. Invigoration, rejuvenation, resuscitation, extended life, immortality are sometimes combined, sometimes confused in various legends; the concepts are after all closely related.[29] Mandeville's direct source for this passage in his *Book* is the twelfth-century *Letter of Prester John* in which the fountain, in India, is identified as the Fountain of Youth and explicitly associated with the Christian living waters: it heals any infirmity and — with notable specificity — keeps the drinker as if *thirty-two years old* (the prime of life) for as long as he lives.[30] But in fact all the source material on which Mandeville draws mixes and blends a range of temporal effects on the body, literal and metaphorical. Alexander the Great, in the mass of legendary materials elaborated around him, is said to have come to India to seek the well of life but found instead apples that granted Hindus a four-hundred-year life span.[31] In the *Roman d'Alexandre*, another of Mandeville's twelfth-century sources, Alexander finds the fountain that restores people to thirty years of age, actually reversing the stream of time.[32] Charlemagne legends, geographically far flung, also include episodes at the fountain: the chanson de geste *Huon de Bordeaux* splits the effects between the Fountain of Youth (which heals) and an apple tree growing beside the fountain that turns back the clock (which makes an eighty- or one-hundred-year-old man as young as thirty again).[33]

In his account of his experience, by specifying this legendary fountain as such, Sir John puts himself in the company of those legendary people. He thus entertains the wish that his life course, with its expected trajectory from health to sickness, could be slightly altered. Of course he could have tossed off this comment about having drunk of the well merely to bolster his claim to authentic traveler status; it would in that case function like his other claims to have seen relics or wonders, like the head (in Constantinople) of the spear that allegedly pierced Christ on the cross or the magnetic sea (ch. 2, p. 9; ch. 31, p. 180). But I hear something additional here: his brief remark about the drink's effects — "still I feel I'm doing better" — not only acknowledges the legend but also expresses an aspirational belief in — a desire for — a shift in his lot. A few sips of this fountain, whose source reputedly is the Earthly Paradise, might have slowed the relentless effects of time in his life. It could indeed happen, he is saying, in fact I believe it did: his ordinary earthly temporality has been touched, just slightly wetted, by the waters issuing from Eden.

BACK TO THE GARDEN

We turn finally to the well's putative source in Eden, the Earthly Paradise. Sir John has already told the story of the paradise created in India by the Old Man of the Mountain: he keeps maidens and young men under the age of fifteen years there and promises such youthfulness to anyone who dies in his (homicidal) service. This paradise offers perpetual youth but is patently false (ch. 31, p. 184, l. 35–p. 186, l. 33). But the real Earthly Paradise is the source of the fountain from which Sir John drank.

The *Letter of Prester John* specifies, "It changes its taste every hour by day and night, and is scarcely three days' journey from Paradise, whence Adam was expelled" [*Variatur autem sapor eius per singulas horas diei et noctis, et progreditur itinere dierum trium non longe a paradiso, unde fuit*

Adam prothoplastus expulsus]: the happy powers of the fountain, precisely clocked in earthly time, are almost overwhelmed in that sentence by the grievous historical significance of Eden.[34] Expulsion is the key element in the myth of the Garden: loss is Eden's affective core, in the Mandeville book as well as in the *Letter of Prester John*. Humans cannot get to Eden now, and could not enter without God's special grace even if they could reach it, it is so off-limits to mortals. But that wrenching postlapsarian fact of life remains: paradise is *on earth*. Connected to the rest of the world by the four rivers that issue forth from it but distinctly set off from the rest of the orb, it is a place powerfully "present," Scafi asserts, "in its very loss."[35]

A powerful mix of presence and absence, nearness and distance characterizes the treatment of Eden in the *Book of John Mandeville*. Beyond the far-flung Prester John's Land there is a desert of darkness. Even beyond that, finally at the round earth's imagined corner, is the terrestrial Paradise: "And that desert & that place of derknesse duren [*extend*] fro this cost [*edge*] vnto paradys terrestre, where that Adam oure formest fader & Eue weren putt that dwelleden there but lytyll while [*where Adam our first father and Eve were put who dwelled there but a little while*], And that is towardes the EST at the begynnynge of the erthe" (ch. 34, p. 201, ll. 31–35). Time begins in this Garden — our first parents stayed there only a "lyttyl while," as Sir John, following Augustine in the *City of God*, says. Augustine doesn't specify exactly how long the couple was there, but he does insist that human history started here with Adam's creation, and maintains that the little while in question was not time enough for procreation.[36] Later exegetes get much more specific: Dante, following Peter Comestor, famously has the couple stay there only a bit more than six hours, and Sir John himself earlier had noted in his book that Adam was put into Paradise and left it on the same day.[37] But Sir John's "little while" in this sentence also recalls that resonant phrase from the Gospels that we considered in chapter 1: in the sermon on that Gospel phrase, "a little while" betokens both a measurable time in Christ's life on earth and also the boundlessness of eternity. It is complicated: that "little while" in the sermon is a mundane, linear time that touches on eternity.

The character of time in the Garden of Eden is similar. It was in fact contested among early exegetes. What *would* time be, in this place — this "'nowhere' that [is] 'somewhere,'" as Scafi puts it, a locale that is "different from the rest of this world" but "part of real geography," utterly separated from the rest of the world yet tightly connected to it?[38] Isidore of Seville maintained in his *Etymologiae* that it doesn't have seasons but contains real plants.[39] Augustine had argued for the existence of mundane, historical time in this place; but in the era of the earlier commentator Eusebius, Adam and Eve's time in the Garden was thought *not* to move in the usual sublunar way.[40] Augustine's view was vastly preferred by commentators and mapmakers through the medieval period, yet the puzzling nature of Edenic temporality—the earthly mixing with the divine—still remained in legends from the twelfth and fourteenth centuries, wherein time in Eden is shown indeed to pass (the Earthly Paradise is not eternal) but pass *differently* from all other earthly time.[41]

Thus the fourteenth-century Italian legend in which three monks are vouchsafed entrance to Eden and actually experience firsthand its extraordinary temporality, finding that time passes much more slowly in the Garden.[42] Let me turn to this legend for a moment, both because it makes an interesting comparison with other asynchrony stories we've read in chapter 1 and because it gives a keen impression of Edenic time and the kind of desire that reaches its fulfillment in such extraordinary temporality. In a convent beside the river Gihon (one of the four rivers issuing from Paradise), three monks lived a holy life. One day a marvelous bough drifted downstream while they were bathing, and they purposed to find its sacred origin. After a yearlong upward journey, they reached the gates of the earthly Paradise, guarded by an angel of the Cherubim; they contemplated his dazzling beauty for five days and five nights. And that is the end of mundane time for them; they are admitted to the Garden, whose chronology is completely different. Upon entering they see and hear the most delightful things: heavenly music, a "living spring," the Tree of Good and Evil, the Tree of Salvation, the tree of glory, other wondrous fountains and trees. They are led through this dazzling place by Enoch and Elias; eventually these two take the monks back to the gates and tell them to return to their convent.

Lo and behold, it's "The Monk and the Bird" all over again. "O Sirs," say the monks, "have mercy upon us! We beseech you, vouchsafe to let us tarry fifteen days here!" "Therewith they wept and wailed and fell on their knees, and said to those holy fathers: 'We have not yet been eight days here!' Then they made answer: 'Ye have been here seven hundred years.'"[43] The comparison to earthly chronology is made explicit: Edenic time passes much more slowly, eight days in Paradise equaling seven hundred earth years. Both chronologies are intelligible to Enoch and Elias. Having experienced this temporal bounty, the monks want eternity: they apprehend that the delights of the Earthly Paradise are an inkling of what is to come in the kingdom of heaven, and they want to go there. But being human they must return to earthly life; Enoch and Elias send them back to their convent: "Go now with God's grace, and in a brief space ye shall come to that realm of eternal life."[44]

As in "The Monk and the Bird," once they return to their former monastery, a book must be consulted in order for the three monks to be identified properly. Of course all their human companions there are long, long gone. Again, the comparison with mundane time is sharp: the books record the exact "hour and day and month and year" of their departure. And then after forty days they turn to dust and enter the eternity of heaven.[45] The persistent comparison of earthly and Edenic times befits the locale of the Earthly Paradise: for Edenic time is an earthly time that is, after all, different from earthly time. And so, even though their asynchrony back at the monastery plays out in the same way as that of the aged monk I discussed in chapter 1, it does draw attention to something different: it is not the eternal joy of heaven itself they have experienced, though they have seen something that gives a sense of the eternal. Paradoxically both mundane and not, their mortal experience takes them beyond all mortal bounds.

Crucially, in this legend we learn that in the Garden the three monks have drunk from the Fountain of Youth. Hearing about the vast amount of time that has passed since they entered the Garden, the monks ask, "'How can it be that we have been here seven hundred years? for we seem to be of that same age whereof we were when we came hither.' Then said the holy fathers, 'Ye have eaten of the fruit of that tree which suffreth not old age, and ye have drunken of the sacred water of the Fountain of Youth, and have dwelt in this most holy place wherein ye have heard somewhat of the glory of eternal life.'"[46] Beside the fruit tree it is much like the fountain in *Huon de Bordeaux*, "a living spring, whereof whoso drinketh can never grow old, and whosoever is already old, he turneth to the age of thirty years."[47] But this spring's powers are not limited by the cautious voice of Sir John: they stop time, they even turn back the clock, they touch on eternity itself. This spring, that is, *works*.

It is no surprise, then, that Sir John would want to experience Paradise. In his travels he has seen just about everything else on earth. He has already tasted the fountain outside the Garden, in India; he is now ready for the ultimate earthly experience. And he has finally reached the gates of Eden near the end of his long narrative, so now is his chance. Paradise is the highest place on earth, he points out, so high that it escaped Noah's flood; it is encircled by a strange mossy wall with an entrance enclosed by fire, "so that noman that is mortall ne dar not entren" [*so that no mortal man dare enter*] (ch. 34, p. 202, l. 27). Sir John's description focuses on the perilous landscape rather than the ferocious angels guarding the gates. In fact, there are no angelic guards at all.[48] Instead, forbidding natural features remove Eden from mortal reach. Many humans have tried to navigate the treacherous waters of the four rivers that issue from Eden — wild beasts and impassable mountains make an overland journey impossible, he notes — and have ended up blind, deaf, dead. Sir John's description of the attempts of "grete lordes" to row to Paradise is particularly vivid, lingering on the auditory hazards of any attempt: not only are the waves enormous but also "the water roreth so & maketh so huge noyse & so gret tempest that noman may here other [*no man can hear another*] in the schipp, though he cryede [*cried*] with all the craft that he cowed [*could*] in the hieste voys [*highest voice*] that he myghte . . . And manye dyeden for weryness [*died of weariness*] of rowynge ayenst tho stronge wawes [*against those strong waves*], And many of hem becamen blynde [*became blind*] And many deve [*deaf*] for the noyse of the water" (ch. 34, p. 203, l. 30–p. 204, l. 3). Without a special dispensation from God, "no mortell man may approche to that place" (ch. 34, p. 203, l. 30–p. 204, l. 4).

Paradise is close. It just about roars in his ears. So even though he dutifully, doctrinally, acknowledges that he is not worthy of Paradise on earth — because he, as a mortal, has not been purged and glorified — and he admits that he has not been there, Sir John sounds a frustrated note: "Of paradys ne can I not speken propurly for I was not there; it is fer beyonde & that forthinketh me. And also I was not worthi" [*Of Paradise I cannot speak properly for I was not there; it is far away and that displeases me. And also I was not worthy*] (ch. 34, p. 202, ll. 10–12). The syntax here is striking. In the Egerton version the affect expressed is more obvious: "Off Paradys can I noght speke properly, for I hafe noght bene thare; and that forthinkez me" [*Of Paradise I cannot speak properly, for I have not been there and that displeases me*].[49] But here it is the very location of Paradise that galls him: "Paradise is far away and *that grieves, vexes, bothers, angers me.*" Eden is on earth, and thus Sir John should be able to visit it; but he cannot, and the traveler backs away, ending his narrative not with this furthest place on earth but with a pedestrian account of Tibet and other lands surrounding the land of Prester John. His curiosity, his attraction, indeed his desire has overwhelmed the requisite theological resignation.

That sentence about Eden is an odd one. Sir John's remark is in fact a bit unusual for a traveler. Scafi maintains that "none of the earlier, thirteenth-century travelers," including Odoric of Pordenone, Mandeville's major source for the second half of his book, "ever suggested that they had actually seen (or had wanted to see) the Garden of Eden itself. . . . Paradise could be approached in the visionary or mystical literature, but throughout the Middle Ages up to the Renaissance there was never a real claim made to have seen the Garden of Eden, or hope to see it, at first hand."[50] Medieval travelers and geographers understood that Eden existed as a real place but was off-limits to mortals, period. Mandeville's comment here is not a "real claim," no, but neither is it an expression of visionary or mystical desire; in combination with the experience at the Fountain of Youth, where Sir John briefly entertains the possibility of a different, more pleasurable temporality of life on earth, I understand the remark to express a moment of irritation with the Western Christian myth of Eden itself—with its insistence on Eden's hauntingly present absence, with the unavailability of its delights, including its marvelously slowed-down temporality. The final, thumping anticlimax of the book—Sir John does not end his narrative on the verge of Paradise—may be Sir John's way of further signaling his impatience with the myth of inaccessible Eden. Sir John is barred from the unearthly earthliness of Eden. Its unique and lovely temporality, a time that fostered an original human state that was not progressively degenerative, is withheld from him. It is truly a lost time: not only a past era that is gone but also a temporality that he will never on earth know. And that frustrates, grieves, angers him.

Sir John in his book expresses more desire than other travelers to go beyond the theologically imposed limitations of mortal experience, even as his body, eventually creaky and old, stays stubbornly on its forward path. He unwillingly ends his travels because he is plagued by disease, but the temporal desire in his book still radiates forth. In fact, Sir John finally suggests that the act of reading the book might itself put into play a certain asynchrony. At the end of his long narrative he asks readers to pray for him, and he promises to pray for them. Those who pray for him he makes "parteneres" of his pilgrimages and all good deeds that he has done or will do, and grants them "part" of all those activities: his readers, that is, get the spiritual benefits of going on a pilgrimage simply by reading and praying. Indeed, from the twelfth century reading had been associated with spiritual pilgrimage, metaphorical movement in Christian space-time.[51] If this final suggestion mitigates Sir John's frustration, the desire for another kind of time in the book recurs in much later readers. As we shall see, the act of reading the *Book of John Mandeville* proved to be temporally complex indeed in nineteenth-century Britain, when the first serious philological studies of the text were undertaken. If Sir John at the end of his travels expresses frustration with the inaccessibility of Eden, forever lost, readers of the book in Victorian England find in it a vehicle to express their own melancholy for the glories of a lost time.

AMATEURS, PHILOLOGY, AND BRITISH INDIA

HENRY YULE, A.K.A. MARCO POLO

The appeal of Sir John's travel narrative proved enduring: it circulated in more than two hundred fifty manuscripts from the era of its composition — the mid-fourteenth century — until the end of the fifteenth century, was translated into all the major vernacular languages and then some (Danish, Czech, Irish), and its relatively steady publication history thereafter continues unabated. But the luster of its author dimmed considerably when nineteenth-century British scholars determined that Sir John was likely not the eyewitness traveler he had claimed — and they had taken him — to be: under their probing philological eyes the book turned out to be made up of many previous texts.[52] Uncertainties that had simmered softly for centuries boiled over: was "Sir John Mandeville" a knight, as claimed in the narrative? Was "Mandeville" even the writer's name? Was he English, again as claimed? Had he traveled anywhere at all? Samuel Purchas in 1625 had registered some doubt about the book as he trumpeted Mandeville as next to Marco Polo "the greatest Asian Traveller that ever the World had" while he blamed someone else for riddling the volume with fables.[53] Robert Burton in *The Anatomy of Melancholy* (1621) had waved away Sir John Mandeville's "lies"; Sir Thomas Browne had more moderately noted in *Pseudodoxia Epidemica* (1646) that the book might be received "in some acceptions of morality, and to a pregnant invention may afford commendable mythology, but . . . it containeth impossibilities, and things inconsistent with truth."[54] But the full indignation of nineteenth-century editors exceeded these accusations: Colonel (later Sir) Henry Yule in 1866 refers to Mandeville's "wholesale robberies."[55]

The extensive use in the book of source materials for allegedly personal experiences was zealously documented by Yule in the *Encyclopaedia Britannica* in 1883. To "the unveracious Maundevile," Yule had earlier made clear, he preferred "truthful Marco," Polo, that is, whose own book of travels Yule edited in a weighty two-volume work.[56] In fact, Yule's preference for the Italian explorer — "the companion of many pleasant and some laborious hours, whilst I have been contemplating with him ('*vôlti a levante*') that Orient in which I also had spent years not a few" — shaded into profound identification: not only did he often sign his own journalism as "MARCUS PAULUS VENETUS" or "M.P.V," but even his daughter was identified once when travelling in Russia as "Mademoiselle Marco Paulovna."[57] For Yule himself had traveled: he began his career in India as a Bengal Engineer, eventually to become Secretary to Government for Public Works, traveling widely in the region and responsible in part for, among other things, the introduction of the narrow gauge railroad over a swath of the subcontinent.[58] What he understood Marco Polo to be doing in the thirteenth century — traveling, mapping, creating access for others, disseminating information — Yule saw himself undertaking in the mid-nineteenth.

Yule's indignant cross-temporal *dis*identification with Mandeville was comically dramatized by essayist Andrew Lang a few years later. In an 1886 "letter," one of his satirical *Letters to Dead Authors*, Lang addressed "Sir John Manndeville, Kt." himself, bluntly accusing Mandeville of being a liar and a fake, and contrasting him with the real thing in the realm: Henry Yule, who had indeed actually seen the land of Prester John. Lang's "Letter" begins:

> Sir John, — Wit you well that men holden you but light, and som clepen you a Liar. And they say that you never were born in Englond, in the town of Seynt Albones, nor have seen and gone through manye diverse Londes. And there goeth an old knight at arms, and one that connes Latyn, and hath been beyond the sea, and hath seen Prester John's country. And he hath been in an Yle that men clepen Burmah, and there bin women bearded. Now men call him Colonel Henry Yule, and he hath writ of thee in his great booke, Sir John, and he holds thee but lightly. For he saith that ye did pill your tales out of Odoric his book, and that ye never saw snails with shells as big as houses, nor never met no Devyls, but part of that ye say, ye took it out of William of Boldensele his book, yet ye took not his wisdom, withal, but put in thine own foolishness.[59]

Mandeville's fault, according to Lang here, was in taking up the stance of having really been there. In this Yule bests him: Yule has seen the marvelous reality of which Mandeville has only read. Yule actually did report on a "bearded" woman of Burma (now Myanmar), complete with an illustrative plate, in his *Narrative of the Mission Sent by the Governor-General of India to the Court of Ava in 1855*.[60] Andrew Lang's letter sets up a glaring contrast to Mandeville: *Yule* is the traveler with the unvarnished tale; *he* has written the "great booke"; he *is* Marco Polo.

The temporalities are intriguing in this whole imagined scenario. To begin with the obvious: Marco Polo is taken as a prefiguration of the English colonialist; medieval travel is made out to be the prehistory of nineteenth-century colonization. Time moves inexorably forward in the West, from medieval to modern, in the inevitable progress that is colonial expansion. But in eastern places such as Burma, time moves at a different pace, or doesn't move at all: in Lang's letter, the modern colonel has seen the lands that still seem to be in the Middle Ages, filled as they are with wonders and marvels. This temporal situation exemplifies what Johannes Fabian has called the "denial of coevalness": colonialist space-time maps geography on a timeline, so that India in the nineteenth century is seen to be at the stage of development reached by England in the thirteenth century. That is, India is in the Middle Ages while England has developed into modernity.[61] Yule has traveled East, and has thus traveled back in time.

But the affective thrust of Lang's letter and Yule's own pseudonym complicates this temporal distancing. If the East is medievalized, so is Yule. Henry Yule is swept back into the Middle Ages, whence also the "Middle English" voice of Andrew Lang comes. Yule is seen by Lang as, and feels himself to be, a contemporary of the medieval man, his comrade and friend.[62] In the work of the British civil servant and leisure-time philologist Yule, we hear the affectionate discourse of the amateur: Sir John may have been rejected, but Marco is embraced as a boon companion. Love for this friend as well as a desire for the past have motivated the temporal reversal. But as we've seen before, nostalgia works in complex ways: "European colonial commentary" is engaged in "analytical distancing on the one hand — the denial of coevalness to India — and affective identification on the other," as Ananya Jahanara Kabir and Dipesh Chakrabarty have both seen. The temporalities of this "paradoxically intimate otherness" are complex, particularly for the imperial philologist.[63] If, in the reading of the Mandeville book in the first section of this chapter, we have understood Sir John's relationship with Eastern others to be absorbed into his overall view of the once and future Christianization of the world, we shall see something different here: an ambivalence that includes both assertion of imperial superiority and melancholy for what has already passed.

ANDREW LANG, "DIVINE AMATEUR"

Andrew Lang, the well-connected, later-nineteenth-century man of letters, highly educated but not an academic—he was a journalist, novelist,
poet, translator, literary critic, folklorist, and retailer of fairy tales—found
plenty both to ridicule and to love in the *Book of John Mandeville*.[64] Re-
hearsing Henry Yule's accusations that Sir John was a liar and a thief who
ransacked "Odoric his book" and "William of Boldensele his book," he
not only implies that armchair travel is a pathetic imitation, but he also
endorses Yule's assessment that Mandeville is something of a fool: "For he
saith that . . . part of that ye say, ye took it out of William of Boldensele
his book, yet ye took not his wisdom, withal, but put in thine own fool-
ishness."[65] Nevertheless, Lang at last softens, citing "the frailty of Man-
kynde," and seems to join others who hold Sir John to be "a good fellow,
and a merry": "so now, come," he says to his medieval addressee, "I shall
tell you of the new ways into Ynde" (111). Thereupon Lang asynchronously
informs Mandeville of the recent development of the British Empire, cul-
minating in its arrival in India. Lang, self-professed amateur when it came
to reading the medieval text (he insisted he read Malory only for pleasure,
for example) and whom Oscar Wilde dubbed "divine" as amateur because
of the quality of his prose, took a kind of pleasure in Mandeville that Yule
seems not to have been able to (and that Hamelius scorned); his voice af-
fectionately merges with Sir John's.[66]

Lang's letter, updating Sir John on the British Empire's historical
progress toward securing the way to India, is an explicit exercise in amateur medievalism as Orientalism. In a "Middle English" voice that paro-
dically echoes Sir John's—with a tone that is uncannily true to the medieval one—Lang casts his eye on the India of the 1880s and renders his
observations with the kind of rational understatement that we recognize
from the *Book of John Mandeville* itself: "In that Lond they have a Queen
that governeth all the Lond, and all they ben obeyssant to her. And she is
the Queen of Englond; for Englishmen have taken all the Lond of Ynde."
Invoking astrology (as used in the book itself) to justify the English inclination to travel, "for to go diverse ways, and see strange things, and other
diversities of the Worlde"—which apparently describes the impulse to
colonize, too—Lang uses the bulk of the letter to describe routes to India:
"Fro Englond men gon to Ynde by many dyverse Contreyes" (112).

His itinerary accounts for the English imperial conquest of (or at least
bid for) each point on the way to India. "First come they to Gibraltar, that

was the point of Spain, and builded upon a rock; and there ben apes, and
it is so strong that no man may take it. Natheless did Englishmen take it
fro the Spanyard, and all to hold the way to Ynde. . . . And at Famagost is
one of the principal Havens of the sea that is in the world, and Englishmen
have but a lytel while gone won that Yle from the Sarazynes" (112–13). The
itinerary reports the current geopolitical state of "the way to Ynde": Famagost is reputed by some Englishmen to be too hot and barren, but other
Englishmen — those who are proper "werryoures" — "dwell there in tents"
to keep themselves fresh. Egypt is the very "Vale perilous" (114), ruin of
reputations and sink of many British pounds sterling; Muscovy, through
which is an alternate route to India, is held by competitors for India who
compete for the affection of the Emir of the Afghauns and might indeed
make war on the English.

The language of the medieval past is the medium Lang uses to legiti-
mate the geopolitics of empire. His letter is a witty epistolary exercise in
literary criticism with an explicitly political edge. Lang reads the *Book of
John Mandeville* as proto-imperialist, a reading that is not completely un-
founded, given its dominant Christian space-time scheme, as we've seen,
and its admonitions to Christians to take back the Holy Land. Lang's Sir
John is a knight of the Empire even if he has not gone anywhere, and his
book is a stylistic, rhetorical guide to empire: Lang determines that the
British Empire realizes the project of Mandeville, fulfills the past in a glorious neomedieval present. But at the same time Lang suggests in contrast
that the true glories of the Empire have already been lost: at the outset of
his letter, right after the introduction of the Queen of England and India,
he identifies a new generation of meager people who would squander the
imperial gains of old. Informing Sir John of events that postdate his own
book, Lang notes that the Englishmen who conquered India were great
knights indeed:

> For they were right good werryoures of old, and wyse, noble, and worthy.
> But of late hath risen a new sort of Englishman very puny and fearful, and
> these men clepen Radicals. And they go ever in fear, and they scream on
> high for dread in the streets and the houses, and they fain would flee away
> from all that their fathers gat them with the sword. And this sort men call
> Scuttleres, but the mean folk and certain of the womenkind hear them
> gladly, and they say ever that Englishmen should flee out of Ynde. (111–12)

Lang is thus not only fondly backward looking but is melancholy about the
Empire: the loss of India would be a deep threat to England as it under-

stands itself historically. The real imperial warriors are already gone, and with them go the English Middle Ages they so heroically recovered in the East.

The use of amateur "Middle English" here in the voice of Mandeville indicates a complex amalgam of absence and presence, progressive superiority on the one hand and affective identification and desire on the other. You can hear the push-pull even in the mock benediction of this letter that brings up as pitiful the old-age ailments I discussed above: "may the Seyntes hele thee, Sir John, of thy Gowtes Artetykes, that thee tormenten. But to thy Boke I list not to give no credence" (118). If the medieval past is recovered and played out in the Eastern present, as the imperial asynchrony would have it, even so it also can be lost with the East, as Lang's melancholy witnesses. Such affective identification makes it impossible to "disentangle completely colonial and metropolitan intellectual developments"; this structure is characteristic of British imperial attitudes, as Ananya Jahanara Kabir has eloquently argued.[67] What I want to emphasize in this affective structure is the idea that the amateur medievalist — not only "divine amateur" Lang as he addresses Sir John here, but also colonial administrator and leisure-time philologist Yule — has a special relationship to imperial asynchrony. For him, the medieval is not a merely analytical, distanced construct, and medievalism is not simply a medium of distanciation; the medieval is also an affective reality, a presence, whose conflation with and manifestation in the East infuses already complex colonial affect and temporality with especially keen desire.

M. R. JAMES AND GERMANIC PHILOLOGY

A year after Andrew Lang's "Letter" was published in his *Letters to Dead Authors* yet another parody of the *Book of John Mandeville* appeared in England — perhaps because of the influence and notoriety of Yule's work on the book. And this time the Germanic school of comparative philology was the butt, or at least one of the butts, of the joke. In 1887 M. R. James, eventually to become an eminent manuscript scholar himself, wrote a merciless parody of the voice of the philologist. Two years beyond his undergraduate days and just elected Fellow of King's College, Cambridge, he was "mending up" his Fellowship dissertation on the Apocalypse of Peter when he conceived of the idea to create a fake, "lost" chapter of the *Book of John Mandeville*.[68] James, a precocious scholar educated at Eton and King's, had already published scholarly articles as well as formulated an extraordinarily ambitious project; he would go on to catalogue the manuscript collections in the Cambridge University Library and the older colleges, in addition to taking on other estimable editorial projects and administrative posts (as provost of King's and finally of Eton).[69] But his scholarly pursuits never precluded more imaginative and self-reflexive engagements: James would become known not only for his voluminous scholarship on ancient and medieval texts and artifacts but also, and much more widely, for his ghost stories, often featuring antiquarians and their medieval objects of preoccupation.[70] In this amateur fiction (built around protagonists who were for the most part "stand-ins for himself," expressing a strong affective bond to his objects of study) written "at long intervals" mostly as holiday entertainments, James reflected deeply and critically on his own professional preoccupations as manuscript scholar, philologist, archaeologist.[71] So the short parodic piece of juvenile writing to which I shall now turn, brief and written merely as a lark, is nonetheless indicative of James's complex engagement with the medieval.

In a slim satirical pamphlet entitled *Athens in the Fourteenth Century: An Inedited Supplement to Sir John Maundeville's Travels. Published from the Rhodes MS. No. 17, by Prof. E. S. Merganser*, James assumes the voice of "Professor Merganser"—a merganser is a large duck—introducing a critical edition of a heretofore unknown "extra chapter" of *Sir John Maundeville's Travels*. The fragment was supposedly discovered in a privately held manuscript. In germanically clotted English the Professor begins his "Foreword":

> I shall from the upset beg to excuse me, for all these that through misluck and an over-weening forknowledge of the English speech mistakenhoods may befall me, my good-heart readers. Ever must my plea of an amateur be that I have in my studies of the foresaid only so far as the early twelfth yearhundreds beginning bestrided. And this last, is it from our today's times forgettinghood or our much to be bewailed speechshapelearningness's unwisdomship, is to a nineteenth yearhundred period's togethergatheringreceivingsaloon sad unbefitted. Man can hope, the alltimes speechshape will not long—

At this point the "Foreword" breaks off, and a bracketed section follows: "[A temporary indisposition will not allow of Prof. Merganser's completing this sentence; and as he is anxious that his work should go to press as soon as may be, I have undertaken to finish this preface for him, and to supply some little information as to the MS. he used, of which I am the possessor. . . .]" The rest of the bracketed section, signed by "George J. Barker," includes a brief description of the manuscript's physical characteristics as well as contents — shades of James's later scholarly specialty, manuscript description, as Nicholas Rogers observes — and then two short paragraphs of comment.[72] In the first the manuscript's genealogical descent and theological tendencies are noted in a sharp mockery of textual editing:

> The Professor wishes me to say that in his opinion this extra chapter belongs to the "Group B[1] of South-Eastern English Recensions which the so-called Maundeville underwent between the years 1397 and 1399 at the hands of a group of littérateurs of a quasi-archaistic tendency." He discovers in it a decided opposition to the doctrines of the Lollards, and an equally strong bias in favour of the Sacrament of Extreme Unction: both are deduced from the silence of the writer.[73]

The second paragraph of the section remarks on the importance of the manuscript's "description of the Parthenon, then comparatively intact."

The "text" itself (a page and a half) follows all these preliminary comments; it is a pitch-perfect parody of the prose style of "the so-be-called Sir John Maundevile" (238) — so perfect that it fooled the director of the Fitzwilliam Museum at Cambridge, or so James claimed. The text introduces the city of Athens, including an etymology of the name and the religious tendencies of its people, and details the friezes of the Parthenon (the Elgin Marbles in situ), noting that the sibyl prophetically determined the sculptural program, "And al thise ystories ben kytte in whyte stoon wondir fine": the ten plagues of Egypt, the worship of the golden Calf, "and myche matere of deuylles and nakyd men fyghtynge ech with other" (238); the wars of the Jews featuring Gideon, Judas Maccabaeus, and David; the Twelve Apostles, Our Lady, and so on. Because the patron saint Denis the Areopagite was beheaded, many statues were made intentionally headless, which confused one of Sir John's companions. There is indeed no mention of Lollardy or the Sacrament of Extreme Unction.

Beyond the peerless imitation of Mandeville, what interests me here is twofold: the ridicule of the explicitly amateur philologist, and the fact that the *Book of John Mandeville* is the occasion for it. On one level the philological parody is but a recognizable genre production, a jeu d'esprit of a prodigious young scholar steeped in medieval manuscripts; moreover, the parody might reflect a certain English pragmatism in the face of Germanic

theory as well as some English xenophobia to boot. "George J. Barker" is
a persona James created in his school days, eventually well known to his
friends;[74] here, he seems to be M. R. James the professional-in-the-making,
busily abjecting any traces of the amateur whom he competitively imagines as a Lachmannian bungler. "Barker" completes the task that the Professor sets out to do, and he sounds just like the descriptive bibliographer
James was to become: the list of contents seems lifted straight out of one
of James's catalogue entries. But the amateur's words remain there on the
page, and after some chuckles at them we might think about the effect of
their lingering presence. We have here a philologist who is just beginning
his researches and has not gotten past "the early twelfth yearhundreds"; he
is thus "amateur" because his studies are incomplete. But more abstractly,
perhaps James is suggesting that there is something always inexpert about
the philologist, that the philologist is ever amateur. Is it that the science
of philology is phony? (Thus the "evidence" of silence in the penultimate
paragraph.) Or is it too demanding ever to master? (Thus the overwhelming nature of "a nineteenth yearhundred period's togethergatheringreceiv-
ingsaloon.") Is it that philology is not actually realizable in modern times
(due to "our today's times forgettinghood or our much to be bewailed
speechshapelearningness's unwisdomship")? Might the suspicion be that
the "alltimes speechshape" can never be fully known or realized? And the
goal of reconstructing language forms that would demonstrate a definitive
connection between past times, past peoples, and the present must ever
recede? In the little drama of interrupted textual editing enacted here, is
philology itself seen not only as a medium of hopeful idealism but also as
a messenger of inevitable incompleteness and loss?[75]

James's ghost stories, his hobby fictions, offer darkly affirmative answers
to such questions. They take off from precisely the melancholy knowledge I
have inferred from the case of the amateur philologist. In "Canon Alberic's
Scrap-book," one of his best-known stories, a manuscript collector buys at
a bewilderingly cheap price a scrapbook of gorgeous rare pages, treasures
ripped out of medieval manuscripts. The seventeenth-century man who
compiled these magnificent fragments apparently dabbled in the dark arts
and seems to have been haunted by a hairy demon summoned by his own
black magic — but it seems equally plausible (given that James once wrote
of "the Malice of Inanimate Objects") that it is the manuscripts themselves
exacting their revenge for their own despoliation.[76] The latter-day collector is attacked by that hairy demon but manages, with the help of a cruci-

fix, to survive. These stories suggest that loss is not only inevitable but also must be accepted, that curiosity about or desire for the past can be dangerous: such curiosity and desire can not only threaten the stability of your affective and historical self-understanding and positioning but can in fact kill you. Ancient artifacts present a puzzle or abet a mystery that the antiquarian is driven to solve, but they also unleash a fury of malevolence and violence. As readers of these tales over the years have observed, causes and effects in these stories do not clearly add up. But as Michael Chabon maintains, we are left "utterly convinced that such an explanation is possible. . . . [James] makes us *feel* the logic of haunting, the residue of some inscrutable chain of ghostly causation, though we can't — though, he insists, *we never will be able to* — explain or understand that logic."[77] What we do know in these stories, though, is that the past is powerfully present in objects, and he who meddles with them can certainly come to regret doing so; the past is best left lost and obscure, lest its inexplicable and boundless malignity be loosed. Technologies of recovery — archaeology, philology, James's pursuits in his professional life — be damned.

Such a view of philology suggests its conceptual relation to the colonial endeavor, as Andrew Lang expresses it in his letter to Sir John Mandeville. Melancholy about inevitable incompleteness and loss links the colonial, the philological, and the amateur.[78] What James's stories add to this list is the queer in its specifically sexual aspect: desire for a different time, or a different kind of time, becomes all but explicitly, and certainly dangerously, sexualized. Antiquarian poking into the past brings his protagonists into contact with "loathsome" apparitions — "cool, fleshy, pink, protuberant, furred, toothed, or mouthed," as Chabon pointedly describes them.[79] In stories that James wrote from and about the homosocial world of nineteenth- and early-twentieth-century British academia, such apparitions reach out to touch, grab, hug. The past is the realm of sex — one apparition, summoned by a whistle found at the site of a Knights Templars' estate, takes its eerie, horrifying shape from rumpled bed linens, Chabon notes — and antiquaries' desire for that different time is revealed to be queer desire in its most specifically erotic sense. Imperial melancholy for inevitable loss turns into sexual horror at the possibility of recovery; asynchrony exposes possibilities and temptations that are both desirable and terrifying. Moreover, this view of the queerness of temporal desire in James's stories brings out, in retrospect, the queerness of Sir John's desire for another kind of time — his wish for another life course, for embodiment unburdened by the passage of time—as well as of the ambivalent affectivity of Yule's and Lang's connections to the past, crossing time and space to embrace boon companions and good fellows of yore.

ASYNCHRONY AND QUEERNESS

An ambivalence related to that in Andrew Lang's Orientalist amateur medievalist "Letter" is audible in Thomas Carlyle's emphatic essay from 1840, "The Hero as Poet." This is one of the lectures in the series that comprises his volume, *On Heroes, Hero-Worship, and the Heroic in History*. Carlyle, who was a member of the Society of Antiquaries of Scotland, knew Frederick James Furnivall (and Henry Yule joined the society's Honorary Fellows after Carlyle's death);[80] his lecture series precedes by a generation the high philological period on which I have been focusing, but in its affective contours this essay is nonetheless useful in limning colonial affect. Carlyle's lecture series discusses all the guises in which heroism has been manifested in the world—as divinity, as prophet, as priest, as king, and so on. "The Hero as Poet" is a vigorous and passionate discussion of the nature of the poet who, as Great Man, is Heroic warrior, Politician, Thinker, Legislator, and Philosopher.[81] He is touched by the Universal and unites his nation in a way that no mere human can. Dante and Shakespeare are Carlyle's two examples.[82] Shakespeare in particular, Carlyle asserts, is utterly invaluable to England in his ability to pull together Englishmen into a cultural nation, whether or not they live in England, whether or not the British colonies gain independence. To prove this assertion, Carlyle poses a hypothetical question:

> For our honour among foreign nations, as an ornament to our English Household, what item is there that we would not surrender rather than him [i.e., "Shakspeare"]? Consider now, if they asked us, Will you give up your Indian Empire or your Shakspeare, you English . . . ? Really it were a grave question. . . . but . . . Indian Empire, or no Indian Empire; we cannot do without Shakspeare! Indian Empire will go, at any rate, some day; but this Shakspeare does not go, he lasts forever with us; we cannot give up our Shakspeare![83]

Harish Trivedi points out that "more than mere rhetoric or whim" must have motivated this grand comparison, which balances "against each other in poignant mutual renunciation what were clearly in [Carlyle's] judgment the two greatest English glories ever."[84] The assertion of Shakespeare's timelessness (he is from the past, but "he lasts forever") brings out in contrast the merely temporary nature of the "Indian Empire," an empire weakened or tainted perhaps by the putative asynchrony that invited its subjugation in the first place.[85] This assertion drowns out the hint of melancholy about the inevitable loss of an India that is, as the past, already lost.

I learned about this essay from my father. I asked him some years ago what he read in his English literature classes at school in India. With a razor-sharp memory that instantly spanned the fifty-odd years in between, he listed the usual suspects in the early-twentieth-century British curriculum. And he mentioned with great gusto this essay by Carlyle, which he remembers to this day. His British instructor had presented it very memorably; this was during the Second World War, my dad reminded me, and while everyone was captivated by military heroes, here was a writer in stark contrast saying that poets could be heroes and sing for their country, too. *What country was yours, Dad?* I wondered internally. When I read him this passage about Shakespeare and Indian Empire, he laughed, saying he didn't remember it. This was many, many years ago, and that was not something he recalled.

Since I can hardly remember essays I read last semester, I certainly recognize that my explicit question about this passage—do you remember this?—makes quite a demand. But my implicit question was even more demanding and, I now think, unfair: how could you *stand* to read this? I don't know if my father caught my tone of postcolonial indignation; I hope he didn't. But the passage haunts me. I think of my father as a twenty-one year old at a British equivalent of junior college in what is now Pakistan, reading documents of alleged English cultural superiority, turning the pages with his pale Parsi hands, and I wonder: How did it feel to be living, acting out, performing someone else's past? What kind of present did that colonial chronology, that imperial asynchrony make for? I imagine these questions would not make much sense to my father, formulated in this way; after all, even as a colonial subject he had a direct connection to the place of his birth and history that the English could never achieve.[86] But what do I sense, if not that had he not left he would always have felt in a fundamental way behind the times?

The colonial encounter in fact promised a kind of time travel to good colonial subjects, to good Parsis in particular. This light-skinned Zoroastrian people arrived in India in the tenth century when (probably) fleeing persecution in their native Iran, where Muslim Arabs had taken over several centuries earlier. They were allowed to stay in Gujarat after they promised not to take up any room but to sweeten the lives of the native Gujaratis. These Persians were "industrious" and "took care of their own kind," the story goes, and when centuries later the British arrived the Parsis thrived: they were not Indian, after all, and could rise above an India seen as "almost . . . barbaric." [87] As one commentator puts it, some Parsis in the nineteenth century seem to have believed "that the British presence had enabled the basic qualities of Persian nobility to emerge from under the accretion of Hindu custom." [88] Parsis became "the most English-identified, westernized community on the subcontinent," disidentifying with Hinduism, embracing their difference as racial superiority, and seeing themselves as more European than Indian, indeed, "almost-English" gentlemen. Parsis were modern in a primitive land of Hindus. "The Parsis are the one race settled in India . . . that could for a moment be called white," wrote a Parsi in 1906: that "moment"—which makes the racial politics of this Orientalist timeline perfectly clear—was a temporality no less fantastic than the temporalities in the *Book of John Mandeville*, a fleeting instant in which imperial asynchrony synced up, in which the Eastern past was allowed to catch up and merge with the Western present. [89]

As my father said to me a few years ago as we were standing in Gandhi's house in Bombay (Mumbai), his family was "pro-British" even as they respected Gandhi as the father of the nation and knew it was time for the British to leave. My dad's paleness meant that he was often taken for an Anglo-Indian in India. His Parsiness, his not-Indianness, allowed him to claim as more or less his own the British culture that he prized. For a moment he was *almost* up to date. And once he came to the West, my father stepped altogether into what he saw as modernity and never looked back. Walking with me and my sister in Bombay as we visited India together, he shooed off hawkers and beggars in a brusque Hindi that seemed almost a physical reflex: the hawkers were stunned by the light-skinned American speaking so colloquially ("Nice Hindi!" one startled boy exclaimed) while I was stunned by this verbal—really, bodily—irruption of the past into the present.

India was in fact strangely past and present in our household in California, where he settled with my mother and where I was born and raised. My mother was born in Southern California of Midwestern, ultimately European, stock, and it was America, her native land and my father's adoptive

TEMPORALLY ORIENTED   103

home, that provided the infrastructure, ecology, atmosphere, and interior décor of our '60s suburban ranch house. But India flashed momentarily in brightly colored fragments, sparkling against the wall-to-wall carpet and floor-length drapes: dried mangos pressed with silver leaf that came in the mail from my grandparents, whom I never met; the ruby they gave for my father's marriage to my mother; her jewel-colored sari, bought on her first trip to India with my father when I was about eight; the blue airmail forms that would come with astonishing regularity from my grandfather, the letters signed "Cheerio, and God bless." Their regularity was astonishing because India seemed to me so backward, so far away and far behind my contemporary father, by then a naturalized United States citizen and Christian convert; how could it also be so continuous, so present?

Much of my work as medievalist has tried to answer that query or, more fundamentally, has tried to address the temporal questions that it begs. In the strange "time-knot" in which I grew up (that concept is from Dipesh Chakrabarty), the timeline of modernity stretched forward as the Santa Clara Valley transformed into Silicon Valley and orchards yielded to semi-conductors, even as there was braided therein a resilient strand of another kind of time.[90] My mother gave me my worker-bee desire for progress, my rigor and striving to move forward. My father of course was deeply invested in forward-moving progress, too, but he also brought another time-line unfolding on a different calendar: even the very day of his birth was a mystery, not because of sketchy documentation in his primitive birth-place, as I once thought, but because the Zoroastrian calendar differs from the Gregorian (the Parsi calendar has thirty days for each month), and so birthdays become moveable feasts in the latter. A different time frame was always subtly but definitely present. It meted out my forward strides a little out of step, a little behind "real" Americans: I was always playing a no-win game of catch up, a not-quite-white, naive beginner lagging behind their fully fledged expertise, a girl inappropriately attached to girls tagging along behind their forthrightly reproductive straight lives. It has made me keenly attuned to the ways cultural differences get turned into temporal distance, the ways sex, gender, race, religion and nation, work and play, West and East get graphed on a timeline. It has made me permanently feel like an amateur.

Thus I can see that geographical distance is temporalized in the *Book of John Mandeville*, for instance, and in British Orientalist discourse, and I can analyze such significance in terms of the writing of world history.

But I have a feel, too, for the kind of desire that Sir John feels — the desire to experience another kind of time, in the body and on earth — or that Henry Yule feels — the desire for the past. I understand, too, the fear of what that desire for the past might entail (like M. R. James's protagonists). I claimed earlier, in my analysis of the Seven Sleepers in chapter 1, that we all began life asynchronously, in a nine-month sleep, and that this experience provides us all with the ground for feeling that other temporalities press upon mundanely sequential chronologies; here, now, I have described how these other temporalities press upon me. If such desire lands James's characters in unspeakable, queer territory, I want to try to speak conceptually and analytically about what, exactly, is queer in a desire for the past. If my not-quite-white queerness makes me feel akin to amateurs I would like to use that sense of kinship as a prompt to consider different approaches to the text, to scholarship. The sense of the inevitability of incompleteness and loss that I have associated in this chapter with medieval travel as well as colonialism, amateurism, philology, and sexual queerness is ultimately useful in orienting me toward the ever-incomplete and unmasterable present. The unassimilable, the unmasterable have become my preoccupation, challenging formulations of Middle Ages and modernity as well as of progress and development, especially in the tightly intertwined realms of gender and sexuality, race, class, and nation.

Dipesh Chakrabarty notes that "the writing of history must implicitly assume a plurality of times existing together, a discontinuity of the present with itself." I insist on what Chakrabarty calls an "irreducible plurality in our own experiences of historicity."[91] My own queer diasporic experience, with its complicated time-knots of past and present, exemplifies this; it places me in the heterogeneity of the present and sensitizes me to its other times.[92] The rewards of living in such an asynchronous *now* are not guaranteed, as the possibilities can be terrifying and potentially lethal: so M. R. James warns and the witness of Indian Empire attests. But in opening different kinds of time such a *now* offers the possibility of a framework — not only for a more vital medievalist practice but also, precisely because of that nonmodern vibrancy, for more life.

THREE

In the Now

Margery Kempe, Hope Emily Allen, and Me

How does it feel to be asynchronous? In an episode, both riveting and typical, of her book the devout late medieval English laywoman Margery Kempe visits the grave of her loyal supporter and sometime confessor, Richard Caister of Norwich. She makes such a ruckus in the churchyard and then in front of the high altar — weeping, screaming, throwing herself to the ground and writhing in the extreme devotional practice that is her trademark — that people around her are completely annoyed. Suspecting her of "sum fleschly er erdly [*earthly*] affeccyon," these onlookers snarl, "What eylith the [*you*] woman? Why faryst thus wyth thi-self? We knew hym as wel as thu."[1] Among the backbiters Margery finds a sympathetic local woman and proceeds with her to her church. There Margery gets into yet another face-off with a believer less zealous than she: Margery sees an image of the Blessed Virgin Mary holding the dead Christ — a pietà — and is absolutely overcome by this sight: "And thorw [*through*] the beholdyng of that pete [pietà] hir mende was al holy ocupyed in the Passyon of owr Lord Ihesu Crist & in the compassyon of owr Lady, Seynt Mary, be [*by*] whech sche was compellyd to cryyn ful lowde [*loud*] & wepyn [*weep*] ful sor, as thei [*though*] sche xulde a [*would have*] deyd" (148). The good lady's priest holds a more distanced perspective, however: "Damsel," he says to the convulsed Margery, "Ihesu is ded long sithyn" [*Jesus is long since dead*] (148). Provoked by this dismissal, Margery responds to his cool detachment with a scorching rebuke: "Sir, hys deth is as fresch to me as [*as if*] he had deyd this same day, & so me thynkyth it awt [*ought*] to be to yow & to alle Cristen pepil. We awt euyr [*ever*] to han mende of hys kendnes [*kindness*] & euyr thynkyn of the dolful deth that he deyd for vs" (148).

In this striking confrontation, we hear a clash of temperaments, of estates, of spiritual commitments: the moist, restless, righteously angry laywoman versus the dry, satisfied, and complacent clergyman. This contrast is structured by Margery's point of view, of course, which produces the narration of this episode: it is all part of what has been called her "active propaganda," her angling for sainthood via her book.[2] But can a priest really have said that — "Jesus died a long time ago, young lady"?[3] How can Margery have even imagined such a confrontation?

Radically different experiences of time divide Margery from this cleric and inform the narrative construction of this episode. His words sound secular, almost incredibly so, but they are not necessarily as disenchanted as they might at first seem. Perhaps he is making the implicitly reassuring point, in the face of Margery's grief, that the Church (and he himself as the embodiment of that Church) has been able to conserve access to the body of Christ over the centuries. In the priest's world, time passes but the Church reclaims it; his words separate the past from the present but also assert that access to the past is possible in the present through the Church. His words brandish access to the past in an affirmation of institutional power. Margery, in his view, is a pathetic anachronism — a creature stuck in the past and not availing herself of the comforts that the Church can provide in a present otherwise defined by inexorable loss.

His is a temporal multiplicity tightly controlled by institutional structures. For Margery, in loud contrast, the point is immediate personal access to Christ now. The conflict with the priest in front of the pietà goes to her core and tests the immediate reality of her being. Her response is ethical and moral, focused in the *now* and distanced neither by institutional structures nor by the chronological time they seek to control. Her time, her present, her now, is invaded or infused by the other: the pietà out there becomes the pity in her. That's what it feels like to be asynchronous; she is a creature not merely in another time but rather with another time *in* her, as it were. No reading of this episode as a historical allegory of theological conflict, or as part of a chronological, periodizing narrative about the institution of Catholicism and the challenge of emergent Protestantism can account for this; revealing the shortcomings of periodization, a historical narrative that links her with holy women of the European continent such as Saint Catherine of Siena marks Margery as living in the wrong country and a generation late.[4] There's something about Margery that will not be assimilated into these paradigms; there's something out of joint.

This clash of temporalities — the priest's pragmatic observation of a progressive historical chronology, Margery's absorption in the everlasting *now* of divine eternity — is what piques my interest here. The narrative sequence of this chapter in Margery's book is in fact more disrupted than I have yet mentioned. By the end of the scene the prophecy that prompted Margery's visit to Norwich in the first place proves on her return home to Lynn to be true. That is, Margery has foreseen her current priest's recovery and goes to the grave of Richard Caister, her (past) priest confessor, in a gesture of thanks to God for that (future) recovery. In Margery's narrative world, past-present-future times are collapsed into a capacious *now* constituted of multiple times and attachments: the whole book is itself a memorial construction — dictated by Margery to several different scribes — in which not only chronological time but also thematic associations order the narrative sequence, and intensification (of themes, of Margery's own being) interrupts chronological progression.[5] Margery seems in this particular episode to inhabit a time zone, an asynchronous *now*, different from that of the other people whom she encounters in Norwich. Roaring and weeping when that priest approaches her, she does not stop her conniption just because of his remark that may well be an attempt at consolation. She takes her time, as it were: and "Whan hir crying was cesyd [*ceased*]," when she stops crying, when the pressure of Christ's presence subsides, then she rebukes the priest for his apparent indifference (148). It is as if she is in another temporal dimension even from the people who take her under their wings; others insist that Margery eat, others speak for her ("the good lady was hir auoket [*advocate*] and answeryd for hir," as if Margery is elsewhere), others take her as an "exampyl" (148).[6] They put her into, or connect her to, the stream of mundane, everyday life, out of which she has precipitated.

These complex temporal reckonings, and especially an expanded understanding of contemporaneity, the *now*, begin this investigation of the *Book of Margery Kempe* and nonmodern temporalities, not only the temporal encounters represented in the book but also the temporalities of readers' encounters with the book in turn. My hypothesis is that reading the book's multiple temporalities opens up temporal avenues for postmedieval readers in turn, but already we have encountered something like temporal bullying in the text itself. How can we, as readers of the *Book of Margery Kempe*, avoid recapitulating the priest's condescending gesture of temporal control? What are other ways of experiencing time besides objectifying it, segmenting and claiming it, deploying it in an exercise of interpretive power or defense of some institution? If this is what the priest in Margery's book does, as he would control time past and access to it, what else is there? How can we engage the complex temporalities of the *Book of Margery Kempe* rather than merely identify them in advance with preexisting temporal systems? What might it mean for us as readers to take seriously Margery's claims to experience a kind of time different from those around her? How does the book—with its temporal multiplicities—draw us in? What might it feel like to experience a *now* that includes Margery as well as other readers of her book? And what will allow us to analyze these experiences?

The following remarks don't provide an exhaustive answer to such questions, I hasten to note before my claims get ahead of me. Or maybe that's exactly what I should be promoting, claims that race out ahead, arguments that disrespect the temporal and causal demands of conventional historically minded analysis. I do not intend to do a full reading of the *Book of Margery Kempe* in these few pages; I offer, rather, an exploration of temporal experiences of being out of joint, using the examples of Margery Kempe and her first modern editor, Hope Emily Allen, and, finally, me. The exploration proceeds by juxtaposing three temporally unruly phenomena: first, the heterogeneous times of Margery's life, at moments thrillingly, achingly touched by the extraordinary irruption of the eternal, but often as ordinary as Simplicius (in his commentary on Aristotle's *Physics*) saw time to be, passing quickly or slowly according to one's moods;[7] juxtaposed with, second, the struggles of Hope Allen—independent scholar whom I see as amateur not merely because she worked outside the academy but mainly because of the particular bond of contemporaneity she felt with Margery as she tried to edit an ever-expanding history of Margery and lost the battle against the *lack* of deadlines; juxtaposed with, third, my research into Hope Allen's archive, which took me to places deeply familiar and unfamiliar. I read Allen's papers on the Bryn Mawr College campus where both she and I were undergraduates, both of us earnest students in the process of becoming medievalists: we were both reading about a past that would become for each of us — as the past was for Margery — part of an absorbing *now*. But the truly transformative moment occurred not in that place but at the Bodleian Library in Oxford where I could not have felt my out-of-jointness — my own amateurism — more.

THE TIMES OF MARGERY KEMPE

The monk of "The Monk and the Bird," as we saw in chapter 1, longs to experience the joy of heaven in this life. This seems in fact to be something like his last wish: "euer [*ever*] was his thoght on this: / To se sum point of heuyn blis [*bit of heaven's bliss*], / Out of this life or he ferd [*before he left this life*]."[8] The narrative drama of the exemplum depends on this everyday worldly orientation: its poignancy emerges when eternity is contrasted to the here and now. Such a this-worldly framework is also present in the *Book of Margery Kempe*: the power of Margery's witness to the divine is constantly calibrated in relation to the mundane life around her. Her everyday life is punctuated by eternity, which touches her, however, not in response to a specific request (as it does the monk) but as God moves. As interruptions unwilled by her, these divine visits can be deeply unsettling to her, at times unwanted because so alien and exalted, and are often viewed dubiously by those around her.[9]

Thus like the monk Margery hears beautiful music emanating from its eternal source, but she receives scorn after hearing and speaking of it instead of — as in the monk's case — an eventual embrace as a long-lost community member. Heavenly melody first bursts forth in her intimate domestic space, when she is in bed with her husband one night; this is not the open, unbounded forest of the monk's fable landscape. "On a nygth, as this creatur lay in hir bedde wyth hir husbond, sche herd a sownd of melodye so swet & delectable, hir thowt, as sche had ben in Paradyse" (11): she hears delightful music and it seems to her as if she is in Paradise. "This drawt" (11) — this draught, this pulling into the divine, this mystical ecstasy (according to the *Middle English Dictionary*) — is a very private experience; it opens up a gaping difference between her and those around her in her everyday sphere. There are no authoritative books to consult, there is nothing to confirm the power of her experience in this place where she still remains subject to her husband's carnal desire. But the experience of that music changes her forever: she can't hear any mirth or melody thereafter without weeping, sobbing, and sighing after the bliss that is in heaven, and she becomes the object of such doubting and peevishness as we have already seen in the scene with which I opened this chapter: "Why speke ye so of the myrth that is in Heuyn," sneer her neighbors. "Ye know it not & ye haue not be ther [*been there*] no mor than we" (11).

These neighbors insist that Margery couldn't have seen heaven, but aren't they in some fundamental way wrong? Margery's narrative, of course, intimates that they are. They are frustrated with her because she will not be social with them anymore, will not speak of worldly things as they do and as she used to do; but from Margery's point of view they are petty and banal, caught in the narrowness of their meager *now*. Perhaps she *has* been to heaven, Margery's book suggests; that phrase, "as sche had ben in Paradyse," *as if she were in Paradise*, works to bridge the gap between earth and heaven, as Nicholas Watson puts it. That *as if*, he writes, "annihilates time."[10] When she later adopts the white clothes of a virgin (following Christ's command, and despite the fact that she has borne numerous children), Margery may not only demonstrate her obedience to Christ but also claim that she is in heaven already. As the thirteenth-century prose treatise on virginity, *Hali Meidhad* [*Holy Maidenhood*] repeatedly asserts, virginity on earth in itself foreshadows the angelic life in heaven: it *is itself* an angelic and heavenly life.[11] Julian of Norwich, whose spiritual authorization Margery solicits, further explains in her own *Showings*: "we be more verely [*truly*] in hevyn than in erth." That is, when our lives are fulfilling their mystical promise, we *are* in heaven.[12] Margery may be making just this temporal argument for herself.

This is not to say that the community members around Margery, dubious of her claims to eternal experience, lack temporal complexity themselves. They participate in liturgical Palm Sunday processions, for example, "by the end of the Middle Ages the most elaborate and eloquent of the processions of the Sarum rite," according to Eamon Duffy, in which the life of Christ on earth is recapitulated in the here and now.[13] This yearly ritual, which celebrates and symbolically reenacts Christ's entry into Jerusalem to begin his Passion Week, is described in loving detail in Margery's book as she notes that she was celebrating along with others: she "was at the processyon wyth other good pepyl [*people*] in the chirch-yerd [*church-yard*] & beheld how the preystys dedyn her obseruawnce [*priests performed their rite*], how thei knelyd [*kneeled*] to the Sacrament & the pepil [*people*] also" (184). Such a churchyard procession with the sacrament was dramatic and visually arresting, including reading the story of Christ's entry from the Gospel of Matthew; singing anthems (sometimes in Old Testament prophet costume), invocations, and hymns; strewing flowers; and, it seems from Margery's account, a sermon. When the procession moved toward the church's western entrance, the priest knocked with his processional cross on the door, symbolically replaying the harrowing of hell: Margery recalls the moment when "the preyste toke the crosse-staf [*staff of the processional cross*] & smet [*smote*] on the chirche-dor & the dor openyd a-geyn hym [*the door opened to him*], & than the preyst entryd wyth the Sacrament & al the pepil folwyng in-to chirche" (186–87). Once inside the church the people see the veil that has been covering the cross during Lent lifted in a breathtaking ceremony: "thei wer comyn in-to the cherch & sche beheld the preystys knelyng be-forn the Crucifixe, and, as thei songyn [*sang*], the preyste whech executyd the seruyse [*the priest who celebrated the service*] that day drow [*drew*] up a cloth be-for the Crucyfixe thre tymys [*times*], euery tyme heyar [*higher*] than other, that the pepil xulde se [*so that the people should see*] the Crucifixe" (187). The liturgical compression of time that I discussed in chapter 1 is enacted here for and with the entire community, as the events of Christ's life are blended into a complex *now* comprehending past and future times.

But Margery's narrative always implies that for her such events are more intense than they are for others around her. Here the event is at once more deeply implicated in the everyday and more intricately extended into multiple times; it is more intimate with the divine. In response to the Palm Sunday sermon, when the priest repeats the phrase "Owr Lord Ihesu langurith for lofe" [*Our Lord Jesus languishes for love*], Margery breaks out into screeches and yelps — at which the Lord is pleased, though not her fellow worshippers — and, moreover, "Sum-tyme sche herd gret sowndys & gret melodijs wyth hir bodily erys [*ears*], & than sche thowt it was ful mery in Heuyn" (185). More celestial music, as before in her bed; more witness to the divine *now*, which only increases her outsized longing to be there forever. When the priest knocks and then enters the church, Margery thinks

on Christ's harrowing of hell, which is the traditional, communal significance of this Palm Sunday ritual, but the narrative energetically asserts
that her thoughts and desires at that moment were more than her tongue
(and perhaps by extension *any* tongue) could tell (187). And toward the
beginning of the ritual celebration, when Margery watches the priests in
the churchyard kneel in front of the sacrament, and the people also, she experiences a temporally multiple inner vision: "it semyd to hir gostly sygth
[*spiritual sight*] as thei [*as though*] sche had ben that tyme in Ierusalem &
seen owr Lord in hys manhod receyuyd of the pepil [*received of the people*]
as he was whil [*while*] he went her in erth [*here on earth*]" (184). That is,
prompted by the priestly reenactment, Margery in her inner contempla-
tion is as if in Jerusalem at that moment, seeing Christ enter the city. But
the passage might also be recalling her own actual pilgrimage to Jerusalem,
where she felt the presence of Christ.

Margery's pilgrimage to the Holy Land is recorded in earlier chapters in
her book, having taken place before these yearly Palm Sundays she recalls
in chapter 78, and it is striking indeed to note the temporal dimensions
of her experience there. Certainly for her, traveling east is traveling back
in time, a spatiotemporal scheme present in the *Book of John Mandeville*,
which I analyzed in chapter 2: as Rosamund Allen puts it, pilgrims "find
themselves closer to the long-dead founders of their faith than to the local
inhabitants with whom they negotiate for food, shelter and access to the
shrines."[14] Margery does chronicle some contact with local denizens, especially the "Sarazines" [*Saracens*] who gratifyingly appreciate her more than
do her disloyal fellow English pilgrims; indeed, "sche fond alle pepyl good
on-to hir & gentyl saf only hir owyn cuntremen" [*she found all people good
to her and gentle with the sole exception of her own countrymen*] (75). But
much more significant are Margery's experiences of the presence of Christ
suffering his Passion (Margery sees in her inner sight his crucifixion, 68); of
his mother (at the sepulcher, "than was owyr Ladijs sorwe hir sorwe" [*then
was our Lady's sorrow her sorrow*], 71); of Mary Magdalene ("& sche stode
in the same place ther [*where*] Mary Mawdelyn stode whan Crist seyd to
hir, 'Mary, why wepyst thu?'" 75); of Saint John and others who loved the
Lord (she saw and heard their mourning at Christ's death, 68). As does
Mandeville in his narrative of Sir John's travels, as we saw in chapter 2, she
coordinates her travels with the Gospels. But if Sir John is relatively aloof
from what he sees in the Holy Land, observing others and holding his distance, Margery immerses herself in the density of the *now* in Jerusalem.[15]

So to return to my opening question: what does this feel like? "The mystic is seized by time as by that which erupts and transforms," writes Michel de Certeau of the mystic's temporality, opposing it to the historian's chronological, classificatory handling of time.[16] Whether or not we insist on the label "mystic" with all its baggage for Margery, few accounts of such a physical experience of time are better than that of Margery Kempe in the Holy Land.[17] Time erupts in Margery's body, and the ensuing temporal struggle turns her, in the memorable phrasing of her book, "blue as lead." Used at least three times in the book, this phrase describes Margery's livid, mottled skin, her blotchy, pent-up complexion as she weeps, sobs, and screams in the particularly extravagant performance of devotion that began for her in the Holy Land. "Sche wyth the crying wrestyd [*wrested*] hir body turnyng fro the o [*one*] syde in-to the other & wex [*turned*] al blew & al blo as it had ben colowr of leed [*all blue and ashen like the color of lead*]" (105). "Blue as lead" is a common simile in Middle English, indeed a cliché, as you can sense from the syntax of this line: "turned blue . . . blue as lead." Because of the rhyme word "dead," which appears in numerous other works alongside this simile, and because of lead's associations with heaviness as well as its pale, ashen, bruised color — "My herte is heuy as lede," as one medieval romance character moans (in *Sir Amadace*, c. 1475)[18] — the image carries a feeling of sadness, desperation; being weighed down, as the *Middle English Dictionary* puts it, by sin, by grief; even a feeling of death.

In her desperate agonies of devotion, it seems that Margery will indeed die. Her extraordinary bouts of crying originated at the scene of Christ's death, on Calvary: the actual place triggers her bodily act of compassion, her suffering together with Christ. Chapter 28 tells us that she locates that place in her soul — it becomes "the cite [*city*] of hir sowle" (68), where she sees "freschly" how the Lord was crucified. Her body is thus transfixed by the time and the place — in fact it becomes the space, the physical image of the time — of Christ's death. Christ's death should always be fresh to us, she admonished the priest in the passage with which I began. That event in Norwich occurred chronologically later than this trip to Jerusalem, but no matter: Margery is in the everlasting *now* of the fresh prince of heaven.

Margery tries to resist these intense eruptions of crying, chapter 28 tells us, because she knows that they irritate people.

As sone as sche parceyvyd that sche xulde [*would*] crye, sche wolde kepyn it in as mech as sche myth [*might*] that the pepyl xulde not an [*should not have*] herd it for noyng [*annoying*] of hem. For summe seyd it was a wikkyd

> spiryt vexid hir; sum seyd it was a sekenes [*sickness*]; sum seyd sche had
> dronkyn to mech wyn [*too much wine*] . . . And therfor, whan sche knew
> that sche xulde cryen, sche kept it in as long as sche mygth & dede al that
> sche cowde to withstond it er ellys [*else*] to put it a-wey til sche wex [*became*]
> as blo as any leed, & euyr it xuld labowryn in hir mende mor and mor in-to
> the tyme that it broke owte. (69)

"It" boils in Margery's "mende"—her mind, where, as we have seen in Augustine's *Confessions*, past memory, present attention, and future anticipation pull in different directions—while Margery's body, scarred by past
time, pushes back. Here Margery's experience may be seen as an intense
corporeal performance of the *distentio animi* that Augustine bewails: all
those earthly temporal modalities of past, present, and future are at odds
until the eternal *now* is joined.[19] The use of "it" for her emotion, her compassion, is notable, for "it" is not a thing, despite the apparent reification.
"It" will not be withstood or "put away"; to do so would turn "it" into an
object or event in chronological time, something that can be made part of
the past or deferred into the future. "It" is *now*. The seething, leaden body,
overwhelmed, blue, yields to the *now* that is so powerful that "it" bursts
forth, overtaking any other temporality or causality. This is what it feels like
to experience a totally different form of time: Margery is overtaken by the
eternal *now*. Her crying becomes a performative with no separable content,
the meaning in the movement, enacted in an all-inclusive present.[20] Such
weeping is not subject to historical comparisons: even the Blessed Virgin
didn't cry this much, her companions observe wryly, but that matters not.
Rather, her crying absorbs the temporalities of past, present, and future
into a panoramic *now* where God and all his creatures can, and should,
live. In her wondrous bouts of devotion Margery animates the temporal
principle de Certeau articulates: for the mystic, "time is . . . the question
of the subject seized by his or her other, in a present that is the ongoing
surprise of a birth and a death."[21] In its emphasis on the endlessness of the
present, oriented around the Incarnation and Crucifixion, this neatly describes Margery's experience.

Yet Margery keeps careful count of these incursions of the expanded
now into her days, and thus a strange commensurability is imposed on this
explosive incommensurability, on the moment of *now*. She times these episodes: after frequent occurrences in Jerusalem and Rome, they came sel-
dom, she says, "as it wer onys in a moneth, sythen onys in the weke, aftyr-
ward cotidianly, & onys sche had xiiij on o day, & an-other day sche had

vij, & so as God wolde visiten hir" [*maybe once a month, later once a week, afterwards daily, and once she had fourteen in one day, and another day she had seven, and just as God would visit her*] (69). She cannot know their schedule — "as God wolde visiten hir" is all that can be said about that — but she can count them, she can apply a temporal measure, she can try to express their extremity via an earthly calendar.[22] This language of temporal measurement highlights a paradox, felt throughout the book, in which Margery is indelibly engaged in earthly "quantitative reckoning," as Watson terms it, and just as indelibly convinced of its inadequacy to express the divine *now*.[23] Thus the constant struggle between her neighbors and herself, between ecclesiastical authority and herself, between those "two temporal planes" (as Aron Gurevich puts it) in herself.[24]

Complicating temporal things still further, sometimes the time of Margery's heaven is actually indistinguishable from that of Margery's earth. How separate are the two temporal planes of spiritual and secular? A very revealing passage late in book 1 reminds us of the everyday asynchrony Simplicius discusses: recall from my introduction his contention that no time at all seems to have passed for those who are absorbed in intense thought or action, but in contrast time passes with agonizing slowness for those who suffer. Margery remarks on exactly this characteristic of time — *heavenly* time, that is:

> Owr Lord of hys hy [*high*] mercy visityd hir so mech & so plenteuowsly wyth hys holy spechys [*speeches*] & hys holy dalyawnce [*dalliance*] that sche wist not many tymys [*many times did not know*] how the day went. Sche supposyd sumtyme of v owrys er vj owrys it had not ben the space of an owr [*Sometimes five or six hours seemed to her not the space of one hour*]. It was so swet & so deuowt that it ferd as sche had ben in an Heuyn [*It was so sweet and so devout that it was as if she had been in a Heaven*]. (215)

Time is condensed in her consciousness (five or six hours seem less than one) *not* because time is absolutely different from the earthly in the Lord's realm (two hours are not three hundred years here, as they are in the exemplum of the monk and the bird) but because it is similar — because her dalliance with him is immersive, sweet, and devout: "Sche thowt neuyr long therof ne sche was neuyr irke therof, the tyme went a-wey sche wist not how" [*she never thought the time long and she was never irked by it; it passed she did not know how*] (215). In a grim application of the reverse principle she mournfully remarks in an earlier chapter that fifteen more years of life on earth will feel like "many thowsend" (176). The full complexity of Margery's temporal world cannot, therefore, be encompassed by dualisms between secular and spiritual, subjective and institutional, or linear and nonlinear. And concomitantly, her whole book records not a progression from earthly to heavenly but "an intensification of her being," as Watson observes, an increasing attachment to both heavenly and earthly, to the eternal *now* as well as to mundane time.[25]

Such temporal intricacy, particularly the coexistence — or even, more strangely, the equivalence — of temporal simultaneity in the *now*, on the one hand, and temporal distance in moment-by-moment progression, on the other, is represented in Margery's text. But not only represented: similar temporal possibilities, I now want to suggest, emerge in the experience of reading the book. We can historicize the representations of Margery's *now*, reading them as records of events that take place in relation to other chronologically locatable people and practices, including medieval ecclesiastical institutions and Christian temporal systems; I have been doing just that. But this kind of historical understanding is made possible by a prior experience of contemporaneity between us and Margery: if we did not already in some sense connect with Margery's text, we could not even begin to understand or historicize her.[26] Some connection must already exist (at the least, through our very act of attributing meaningfulness to the text via a mutually intelligible language, which links past and present, creates a contemporaneity) before any connection can be made (any information shared, any understanding reached). This hermeneutic circle is inevitable: in all acts of interpretation, as James Simpson has demonstrated for the medieval context, some such crossing the gap between beings (or between reader and text) is a necessary condition of intelligibility.[27] But the circle need not be vicious: the interpretive gap can be crossed in ways that preserve the otherness of the past (the text) even as mutual intelligibility is recognized in the present. That is precisely the implication of the term "noncontemporaneous contemporaneity," used to describe such an interpretive situation. A hermeneutic connection can in fact be premised on distance.[28]

Hermeneutics, then, is the beginning of one answer to the question I posed earlier about what might allow us to analyze an experience of asynchrony. Hermeneutics is a likely resource for analysis of historically distant works because it has so centrally grappled with the subject/object, self/other relation in the context of reading and interpretation: it is concerned to preserve the alterity of the other in the interpretive enterprise even as it offers techniques of understanding that other from within the other's own horizon — from within his or her "point of view, values, concerns."[29] Hermeneutics can thus begin to illuminate the complex temporal experience that is the act of reading a historical text. Henry Wadsworth Longfellow's experience of reading medieval texts — which I discussed in chapter 1 — comes more precisely into view through a hermeneutical framework, which makes clear the rich productivity of asynchrony, of noncontemporaneous contemporaneity. Recall that John Ruskin in *Modern Painters* claimed that Longfellow "has entered more closely into the temper of the Monk, for good and for evil, than ever yet theological writer or historian, though they may have given their life's labour to the analysis." The modern poet can do this, I understand Ruskin's analysis to suggest, because he has immersed himself in the medieval while he remains "in another element," that is, while he lives in the present day and thus has "*seen* other things" beyond what the medieval person has seen.[30] Hans-Georg Gadamer's explanation of what it means to "transpose ourselves" into a historical situation is useful here: "If we put ourselves in someone else's shoes, for example, then we will understand him — become aware of the otherness, the indissoluble individuality of the other person — by putting *ourselves* in his position."[31] In this fusion of horizons, the modern poet understands the medieval person — better, in fact, than the medieval person him- or herself, because he has "*seen* other things" not available to the medieval person. This is Ruskin's implication, and it is thoroughly hermeneutic: in the fusion of horizons a new time — the noncontemporaneous contemporaneity, the asynchronous *now* — is produced in which "new meanings and possibilities of insight can appear."[32]

What we do with such knowledge of these unavoidably complex hermeneutic conditions, what we do with the awareness of contemporaneity as a heterogeneous present riven with the time of the other, punctuated with the drastically unfamiliar, and edged by the unknown is my concern as we turn back to the *Book of Margery Kempe* and its readers. Margery becomes our contemporary in a complex gesture of closeness and distance, understanding and otherness; such fusion or contemporaneity allows historical understanding, as Dipesh Chakrabarty points out — historical understanding that in fact goes beyond what the text's author says. What Hope Emily Allen did — or, rather, didn't do — with such knowledge is what I shall next explore. Such knowledge attended an ambivalent experience indeed: while noncontemporaneous contemporaneity was a source of considerable joy for Allen, I shall argue, it may as well have underlain conditions that eventually prevented her great work from appearing. Her intense absorption in her objects of study as well as the lack of economic motive or urgent deadlines—both characteristic of amateurism as I have been analyzing it in this book—kept her from ever completing her final magnum opus.

THE TIME OF HOPE

The story of editing the *Book of Margery Kempe* is the stuff of legend, at least for medievalists. Hope Emily Allen's field was early English literature of spirituality. She wrote highly regarded books on the writings of early-fourteenth-century recluse Richard Rolle and had done groundbreaking work on the early English guide for anchoresses, *Ancrene Riwle* (also known now as *Ancrene Wisse*). This scholarly work—as well as familial ties and a bit of good luck—situated her in just the place to be consulted about a newly unearthed manuscript on early English spirituality. In the summer of 1934, as John Hirsh notes, when everyone else had left London on holiday, this American medievalist was in the city and able to make what turned out to be one of the biggest medieval literary identifications of the century.[33] The famous English scholar of mysticism, Evelyn Underhill, had been contacted by the Victoria and Albert Museum about a recently uncovered manuscript, and sensing she was out of her depth, she recommended her distant American relation, who identified the work as a unique copy of the *Book of Margery Kempe*. Hope Allen's career from this point onward changed utterly: an independent scholar whose researches were largely funded by her family's holdings in the Oneida Community, Ltd., she was invited to produce the scholarly edition of the *Book of Margery Kempe* for the Early English Text Society (EETS, Furnivall's organization, which I discussed in my introduction), and "an element of haste" entered her research life which had earlier been temporally unfettered.[34] "It is so exciting it needs speed," she wrote to her chosen collaborator, Sanford Brown Meech, shortly after the identification.[35]

Allen became so "immersed" in Margery's book that her other researches virtually ceased.[36] In compiling the volume, she struggled with Meech—who was on the professional academic track (he soon became a professor of English at Syracuse, and wore a Phi Beta Kappa key, as Allen noted "with horror")[37]—over the scope of their individual responsibilities, particularly over what should be covered in her introduction and notes. (Hirsh maintains that she never would have been treated in this way by Meech if she had been a man; this marks a point at which Allen's socio-economic class privilege as amateur is trumped by her position as feminine within the hierarchy of a distinctly gendered profession.)[38] After tense exchanges and much anxiety, a compromise was found: the edition was completed and published in 1940, with signed notes, a brief "Prefatory Note," and two appendices by Allen, but Allen would be allowed to issue a second volume (entirely her own) for what she really wanted to produce, a general introduction synthesizing the mystical elements with social history. For the 1940 edition she worked on her notes until the very last minute before publication, extending the present moment until she could no longer, until her dilations had to give way to the press's punctuality and the present had at last to be declared finished, closed, past. Peppered throughout the 1940 edition, though, are promises of the large work to come: already, in the 1940 "Addenda" section, the past was proliferating: "My research on these topics became too complicated to be summarized now," she wrote, in her characteristically harried style (lxiii). But the time of the second volume never came.

Hope Allen did path-breaking work making connections between late medieval devotional practice in England and on the European continent. She brought to bear Continental women mystics — such as the Blessed Dorothea von Montau, Angela of Foligno, and Margaret Ebner — on the understanding of Margery Kempe's devotional style in East Anglia. Allen was concerned to understand the local life of Margery as well, and to show how those Continental mystical ideas reached Margery; the second volume, "BMK II," as she referred to it in her voluminous correspondence, was to be a "synthesis of Margery, the mystic and the woman."[39] Her approach to Margery was multiple, engaging both the spiritual *now* and the temporalities of everyday life. Allen always historicized; in fact, one of her sharpest scholarly debates about Margery was with a theologian who, she thought, misunderstood her position toward Margery because of his ahistorical disciplinary disposition. But her work on Margery drew on her "literary" as well as her "scholarly" (i.e., historicist) impulses, as she reflected in a letter; John Hirsh has compellingly explained that Allen's interest in "persons," in both her fiction and her work on Margery, meant that Allen found the current academic discourse inadequate.[40] I would extend the thought here: Allen, I want to suggest, felt a complex contemporaneity with Margery. Such a contemporaneity is not a simple counter to that rigorous chronological historicizing, but rather makes it possible and thus shows "the limited good that modern [that is, modernist and academic, professional] historical consciousness is," as Chakrabarty argues.[41]

Thus we hear the affectionate familiarity with which Allen and her scholarly correspondents refer to their subjects of research: theirs is the intimacy borne of "living with" their authors (as Roland Barthes would say).[42] "Dear Miss Allen," wrote Mabel Day, retired secretary of the EETS, "Here is St. Elizabeth, with many thanks for the parcel, which is most delicious. I like her very much indeed, and I like the way the B. V. M. talks to her."[43] A correspondent at Ohio State wrote a few years earlier about the vita of a German saint: "Dear Hope, Many thanks for Dorothea — I bound her and sent her back to you (registered) on Friday."[44] A professor wrote from Mount Holyoke College: "Elizabeth of Schönau has come to life again: I am just sending back my revised article . . ."[45]

The web of association between and among late medieval mystical and other historical figures, places, and ideas was very intimate, and Allen felt deeply, personally implicated in it. She read the *Book of Margery Kempe* as Margery's own scheming for sainthood, as her own "active propaganda" for canonization: Margery's story in the book is the story of her constantly looking for a champion in this cause. In writing her story, Margery, in this sense, desired a reader such as Hope Allen, certainly Margery's latter-day champion of sorts. In a long letter replying to a graduate student, Allen writes, "I have such an even personal interest in Margery Kempe that I was very pleased to have your kind words about her." The student had written not about Margery, per se, but about the *Book of Margery Kempe*.[46] Yet the distinction is too fine; Allen in fact (and not insignificantly) often conflated reference to the manuscript with reference to the woman. Moreover, her own manuscript, her "magnum opus," as she referred to it, would be an incarnation of herself, a self that is multifarious and heterogeneous: in BMK II, she wrote, "all the absorptions of my various incarnations coalesce."[47] In this way, "Margery gives me hope": this sentence in a letter in 1941 alludes to the ongoing horror of the Second World War, but I am tempted to capitalize that last word, suggesting as it does the complicated mirroring and reflexivity of Allen's readerly experience.[48] Expressing precisely the hermeneutic promise of present understanding of a text and author that exceeds the past's, Allen wrote in another letter, "I hope Margery comes to her own in our life-time."[49]

A feeling of familiarity, inspiration, even identification with one's subject is the common, if not seriously acknowledged, passion of many a historian — the enabling passion, Chakrabarty would maintain. When another correspondent of Allen's refers to a friend of his, asserting, "She knows Margery Kempe," we feel that more than textual comprehension is at stake for her, too, in that breezy statement.[50] But Allen's contemporaneity was complex, difficult, even troubled: the pull of the past was at once thrilling, complicated, and problematic for her, as witnessed in much of her writing over the years, literary and scholarly.[51] In an early belletristic essay, "Relics," whose publication she pursued (without success) for more than a decade, Allen wrote that she experienced the past every day in "relics," the old word for material things "surcharged with the personalities of the past" (58).[52] An "antiquary bred in the bone" (54), as she described herself, Allen felt connectedness through such "antiquities developed in indigenous America" (53) in her upstate New York home. She wished to communicate with others beyond her own mortal being, wanting "to transcend the narrow limitations of the individual" by connecting with the past — even while acknowledging the "vital impulse of life" to be "placed in the real immediate present" (55, 58). But she felt that this approach to antiquities and the past isolated her from her fellow citizens, as it later, perhaps, would estrange her from Meech's professionalism.[53] "My inclination for 'relics' is something inscrutable and inevitable in my composition," Allen wrote. "This is a civilization that makes no provision for my own type. . . . I said to [a woman in a nearby hill village], 'I am very fond of all old things,' and she replied in a puzzled way, 'How very queer that is!' " (54, 55, 56). At the end of this essay, Allen finds after all in this village woman's attitude a shared interest in continuities with the past, stressing not the dead but the living. But this resolution in the article comes quickly, too quickly; I have a feeling that Allen's sense of her own singularity, her queerness, her material absorption in the past, may indeed have persisted beyond that perfunctory essayistic ending. Indeed, in another (undated) essay, "Cycles of Time," Allen broaches directly her own sense of asynchrony vis-à-vis the cycle of nature, both reveling in her own temporality and also hoping to synchronize with the seasons at last.[54]

Allen concedes in "Relics" that "life in an environment solidly filled in with memorials from the past might in certain moods and circumstances, be a torment haunted by incessant ghosts" (58). Was Margery Kempe one such ghost? Perhaps; Allen writes — in the informal context of a letter to another medievalist — of being "buried alive" by the *Book of Margery Kempe*, "almost, as it were."[55] As friends and acquaintances pleaded with her to finish ("there must be an end to revision sometime," admonished Albert Baugh of the University of Pennsylvania), BMK II finally overwhelmed her, though she remained hopeful throughout the experience: an old friend had "sent word that she expected me somehow to 'ooze through' what I set out to do and I am optimist enough to agree with her," she wrote, late in the 1950s.[56] Those researches on the past kept proliferating in the present; even Allen's own scholarly past — her earlier unpublished work on recluses and on *Ancrene Riwle*, set aside because of the "advent of MK" — became engulfed in the vast BMK II *now*.[57]

If this fact of the expansive *now* was not the failure, but rather the very condition, as Chakrabarty might say, of Allen's historicizing work on Margery Kempe, nonetheless the form of the book could not accommodate it. As we've seen, in the hermeneutic concept of contemporaneity the relation between intelligibility and difference, connection and distance, is a very delicate one. "I am sorry not to be self-controlled in libraries," she confesses; Harvard's library in particular "sends me into spasms of excited research."[58] To go through her papers is to encounter a staggering number of versions and versions and versions of her work, patiently typewritten, minutely hand-corrected: multiplicity and interpretive open-endedness can be celebrated as representing infinite possibility, even perhaps a modernist literary style, but can also be seen as evidence of infinite delay, which will, without some internal or external impetus toward closure, defeat the project. This is where her difference from contemporary writers in experimental modes — say, British author Dorothy Richardson, producing her enormous, thirteen-volume novel *Pilgrimage*, whose profuse, proliferating details and refusal of interpretive closure Allen's papers might be said to resemble — is crucial: the expansiveness and passion may have been similar in both cases, but Hope Allen had, for better or for worse, chosen a strict form that demanded finality, and an end, or even just words on pages sent to a publisher, were what she did not deliver.[59] "The parts of my introduction are so many, and complicated and I want them to be simple," she writes.[60] About other research she says, "the trouble is to separate out the various elements from the weltering mass of material at hand. To do so will help me much with BMK II."[61] Allen's experience of connectedness bred yet more and more connections, with perhaps less and less distance, so that finally the closed form of the professional, scholarly book was unable to accommodate them.

Allen's felt experience of temporality was in great part fatigue: her early work on the *Book of Margery Kempe* and other projects had fundamentally worn her out. "Over-stimulation," as she put it, left her drained and exhausted as she worked on BMK II; that had always, in fact, been both the condition of and the impediment to her working, and it may indeed both reenact and result from Margery's own modus operandi.[62] From her letters—with their rushes of words on every inch of the page (paper was scarce, at least during the war) and their excited admixtures of scholarly business with domestic news—one gets the feeling of her entire awareness of the past and all its particularities rising up at once in the present. There was pleasure in this, alongside guilt and bewilderment. Unpublished work burdened and embarrassed her, and she rued her lack of "self-control," but listen to the nervously gleeful figures of speech she used to describe her nonprogress and nonmethod—language that Marea Mitchell notes in making the same point: in a letter to Mabel Day, who was helping her try to finish, Allen declared: "I sent you yesterday a fearful budget—to demonstrate my difficulties in composition thro my mind sprouting like a potato brot [*sic*] from the cellar, when anything comes up that interests me."[63] From another letter to Mabel Day: "I realize that if I were dealing with money instead of research, I would be a defaulter who didn't balance my books, I am so much behind." Moreover, shamefacedly but cheerfully: "I am as irresponsible as a child at times in giving way to enthusiasms which only time will dispel."[64] In fact that forward-moving aspect of time, time as discipline, is what Allen was pleased finally to refuse. To the "professional problem" of writing a scholarly book (to recur to the slogan quoted in my introduction) she offered an "amateur solution." She gratefully quoted an old friend's adage: "Forecast is as good as work."[65]

TIME IS ON MY SIDE

Nothing could have fitted me out better to do research on the *Book of Margery Kempe* than the book itself. Its robust depiction of asynchronies has helped me recognize and experience multiple temporalities in my world. The research first took me to Bryn Mawr College, where Hope Allen was an undergraduate, class of 1905, and in whose library's "feminist collection," as she put it, she wanted at least some of her papers deposited.[66] I was an undergraduate at Bryn Mawr, too, class of 1978, and going back there, I found, was inevitably as much about my own past as it was about Allen's. The journey to Bryn Mawr from New York City felt like a journey back in time, to recur to that space-time trope (though Bryn Mawr is to the southwest rather than to the east of Manhattan): the serenity of the campus, in relation to the intense post-9/11 world of New York in which I was living, seemed to be itself part of another chronology. But the hush I perceived at Bryn Mawr was the sound of my own timeline as I stepped back into the formative locus of my young adulthood, rather than anything anyone else was hearing there now. Time present and time past collapsed as I made my way to the archive.

And time future: for when I sat in the archive (in Canaday Library, a modern building on that Collegiate Gothic campus), doing the work of a professional medievalist, I was sitting in the very building where I had started training to become a literary historian and critic a quarter century ago. And I was sitting on the grounds where Hope Allen, her papers now archived there, had herself received training as a medievalist. Our pasts touched in my reading her pages, an experience of bodily absorption into a moment in which time seemed indeed to stop any forward motion. Allen's papers were even more "non-organised" than her notes in her edition, full of fits and starts, beginnings and dead ends, wormholes of optimism in the face of a task threatening to bury her.[67] The multiplicity of times in the archive that day was composed of temporalities that went back to Margery through Hope Allen and up to me (both in my 1970s incarnation and my early-twenty-first-century one), meeting in my *now* that shared with Margery's and Hope Allen's a refusal of the evanescence of chronological time in favor of an expanded present.

My understanding of that brief experience deepened after a subsequent research trip to read more of Allen's papers. It took another encounter with Allen's papers — longer, and in another location — for me to understand what kind of potential was held in that moment of temporal multiplicity at Bryn Mawr College. It was not intimacy I expected when I sat in Duke Humfrey's Library at the Bodleian several years later. If there was a sense of mutual personal belonging at Bryn Mawr, there was a certain "outsider" status that both Allen and I shared with respect to Oxford — both of us Americans, she never having had a university faculty position. But I felt much further removed (the *real* amateur there) by not having worked extensively with medieval manuscripts and never having used the impossibly ornate Duke Humfrey's Library before; Allen, in contrast, was at home there. I rapidly became absorbed in her papers, though, entranced by her letters crammed excitedly with words at all angles on the page. I was drawn into the daily unfolding of her scholarly life, chronicled in dashed-off post-cards and voluminous missives. Her extraordinary erudition was shared generously with students and colleagues; her scrupulous and unwavering attention to detail was moving and inspiring to witness. At the same time, the foreignness, the strangeness of her pre-electronic world gaped in that very unfamiliar place. Her world's slow, drawn-out temporalities in particular were highlighted in the gleam of the Bodleian's polished wood tables. The material resistance of these papers — Allen's sometimes difficult handwriting in particular — reflected the voice therein, its formality and scholarly thoroughness, its punctiliousness at times and at other times its pain. As I read the papers hour after hour in that drafty and dimly lit reading room, my eyes blurred with the strain.

Yet late in the afternoon, several long days into the business, I felt a shift in that delicate balance of distance and connection — a shift or, better, an intensification — when I came upon several letters. They were letters of condolence Hope Allen had written to her closest English friend, Dorothy Ellis, on the death of *her* companion, Mary Caroline Mackaig, known as Skay.[68] Allen was always personable in her letters; she may have sounded persnickety at times, but she was not aloof, particularly with her friends, with whom she maintained lively, domestic communication as well as more somber scholarly exchange. But these letters of condolence were on a different level. As always, familiar yet proper and restrained, Hope Allen nonetheless registered that *she* understood the loss that Dorothy Ellis had suffered, the loss of another woman: "You have so generously shared with me your treasures of friend and home that now I feel a share in your loss. No one can know what Skay was who had not lived with her — . . . I cannot express to you what you both gave to me those several times when you took me in and nursed me during the harrowing period of preparing Margery for the press." Allen goes on: "You and Skay are one of the magical incidents of my life . . ." The intimacy borne of living with someone; the magic of that closeness that nurtures and reproduces. Allen knows these things. "How cruelly you will miss her I can imagine," Allen wrote simply. "I can *imagine*"; "*I* can imagine" (my emphasis). Fusing horizons, putting herself in Dorothy's place, Hope imagines, and feels, and now must go on: "I shall have to continue to hope that in some altered way we can resume."[69] She will hope: that is, she will be Hope, but changed.

When I read these lines I felt a shock of recognition — and, more intensely, the shock of *being recognized*. The depth of this kind of loss is so rarely acknowledged because the depth of such a relationship is so rarely acknowledged: in this case, two women in an unofficial, ad hoc love relationship. Hope Allen was recognizing it, and in reading her act of recognition I recognized myself, even as I observed the particularity of her own situation and the traditional forms of her propriety. In a complicated hermeneutic mirroring and reflection Hope Allen was recognizing Dorothy Ellis's love, and I was recognizing her recognizing; I was mirroring her mirroring. Wrong kind of scholar, wrong kind of lover, and American to boot, but I recognized and was recognized there in a transformative act of reading and self-recognition in Duke Humfrey's Library. This unexpected queer intimacy challenged me to rethink what I thought I understood about amateurs and archives, about who can and should work there, about what and who exists *in* there, and how. What other voices are speaking in there, to those readers of texts who can hear the question, answer the call?

Such a transformative moment blazes out in my mind even now. It includes the resistance of Allen's voice and my resistance to Allen's voice. My experiences in the archives were certainly structured by ambivalence, and not only a hermeneutic ambivalence between connectedness and distance such as I've been describing. There was also the ambivalence generated by the differing temperaments of the historical subjects themselves. On the one hand, there was the desiring call of the medieval figure — Margery Kempe, who was by all accounts desperate for a cult to follow her death and proceed with her canonization — and, on the other, there was the unknowability of a person as nervous, prickly, and radically centripetal as Hope Allen apparently was. Not to mention, moreover, the disoriented and scared undergraduate that I was in the '70s. My experience of non-contemporaneous contemporaneity in the archive — for me, queer intimacy — necessarily included the ambivalences, awkwardnesses, abrasions that accrued to those bodies so temporally out of joint in the world: as the *now* invades Margery, there is the resistance of her own body, scarred and "blue," as well as the constant irritation of onlookers; as the *Book of Margery Kempe* buries Hope Allen, there is her own outrage at her co-editor for the 1940 edition as well as the frustration of her colleagues about BMK II; as I opened boxes at Bryn Mawr, there was all of that plus my own guarded defensiveness as a displaced kid from San Jose at Bryn Mawr College, a guardedness that was particularly resurgent as I worked at the Bodleian.

What does it feel like to be asynchronous? It can have its downside:

Margery Kempe, pierced by an eternal *now*, remained an outsider, albeit an outsider with social usefulness and a righteous sense of salvation.[70] Hope Emily Allen, outsider to the academy, never finished her work, absorbed as she was in an uncontrolled, indeed uncontrollable, past. There's nothing intrinsically positive about the experience or indeed the condition of multiple temporalities — which condition, I have been arguing throughout this book, is characteristic of life on this earth. As I demonstrated in chapter 1, the persistence of the past in the present, in the disorienting genealogy of King Herla in the court of Henry II, threatens the viability of the whole courtly life; in chapter 2, I showed how British colonists exploited the concept of asynchrony in their efforts to advance empire, temporally subjugating natives of India in an already conquered, already known past; and as I shall suggest in the next chapter, asynchrony can provide the basis for painful social exclusion, of which ghosts are the haunting reminders. Nonetheless, the recognition of temporal multiplicity and the break with discipline are themselves exhilarating. At the least, we can use a queer appreciation of temporal heterogeneity to contest and enlarge singular narratives of development, and to begin to imagine collective possibilities for a more attached — that is to say, queer — future.

FOUR

Out of Sync in the Catskills

Rip van Winkle, Geoffrey Crayon,
James I, and Other Ghosts

LONG EDDY, NEW YORK

I spent much of a sabbatical year not long ago in upstate New York, in a house that I owned with my girlfriend. Our land lay in the remote southwest corner of the Catskill mountain range, home of trout fishermen and deer hunters. The area has been beset by catastrophic flooding, the experience of which has fundamentally altered my sense of natural contingencies, the passage of time, and my place in the landscape. All this has inevitably seeped into my thoughts on temporality; the flooding has given me a fresh understanding of the concept of "the stream of Time." Johannes Fabian uses that phrase in his critique of evolutionary anthropologists; the metaphor relies on an understanding of streams as unidirectional and evenly flowing, producing a concept of time as smoothly progressive, one moment coming after the last in a steady flow.[1] But — as is implicit in Fabian's deployment of the image, and as I am here

4.1. Headstone of David LeValley, 1820–1893. *Photograph by the author.*

to witness—streams do not always behave in this way. The stream that formed the border of our property rose, raged, and tore up its banks in the flood. Shifting and withdrawing, it cut new channels and created eddies, pools, and branches. And it took things with it, all kinds of things—trees, rocks, coffins. From the small family cemetery upstream a headstone washed up on our banks, a part of the nineteenth century that only now, in the twenty-first century, made its way downstream (see figure 4.1). The rest of that family plot is still upstream. If this creek provides a temporal metaphor, the time it images is far from the measured "homogeneous, empty time" that Walter Benjamin derides in his "Theses on the Philosophy of History" and that Dipesh Chakrabarty elaborates in addition as "godless, continuous"; *this* time is heterogeneous and always already very full.[2]

That moving headstone haunts the writing of this chapter. The ghastly rock provides a powerful figure of asynchrony, realized in a particular moment and in a particular place but also opening up a spectral view of the world, a perspective in which the boundaries between the living and the dead, the material and the immaterial, the real and the fictional, the present and the past are porous. It is a world in which everyday time is itself experienced as wondrous, and the present, unmasterable, is full of other times.

Temporal experiences in this world can be thrilling, or isolating, or painful, or something else altogether; I track several figures — Washington Irving, his narratorial persona Geoffrey Crayon, and James I of Scotland — in acts of encountering medieval or ancient texts, and I follow out the ghostly asynchronies that thereby open up. Geoffrey Crayon, himself a figure of exclusion, leads us deep into the spectral world in which an ancient figure haunts these tales of asynchrony with his old, unacknowledged pain.

"RIP VAN WINKLE"

The strange temporalities of the Catskills are indeed legendary, and when I woke up that morning during the flood to find the nineteenth century at my feet, I could not help but think of the waking Rip van Winkle, finding himself in an entirely different time from that in which he went to sleep. In the story by Washington Irving, first published in 1819, Rip van Winkle slept for twenty years one night in those hills, enchanted by old Dutch spirits.[3] "Rip van Winkle" is the paradigmatic asynchrony tale in the United States: claimed as the first American short story, it is a staple of the American literary imaginary. And not only that, simply googling "Rip van Winkle" reveals how pervasive is this character in the map of the nation itself, in the names of everything from major elements of public infrastructure (the Rip van Winkle Bridge across the Hudson River in New York) to countless motels dotting the highways to real estate agencies to all manner of other enterprises. Rip's fame has traveled well beyond U.S. borders, furthermore, as I learned anecdotally during a visit to Tasmania.[4]

But the story is hardly original, even though claimed as a certain kind of origin. Irving himself (in the voice of his narratorial persona, Geoffrey Crayon) mentions the well-known legend of Frederick Barbarossa sleeping in Kypphäuser Mountain in a "note" appended to the story — a sepulchral tale of asynchrony to which I referred in a note in chapter 1[5] — and he knew at least several other traditional asynchrony tales. Henry A. Pochmann painstakingly details Irving's clear indebtedness, in his composition of "Rip van Winkle," to a collection of German folktales, in particular the tale of "Peter Klaus" (in which a goatherd follows a mysterious guide into Kypphäuser Mountain, witnesses a game of ninepins, drinks a potion, and wakes twenty years later). But Epimenides, the Seven Sleepers, and King Herla, whom we have met already in *How Soon Is Now?*, all form a broader context for Irving's tale.[6]

A little moment in the genesis of Irving's work will reinforce the concept of temporal experience on which all of these asynchrony stories build, and of which Rip's tale is a particularly beloved witness: our experience of time may be of a smooth and unbroken series of punctual moments, but it nonetheless may diverge dramatically from what scientific measurement tells us it should be. A visit to Abbotsford, the Scottish home of Walter Scott—whose work proved crucial to Irving's developing Romantic style in the second decade of the nineteenth century—was not only revelatory of the unexpected charms of Scott and his world but also demonstrated the ordinary marvelousness of time.[7] Just before he set about to write the *Sketch Book of Geoffrey Crayon, Gent.* (the work in which "Rip van Winkle" appeared), Irving met Scott and wrote to his brother from Abbotsford enchantedly:

> The glorious old minstrel himself [i.e., Scott, author of *The Lay of the Last Minstrel*] came limping to the gate, took me by the hand.... I had intended certainly being back in Edinburgh today (Monday), but Mr. Scott wishes me to stay until Wednesday, that we may have an excursion. . . . I cannot tell you how truly I have enjoyed the hours I have passed here. They fly too quick, yet each is loaded with story, incident, or song: and when I consider the world of ideas, images, and impressions that have been crowded upon my mind since I have been here, it seems incredible that I should only have been two days at Abbotsford.[8]

Recall again from the discussion in my introduction Simplicius's commentary on Aristotle—particularly, his commentary on Aristotle's reference to the myth of the nine heroes of Sardinia: time flies by quickly when we are absorbed in thought or action, Simplicius observes, and creeps slowly when we are in pain.[9] Irving feels firsthand this relational quality of time. And though it is an everyday fact, absolutely mundane, it nonetheless leaves him incredulous: "it seems incredible that I should only have been two days at Abbotsford."

The way time passes can be hard to believe, and Irving's letter goes on to narrate the adventures at Abbotsford that only heighten his sense of temporal wonder. His host and he wander in an asynchronous realm that suggests not only a medieval tale but also positions Irving himself as something like the wandering, dreamy Rip van Winkle: "I have rambled about the hills with Scott; visited the haunts of Thomas the Rhymer, and other spots rendered classic by border tale and witching song, and have been in a kind of dream or delerium [*sic*]."[10] The medieval tale of Thomas the

Rhymer includes Thomas's dream of a fairy queen and trip with her to an otherworld.[11] Scott recited lines of the ballad as they walked in those very hills: "'We are now,' said Scott, 'treading classic, or rather fairy ground. This is the haunted glen of Thomas the Rhymer. . . .'" Scott apparently suggested to Irving that the ballad would make the basis of an excellent narrative: "'It is a fine old story,' said he, 'and might be wrought up into a capital tale.'"[12] Though Irving did not work it into a narrative after all, some basic gestures of that old medieval story appear in this epistolary description of his experience with Scott at Abbotsford, and are seen, moreover, in "Rip van Winkle": the medieval is part of the asynchronous present. Not only is there a haunted glen and wondrous temporality both at Abbotsford and in Rip's story, as in the ballad, but also we recognize in Rip's experience the dream quality about which Irving writes explicitly at Abbotsford (he was in "a kind of dream or delerium"), and which characterizes Thomas the Rhymer's experience on Huntley Bank, on which he "lay musing and sleeping when he saw, or dreamt he saw, the queen of Elfland"[13] —and there is even the suggestion in Irving's letter that the medieval may be experienced by Irving as itself a present-day dream. Dreams of course multiply the possibilities of asynchrony as they interrupt already nonlinear everyday time with their own inscrutable temporalities; they can invert or otherwise alter cause and effect; they can presage the future; they can bring back in figural imagery people and things long gone; they take place in a *now* of indeterminate duration, lasting who knows how long. Irving's *now* at Abbotsford, breathlessly experienced and described, and in a way prefiguring the times of the *Sketch Book*, is dense with times.

Not long after these magical days spent in Scotland Irving began to write the pieces that made up the *Sketch Book*. Let me recall the particulars of Irving's most famous story in order to highlight its temporal imaginings. Rip van Winkle lives in a village on the Hudson River and roams happily throughout the mountainous area. Beloved of his fellow villagers, he shirks familial duties and his wife's nagging to wander, to play, and to attend to any other household's needs but his own. Walking deep into the woods one afternoon, he indulges his passion for shooting squirrels, thus successfully avoiding Dame van Winkle and his own domestic obligations. The rest is, as they say, history: as evening starts to fall on his little hunting adventure, Rip hears his name cried out in the twilight air. He sees a stranger, dressed quaintly, carrying a keg up a steep mountainside; he helps this "old man of the glen" (776), and together they approach "a company of odd looking personages playing at ninepins" (775). The group is solemn and mysterious, and Rip is puzzled by it. The short and stocky characters partake of the liquor of the keg, and so does Rip, whose senses are gradually overpowered. He wakes up later, stiff in the joints, to find his dog gone, his gun oddly aged, and his beard grown a foot long.

Overnight, it seems, Rip has become a walking anachronism: everything, including his own body, has aged considerably, but he is cognizant of only one night's passing. His experience seems not to have been a dream—though it has a dreamlike, figural, asynchronous quality—because a marvelously long time has in fact passed, and the details of the spirits' visit will be eventually corroborated by another person. To adapt Simplicius's analysis of the fabled sleepers in Sardinia here, Rip does not immediately apprehend the extraordinary passage of time on waking because he does not immediately perceive any great change between the *now* of his falling asleep and the *now* of his waking.[14] Rip fell asleep at night, and wakes on "a bright, sunny morning" (776). He worriedly assumes that he has slept there all the night, because that is what the change from night to morning ordinarily signals. But he soon becomes conscious of enormous and inexplicable shifts, and "Rip van Winkle" comes to resemble other traditional asynchrony stories (say, "The Monk and the Bird") in its attention to the protagonist's growing awareness of, and bewilderment at, his own noncontemporaneity. Rip descends the mountain he knows so well but doesn't recognize much of his village, so "altered" is it (778); the villagers don't recognize him either, and the whole experience becomes more and more alarming until it provokes an out-and-out identity crisis. The monk in "The Monk and the Bird" doesn't know what to make of himself when everything around him has changed so quickly, and neither does Rip. Soon, though, the temporal basics and his identity are reestablished, and Rip, the fittingness of whose name is now clear, settles back into life around a two-decade lapse. The monk must die and proceed to heaven, having been summoned, as it were, by eternity, but Rip mundanely lives on, as if to say that this is just the way time is, this is how everyday sublunar time works. Quotidian time is multifarious. Rip lives with temporal disparity and heterogeneity because asynchrony *is* the everyday.

So time has passed, but Rip, asleep, did not consciously experience it. His present, his temporality differs from that of others around him: he prefers younger people to "his former cronies . . . all rather the worse for the wear and tear of time" (783) which he has not, after all, consciously gone through. Nonetheless, his body has aged: unlike the monk or the Seven Sleepers or King Herla, who have no wrinkles after hundreds of years, Rip has a "long grizzled beard" (779) and rheumatic joints, and he hobbles along at a slowed-down pace (777). He is the very somatization of temporal asynchrony, his flesh in one temporal framework and his mind in another. Neither did he experience the Revolution, that great rupture in the narrative of American origins through which he snoozed. Like King Herla, who missed the Saxon conquest of the Britons, like the Seven Sleepers, who slumbered through the triumph of Christianity over the pagans, Rip has nodded during a signal event that marks a shift in world history and a transition in its period framework.[15] But unlike those other temporal lacunae in which catastrophic changes occurred and are registered as such (conquest, triumph) by our nonparticipants, the Revolution seems to Rip after the fact to be nothing but a matter of minor adjustments. As Rip makes his way back to his village after his twenty-year night, he recognizes the sign outside his favorite inn: the face on it was the same — it was King George's — but the color of the coat had been changed from red to blue and buff, and "GENERAL WASHINGTON" had been painted underneath. Irving here smirks that for all the self-importance of the new nation there was simply not much difference between it and the former regime, but he is also suggesting a more abstract point about the relativity of historical periodization. The permanent deposition of his wife's rule is the regime change that brings Rip joy: if historical periodization were up to Rip, all history would be divided into the years before, during, and after Dame Winkle. He happily resumes the old habits formerly begrudged him, occupying "his place once more on the bench at the inn door" (783).

Everyday time is incredible, it is multifarious, and Rip's experience brings into view — realizes, makes real — the queer potential of the mundane. In Rip, the "queer" that means "strange" meets the "queer" that means "outside of normative reproduction," and it all goes to show just how queer quotidian time can be. Rip has previously refused his obligations as husband and family man: he avoided the tasks of the nuclear family (helping anyone else but his own household), ducked the demands of his wife, and virtually orphaned his children — they run around "as ragged and wild as if they belonged to nobody" (771). Once the twenty-year night has elapsed, his wife is dead and he can finally prosper, in his own way, as the bachelor, idle and revered, he always psychically was. His incredulous shrug of the shoulders whenever the dead Dame van Winkle is mentioned perfectly expresses the simultaneity of the magical and the ordinary that characterizes his queer present: "Whenever her name was mentioned, however, he shook his head, shrugged his shoulders and cast up his eyes; which might pass either for an expression of resignation to his fate or joy at his deliverance" (783). This complex pantomime, for all its misogyny, nonetheless acknowledges the enduring power of the dame: it acknowledges the porousness of the present; it hails the possibility of specters, spirits, ghosts, revenants.

"Rip van Winkle" expresses the constant pressure of other temporalities on our ordinary image of time: it is, in this sense, realistic.[16] Such incredible realism perhaps explains why "Rip van Winkle" seems almost immediately to have been taken seriously in the region itself.[17] The supernatural stratum of the narrative brings out exactly that queer potential of everyday time, the noncontemporaneity of the *now*: "Hendrick Hudson, the first discoverer of the river and country" (782), and his crew reappear every twenty years, with a regularity that ironically heightens the asynchrony of their ghostly presence. Spirits, ghosts, specters and apparitions, gods and the divine: the supernatural can irrupt at any moment, refusing to let us forget the unsettling, marvelous, fearsome asynchrony of life that the hold of classically scientific time-as-measurement would lead us to discount. If the spookily moving headstone with which I began reveals the nineteenth century in the twenty-first, such "disjunctures in the present," as Dipesh Chakrabarty puts it, "allow us to be with" gods and spirits, such manifestations of nonmodern temporalities that can prove to have paradoxically ordinary (because ever potential) queering effects.[18]

Such figures — gods, spirits — are nonrational and learning to live with them — "*I would like to learn to live finally,*" writes Jacques Derrida in *Specters of Marx* — means learning to live in a world in which no opposition between death and life can hold.[19] And with the deconstruction of that foundational opposition, related foundations crumble: the oppositions between inside and outside, presence and absence, materiality and ideality, reality and fiction, true and false, present and past, subject and object — the oppositions structuring the whole modernist settlement, as discussed in my introduction.[20] "Learning to live without all of these props," writes Wendy Brown, whose reading of Derrida has informed mine here, means learning to live in a world permeated by "an elsewhere" and another time, permeated thoroughly but in no permanent or totalizable way. The divine may appear, unfolding its temporality like a luminous peacock, but in such a "postmetaphysical" frame it is as one such ghost among many. In such a world neither the past nor the present can be mastered; indeed, the effects of past on present are not only "unmasterable," but they are also "uncategorizable, and irreducible."[21] Queerness is the ordinary potential of the everyday.[22]

Time can queer you: the present is nonidentical to itself, and it thus constitutes a field in which varying kinds of temporalities get lived out. Within this field some events or conditions—some wrinkles in laminar time—are particularly motivated by specific, unfinished business; some ghosts figure anxious exclusions from the present—unheard voices, unacknowledged bodies, foreclosed potentials. The ghost of Dame van Winkle, for example, has been understood as haunting a masculinist canon of American short stories because of her necessary death at its putative origin.[23] We have a responsibility to such specters who not only figure our inability to master the past or the present but also offer a case for the ethical necessity of doing justice to those excluded. Derrida asks, "Without this *non-contemporaneity with itself of the living present*, without that which secretly unhinges it, without this responsibility and this respect for justice concerning those who *are not there*, of those who are no longer or who are not yet *present and living*, what sense would there be to ask the question 'where?' 'where tomorrow?' 'whither?'"[24] Our responsibility is not only to individual phenomena but also to the very nature of "the living present" itself: such asynchronies as in Rip van Winkle's world—the human body and mind striated by diverse times, spirits returning and drawing the living to them, people existing in different temporalities in the same present moment—present "incredible" potentialities in the *now*, and, further, urge us on toward our responsibility to acknowledge their presence, to restore them to view, to bring out their vitality, to learn to live with them.

"A ROYAL POET"

That time is wondrous and has queer potential does not mean that the *now* is an undifferentiated free-for-all. It means that there are far more possibilities for living than time-as-measurement would lead us to believe, but it does not mean that there are no constraints operating in this temporally multiple world. We will consider further the idea that some specters lurking in the *now* are created by exclusion, like the death of Dame van Winkle. I want to turn now to another figure of exclusion in Washington

Irving's work, an example that will eventually take us further into the spectral world of the *Sketch Book*. The figure is the narrator Geoffrey Crayon himself, and he will in fact turn the logic of spectral exclusion inside out. Amateur and queer, Crayon is excluded from the modernist temporality of the professional and of family life; but when he turns to the medieval past in order to feel whole, we find that he is isolated from that realm as well.

Washington Irving, who eventually made his home in the Hudson Valley, was a dedicated reader of medieval and early modern English literature, an Anglophile and enthusiastic antiquarian at the dawn of the age of the professional historian. We have already seen him tramping around the legendarily enchanted Scottish hills, listening to an old ballad. The temporal weirdness of "Rip van Winkle" appears side-by-side with medieval reenactments and longings recorded in the *Sketch Book*; that association between Rip, Thomas Rhymer, and Irving that I noted above is elaborated in the very structure of the book. The presence of the medieval in a dreamy, ghostly, asynchronous *now* comes to the fore in other pieces in the *Sketch Book*, and engagement with the medieval is now what I want to track.

Geoffrey Crayon, the narrator of the *Sketch Book*, is Irving's fictionalized self—a bachelor New Yorker who reads of and then visits locales important to British literary history, producing "sketches" of them. There are sketches of Westminster Abbey, the Reading Room of the British Museum library, Stratford-on-Avon, and so on, appearing among sketches of American settings and characters as well; spanning both continents and a bit of a hodgepodge, as various critics have seen, they are all united by the narratorial voice of Crayon.[25] In "The Author's Account of Himself" introducing the *Sketch Book*, Crayon characterizes himself as an American, belated and derivative: the contrast between America and Europe is charted along the stream of time. "My native country was full of youthful promise; Europe was rich in the accumulated treasures of age" (744), Crayon remarks; "I will visit this land of wonders, thought I, and see the gigantic race from which I am degenerated" (744). But his belatedness is not only American; it is also dilettantish.[26] He likens his roving, idle gaze to that of an amateur antiquarian window-shopping: "I have wandered through different countries and witnessed many of the shifting scenes of life," he writes. "I cannot say that I have studied them with the eye of a philosopher, but rather with the sauntering gaze with which humble lovers of the picturesque stroll from the window of one print shop to another" (745). Irving's choice of this very form (the sketch) and style (the picturesque) was itself anachronistic, as Susan Manning notes: the picturesque already "had had its fashionable day."[27] Once again we find the amateur in the "wrong" time, belated, out of sync with the chronological present.

Narratorial self-consciousness about his own belatedness is a guiding principle of the work. This American dilettante associates himself with the medieval past: he is an amateur medievalist who in his very name conjures the spirit of Geoffrey Chaucer. Like Chaucer's ever-belated, self-deprecating poetic persona, Geoffrey Crayon, too, is an outsider in relation to love, bookish and unattached to, as well as in, the world. Belatedness is American, it is amateurish, and it is queer. The *Sketch Book*'s epigraph from Robert Burton's *Anatomy of Melancholy* (later than Chaucer, but still antiquated) makes this queerness utterly clear: "I have no wife nor children, good or bad, to provide for. A mere spectator of other men's fortunes and adventures, and how they play their parts; which methinks are diversely presented unto me, as from a common theater or scene." Crayon is radically distanced from all, not merely from the family but even from men who have families. And his queer temporality is played out in a wide range of ways: in the choice of outdated genre, in the narrative structure of flitting from scene to scene, in the hovering presence of the medieval Chaucer, in the "loitering," "lolling," "languid" idleness of the narrative voice (808), and in such thematics as a night that lasts for twenty years as well as a conjuring, as we shall see, that is much wished for but (even queerer) only *sort of* works.

American, amateur, and queer, out of sync and desiring another time. Crayon is certainly nostalgic, yearning for a past era; in fact his sketches of English life irritated some English readers for that very reason. William Hazlitt complained, "Instead of looking round to see what *we are*, he sets to work to describe us as *we were*—at second hand," he adds, since Irving derives his knowledge from books. Despite this round condemnation of Irving's "literary anachronisms"—Irving fails, according to Hazlitt, by "giving us credit for the virtues of our forefathers"—Geoffrey Crayon's relationship to another time, to the past, is actually more complex: he is distanced even from his own nostalgia.[28] We've already heard his voice in the *Sketch Book*'s introduction; let us listen again to what is a complicated mock abjection. Crayon explains the lure of European travel for him as an American, remarking, "My native country was full of youthful promise; Europe was rich in the accumulated treasures of age. . . . I longed to wander over the scenes of renowned achievement—to tread as it were in the footsteps of antiquity — to loiter about the ruined castle — to meditate on the falling tower — to escape in short, from the commonplace realities of the present, and lose myself among the shadowy grandeurs of the past" (744). He seeks an escape from the banal "present" into a richer, grander time. But in the next paragraph something like nostalgia's critical edge cuts in — his tone is ironically self-deprecating: "I will visit this land of wonders, thought I, and see the gigantic race from which I am degenerated" (744). In that mocking voice Crayon puts a little wedge between himself and the simplistic discourse of the Old World, the discourse of English superiority (and the trope of traveling eastward as traveling back in time, whose operations I examined in chapter 2); he distances himself from the discourse of a return to origins that would supposedly complete oneself. While there are sketches (particularly in the "Christmas" section) drenched in sentimental reflections on traditions dating back to the Middle Ages, even there Crayon is the outsider, aware that he cannot quite lose himself in those "shadowy grandeurs," though that losing is exactly his impulse.[29]

Thus his special take on the pervasive air of "melancholy" hanging over the ruins of the past, those crumbling piles he finds both decayed and glorious. Crayon is impressed by their "picturesque" beauty and shivers in their "mournful" atmosphere of loss, but he remains nonetheless detached, in his own temporality, ever belated. He wants this to be a realm of ghosts and specters: in the library at Westminster Abbey, for example, which seems to him "a kind of literary catacomb, where authors, like mummies, are piously entombed," he experiences a vision of books as animated spirits. But mysterious magi-like figures at the British Museum library deflatingly turn out to be nothing more than authors reading and taking notes.[30] And in the sketch called "A Royal Poet," Geoffrey Crayon narrates his visit to Windsor Castle, where he eagerly follows the steps of King James I of Scotland, the late-medieval figure imprisoned there who finally triumphed over adversity to win his lady love and assume his rightful throne. Crayon tries to conjure James but remains detached and isolated in his own time.

Crayon in "A Royal Poet" tells us he has read and loved the famous poem by James, the *Kingis Quair*. James wrote the poem, says Crayon (following the received wisdom in Irving's time) while imprisoned in the keep of Windsor Castle for eighteen years before he became king. Crayon has found in the *Kingis Quair* an inspiring message of aristocratic fortitude in the face of adversity, and a touching expression of a man's romantic love of a lady: James first saw his future queen, Joan Beaufort, while he was imprisoned in the castle tower, and he writes about that experience in the poem.[31] James had a deeply poetical nature, Crayon muses; his imagination could create a "world for itself, and with a necromantic power" could conjure up even in the gloom of long captivity "glorious shapes and forms, and brilliant visions" (817–18). James is so readily able to communicate "his immediate thoughts concerning his situation" that the reader of the *Kingis Quair* is made "present with the captive in his prison, and the companion of his meditations" (818): Crayon, having read the poem, has already felt drawn into James's presence.

But now, in the actual place, Crayon records his own steps through the castle halls and grounds. Looking out at a garden "at the foot of the tower," he's delighted, indeed charmed, and he contends that time has more or less stopped there. The poetry that was written there worked a kind of magic, halting the chronic movement of loss and desolation.

> Time, which delights to obliterate the sterner memorials of human pride, seems to have passed lightly over this little scene of poetry and love, and to have withheld his desolating hand. Several centuries have gone by, yet the garden still flourishes. . . . It occupies what was once the moat of the keep; and though some parts have been separated by dividing walls, yet others have still their arbours and shaded walks, as in the days of James, and the whole is sheltered, blooming, and retired. (827)

The enchanting spot inspires "poetical devotion," a contemplative "musing over the romantic loves of the Lady Jane [i.e., Joan Beaufort] and the Royal Poet of Scotland" (828) that moves Crayon toward communion with the spirit of the dead poet. Crayon walks where James had walked and feels the "voluptuous vernal" weather that James had felt, in "the same genial and joyous month" as that in which James had written his poem (815, 827). The sight of a suit of armor, "richly gilt and embellished as if to figure in the tournay," Crayon writes, "brought the image of the gallant and romantic prince vividly before my imagination" (827). But not just an image: Crayon compares the spot to a shrine, because James's physical presence itself seems to pervade the place.

Crayon is drawn into a copresence of times in the charmed, dreamlike *now*. "I paced the deserted chambers where [James] had composed his poem," he reports. "I leaned upon the window, and endeavoured to persuade myself it was the very one where he had been visited by his vision; I looked out upon the spot where he had first seen the Lady Jane" (827).

He and James are communicating; they are both there, they are at one—
almost, that is. For between the pacing of the selfsame chambers and the
gaze upon the glorious spot, Crayon must work to convince himself of
authenticity, presence, union. His effort is registered in that anomalous
phrase in this otherwise rapturous sketch: *I endeavoured to persuade myself.* I labored to believe that it was the very same window as that in which
James had gazed on his lady for the first time; the admission of effort opens
a suggestion of failure. I wanted to believe, Crayon might as well have said,
that the future king and I, the inspired lover and I, were so near. But I
didn't.[32]

    This hitch at the heart of Geoffrey Crayon's passionate reenactment at
Windsor attests to something of his ineradicable alienness, even to himself.
Despite the intensely contrived reenactment framework, Geoffrey Crayon
remains out of sync both with the present *and also* with the past he so desires. James is not after all there with him. The past and its ghosts are finally
elusive. Crayon is of course not a historian beginning from a posture of remove and confirming his distance from his object of inquiry; he is a dilettante expecting connection, attempting to convoke the spirit, but what
he ends up confirming is that ghosts might well have their own agendas.[33]
We feel the unsettling nature of the noncontemporaneous *now*, and it is
the American amateur, belated and nonreproductive, the queer in his own
temporality cut off from both a socially normative time of work, family,
and reproduction, on the one hand, and a desired past time, on the other,
who brings it out. Times might be multiple in the *now*, but, unmasterable,
they are not equally accessible to all.

THE CONSOLATION OF PHILOSOPHY

So Geoffrey Crayon is a figure of exclusion, and because he is such a figure,
his experience tips us off to the whole logic of spectrality operating in the
world of "A Royal Poet"—a logic whereby the excluded voices, the unacknowledged bodies, the abjected others return to haunt present formations and try to get the justice due them. For the ghost of James I itself
has a ghost, a fact that not only underscores the condition of the multiplicity of the *now* but also suggests that the *now* may be populated by restless spirits seeking to be heard. James, writing the *Kingis Quair*, had many
ghosts (Geoffrey Chaucer and John Gower are named in the poem), but
I focus on an ancient one lurking in his poem and in the account of his
poem in "A Royal Poet." At the very beginning of the poem, James the

poetic narrator tells of his insomnia one night in his prison rooms: he can't sleep, and to wile away the "tedious hours" he reaches for a book, Boethius's *Consolation of Philosophy*. But the book in fact agitates rather than lulls James; he "falls into a fit of musing" (as Crayon describes it) about what Boethius has said concerning the fickleness of Fortune, lingering in "melancholy fancies" until the break of day, when he is startled by a bell striking matins (819). This bell acts on him like a voice urging him to set his experiences down with pen; it is as if the sixth-century Boethius, present, calls out to the fifteenth-century James.

In this atmosphere of visions and dreams, in which spirits linger, Boethius haunts James, who haunts Geoffrey Crayon. But these relationships are more porous than that sequential statement allows; these spirits move in and through the asynchronous worlds of the *Sketch Book* and the *Kingis Quair*, as I shall show. A traditional literary source study would demonstrate how James I in his poem appropriates Boethius's text, and then how Washington Irving (in the voice of Geoffrey Crayon) appropriates James's. But viewed in a spectral light, the *Consolation of Philosophy* and the *Kingis Quair* are less solid and unitary sources, less origins founded in a self-identical present, than part of a heterogeneous *now* in which the divide between living and dead, material and ideal, reality and fiction, text and spirit, present and past, is upset, where traces of signs and tracks of the living function in the same way: "Mark, gramma, trace, and *différance* refer differentially to all living things, all the relations between living and nonliving."[34] In the far recesses of James's text and the text recounting his text, the voice of an ancient writer echoes, sounding the pain of untimeliness. It is not a voice whose wounding has been sufficiently recognized; in fact it is ultimately silenced in the rational philosophical discourse of which it is a part. In this section I take a long look at Boethius's text, analyzing its discussion of temporal issues and tracking the unacknowledged pain that haunts the tales of asynchrony in this chapter. Let me turn now to that "talisman," that magical charm, as Geoffrey Crayon calls it (819), the *Consolation of Philosophy*, in order to begin to apprehend the ghostly workings of these texts, the asynchronous energies that radiate from this work into James's and Geoffrey Crayon's and my own worlds, and back again, creating a dense and dynamic *now*.[35] Passing in and out of the worlds of these texts, excluded by the discourse of rationality—philosophy—but conjured by my own discourse in an effort to do justice, is an asynchronous figure split apart by time.

Boethius's *Consolation of Philosophy* is a work originally in Latin, written in the early sixth century and subsequently translated by numerous writers through the ages, including Alfred the Great, Jean de Meun, Chaucer (whose translation James may have used, and whose version I shall take up here), and Elizabeth I (who accomplished the task with lightning speed).[36] It was indeed a deeply influential work in prose and poetry, celebrated for its bracingly rational approach to enduring questions: Why do bad things happen to good people? Why do the wicked prosper? Is there any justice in the world? What is true happiness, and how can we attain it? Boethius found himself asking such questions after he was imprisoned and exiled, condemned by the very Roman Senate to which he had dedicated his adult life of public service: "in so many ways," John Matthews writes, "Boethius was in reality, as he saw himself, a living representative of Rome, and of the Roman tradition" before its "occupation by barbarian rulers," out of sync in a Rome ruled by Theoderic, King of the Ostrogoths.[37] That is, he was something of an anachronism in his own day—like other writers and readers I have discussed in *How Soon Is Now?* Boethius was a Christian, moreover, as were many, perhaps most, in his day in Italy, and he wrote for a Christian audience.[38] He nonetheless chose to write the *Consolation of Philosophy* in a non-Christian philosophical tradition that was, for all its neoplatonizing, marked by Christianity as part of the past. Anna Crabbe corroborates these observations with her characterization of Boethius's "pleasantly anachronistic prose style."[39] He wrote the *Consolation* not only for specialist philosophers—the audience for other works in his large oeuvre—but for general readers, for future amateurs.[40] And its influence, befitting its amateur target, was belated: not until the ninth century did the first manuscripts surface and the important translation into Old English appear, and only about seven hundred fifty years after its composition did its influence begin to spread widely in the vernaculars.

Boethius was in his forties when he suffered the reversal of fortune that eventuated in his exile and imprisonment in (or near) Pavia, but in his prisoner persona he speaks as an "olde man" as the text opens, prematurely grey and ruefully recalling his earlier days of "youthe," when "in florysschyng studie" he wrote "delitable ditees." The Muses were his glory once ("whilom") in his "weleful and grene" [*healthy and robust*] youth (bk. 1, meter 1, lines 1–13). Echoes of Virgil sound in these opening lines—the Virgil who in turn had "harkened back nostalgically to his earlier bucolic verse": haunting echoes of past selves resound in these lines.[41] The asynchrony here may be pleasing on the level of literary style (as Crabbe suggests) but it *feels* horrible: the prisoner Boethius laments, "For eelde is comyn unwarly uppon me, hasted by the harmes that Y have, and sorwe hath comandid his age to ben in me" [*Old age has come unexpectedly upon me, hastened by the harms that I have experienced, and sorrow has commanded his/its age to be in me*].[42] It is not just that the prisoner was once young and he is now old; it is not even that sorrow has taken over his life; the "age" [*aetas*, "ses aages"] of "sorwe," sorrow's duration, sorrow's own particular temporality, has forcibly occupied the prisoner. This is not simple nostalgia. The man in his forties is taken over by another time: another time takes up residence in this man. In the Boethian poems of Charles of Orleans (written a little after the time of Chaucer's *Boece* translation), the allegorical figure of Age appears; he is duration itself, responsible for the lover's development from youth to maturity. Charles's Age is a benign source of good advice about advancing age, but in the *Consolation* duration and sorrow walk hand in hand. The prisoner's body with its own rhythms has been hollowed out and filled by sorrow's time: "Heeris hore arn schad overtymeliche upon myn heved, and the slakke skyn trembleth of myn emptid body" [*Hoary grey hairs are scattered prematurely on my head, and the slack skin of my hollow frame trembles*].[43] Another kind of time invades and settles into the prisoner's body, which is thus split, heterogeneous, and temporally out of joint: "Myn unpietous lif draweth along unagreable duellynges in me" [*My wretched life drags out hideous delays* (or, *incommensurate intervals*) *in me*].[44] The sentiment in this statement may exceed the notion—presented in Chaucer's source texts—that life is a drag and death will not come soon enough; if we take that phrase "unagreable duellynges" to mean "incommensurate intervals or durations," Boethius the prisoner is complaining that his cursed life proceeds via inner temporal clashing, inwardly colliding times: he experiences his asynchronous physicality as excruciating.[45] Present sorrow tears against the past in the *now*.

The prisoner specifically blames Fortune, the "unfeithful" goddess, for this out-of-joint condition. Fortune once favored him with her transitory goods, but now he laments, "Fortune cloudy [*frowning*] hath chaunged hir deceyvable chere to meward" [*her deceptive countenance toward me*]. These shifty workings of Fortune are in the prisoner's eyes precisely correlated with time: "the sorwful houre (*that is to seyn, the deth*)" threatened him when Fortune was being good to him, but now, when Fortune has turned away from him, death—the end of his time on earth—will not come soon enough (bk. 1, meter 1, lines 24–28); Fortune's change toward him has instantiated those temporal upheavals in his body just mentioned. Fortune plays a major role in the dialogue to follow, though, significantly, she never actually appears in the text; her absent presence, as Andrea Denny-Brown compellingly argues, reflects the lingering aura of the material things the prisoner has lost and to which he still remains attached, things that include his own former body.[46] The past, even himself as past, lingers in ghostly ways. Fortune works cannily and cruelly in time; the experience of living under her capricious, whimsical reign resembles the destabilizing experience of living in time as expressed in Augustine's *Confessions*. It *feels* similar: in late medieval iconography the effects of Fortune are pictured as precipitous climbs and headlong falls, bodies grasping upward and thrusting downward, flung off and outstretched on her ever-turning wheel. The figure of Time in fact rotates a wheel, Fortune-like, in fifteenth- and sixteenth-century literary and visual imagery.[47]

Augustine's term for time is *distentio animi*, as I mentioned in the introduction, *distentio* denoting a stretching out on a rack — or, perhaps, even a wheel.[48] This view of the stressful experience of human temporality presented in the dialogue's beginning — picturing Boethius's own situation but generalizable to all humans caught in time and feeling its constraints — is reminiscent of Augustine's in the *Confessions*, and just as Augustine in book 11 counters the strain of human temporal life with the joy of eternity, so does Boethius's text counter sublunar sorrow with the eternal view from above.[49] As he is penning his first lachrymose lines, Philosophie, an august female figure, appears to the captive in distress and seeks to console him by virtue of her rational approach to his situation. Philosophie is an epiphany or a vision, something like the spirit of classical philosophy conjured by the prisoner to try to assuage his grief and recall him to himself.[50] Philosophie herself appears to be both young and old at once — with "swich vigour and strengthe that it ne myghte nat ben emptid, al were it so that sche was ful of so greet age that men ne wolden nat trowen in no manere that sche were of our elde" [*boundless vigor and strength, though she was full of such great age that no one would believe at all that she was of our age* (i.e., era, time)] (bk. 1, prose 1, lines 8–12) — but though the prisoner cannot comprehend her temporality, as it were, her most penetrating understanding is of the nature of eternity and time.[51] And she has that to teach him.

First, though, Philosophie diagnoses the prisoner's devastated condition as a sickness of the mind and undertakes to heal him as his physician, administering first mild but then increasingly harsh medicines in order to bring him back to what he already knows: that humans incline to the *summum bonum*, God.[52] Fortune, she eventually argues, is just a figment of perspective; to think that events are caused by Fortune is just a bad way of understanding fate, that is, human events in time. Nothing is random, she avers, and Fortune has no independent power: everything that happens happens because God has in his providence planned it. Philosophie's healing gestures include expositions of "the symplicite of the purveaunce of God, and of the ordre of destyne, and of sodeyn hap, and of the knowynge and predestinacioun devyne, and of the liberte of fre wil" [*the oneness of providence, the course of fate, the haphazard nature of the random events of chance, divine knowledge and predestination, and the freedom of the will*] (bk. 4, prose 6, lines 25–29).[53] At the end of this sequence the rational, philosophical consolation Philosophie offers will be complete: everything tends toward the good, even if we cannot know the plan according to which all will happen. The most puzzling crux of all — how humans can have free choice and events can be contingent when God is omniscient — hinges on a distinction between time and eternity; in order to complete the consolation Philosophie must explicate for the prisoner, temporally stressed as he is, the true nature of time. For then she can argue that because God exists eternally his knowledge does not impinge on the human freedom of will or the contingency of events that unfurl in time.

So God is eternal, and eternity, Philosophie asserts, is "parfit possessioun and al togidre of lif interminable" [*perfect simultaneous possession of endless life*] (bk. 5, prose 6, lines 13–15).[54] It is not a perpetuity extended in time but is, rather, a way of living *simultaneously* ("al togidre"): self-present, self-controlled, self-possessed, and ever in the present. Nothing that exists in time, in contrast, "mai enbrasen togidre al the space of his lif. For certis yit ne hath it nat taken the tyme of tomorwe, and it hath lost that of yusterday, and certes in the lif of this dai ye ne lyve namore but right as in this moevable and transitorie moment" [*can embrace simultaneously the entire extent of its life. For indeed it has not yet possessed the time of tomorrow, and it has lost the time of yesterday, and certainly in the life of this day you do not live more fully than in this moving and transitory moment*] (bk. 5, prose 6, lines 21–26).[55] Yet she also emphasizes that the "infinit moevyng of temporel thinges . . . semyth somdel to us that it folwith and resembleth thilke thing that it ne mai nat atayne to ne fulfillen" [*infinite changing of temporal things . . . seems to us in some measure to follow and resemble that which it cannot attain or fulfill*] (bk. 5, prose 6, lines 68–82).[56] Humans live in their present the way God lives in his. But ours is an "unsuccessful" attempt at imitation, as John Marenbon terms it; humans must make "the infinite journey through time." Though "the ordinary, human present provides a comparison by which we can understand something of God's eternal present and so of God's way of knowing," Marenbon sees, there is nonetheless a felt gap between eternity and time.[57] Temporality, as a consequence of its incapacity to confer presence onto the present, is a condition that a thing "suffreth" (bk. 5, prose 6, line 27).[58] Temporal sequence is something that is in experience — and in Philosophie's own expression — characterized by lack: Where, exactly, are we? What do we have, in the present? Not the past, which has been lost; not the future, which hasn't arrived. Philosophie's words resonate with Augustine's as he puzzles out the nature of time in his *Confessions* — the present has no duration at all (11.15) — and as he contrasts time with God's eternity.

Boethius the prisoner is stuck in time, and time sticks in him. Philosophie has led him (back) to knowledge of the supreme good and its glorious, eternal *now*, but "what she cannot supply, or even acknowledge, is . . . a *way* for Boethius to grasp and gain the highest good to which she has led him," as Marenbon puts it.[59] That incapacity weighs at the end of the dialogue. The transcendence of earthly attachments, those ties in and to time, is enormously difficult; lingering attachments register as rifts in the body, as in the first poetic lines of the work, or as backward glances, as in the poem that closes book 3: after Philosophie has led the prisoner to knowledge of the supreme good, she sings a long song about sorry Orpheus and the necessity of fixing one's mind on the "sovereyn day" above. Orpheus with his "weeply songes" provides a wrenching example of earthly love and irreversible loss. That poem registers the present power of past things, past bodies, past lives: "Orpheus lokede abakward on Erudyce his wif, and lost hire, and was deed" (bk. 3, meter 12, lines 62, 6, 58–59).

The remaining poems in the *Consolation of Philosophy* are the place where the temporal problems of past attachments as well as "corporeal depths and energies," as Sarah Kay writes, are felt most acutely: "Though they still aspire to be consolatory, the verse passages also resonate to a pulse of distress."[60] At times they suggest a specifically temporal distress: following the poetic imagery of churning waters and rivers through the work, the rushing streams appearing late in the *Consolation* (bk. 5, meter 1), suggesting the stream of life, prove strange and overwhelming.[61] It is significant, therefore, that Philosophie's last prose statement about divine knowledge ends the work without any poetic elaboration or any response from the prisoner. Seth Lerer argues that this ending is an index of the philosophical dialogue's success: embodying a philosophical problem, the prisoner is consumed by the consolation that has reached its rational end.[62] This may well be the case, but if so, the end—and the consolation as such—leaves unaddressed the disconnect between "knowledge" of the good and "a *way* to grasp and gain" it, the lived gap, that is, between eternity and time. The dialogue's end is forever haunted by a final resolution of this dilemma—an articulation of the way for humans to attain the good, the redemption of time by the eternal—that never comes. The *Consolation* lingers thus somewhere between the said and the unsaid, the dead and the undead. Haunting the overflowing stream with which I began this chapter are the rushing rivers and disordered waters that run through the *Consolation*, signs of the difficulty of human life in time that is unredeemed and unredeemable. Beside the happy Rip in a very heterogeneous *now*, beside the yearning Geoffrey Crayon, the incredulous Washington Irving, the I who kicked that headstone one morning in the Catskills is the temporally rent Boethius.

THE KINGIS QUAIR

And it's just that broken figure that James would conjure away in his poem. The prisoner Boethius, for James, is already and fully consoled at the outset of the *Kingis Quair*, and James reworks the *Consolation* so that Fortune, too, is figured as a positive force in his life. But conjurement always implicates a conjuration, as Derrida would have it: any effort to put the ghost to rest nevertheless acknowledges its continuing power.

Let me turn finally to the medieval poem itself, the *Kingis Quair*. Recall that James says he was reading "*Boece*" (the medieval name for the author and the text) to address an immediate temporal problem: he was awake in the middle of the night and wanted to wile away the sleepless hours. In his description of *Boece*, James immediately names the principals encountered (as we have seen) in that work's opening poem and prose: "that noble senatoure / Of Rome," Philosophye, and Fortune (lines 18–19).[63] But according to James, Boece as he writes his work is already freed of his longing for and attachment to the goods and life he once had; no dialogic process is necessary for him to work through his worldliness. So no need for consolation lingers at the end, nor is there any unresolved temporal dilemma: James

writes that Boece set his pen to work describing his lot and how he began
to comfort himself once Fortune's wheel had turned and condemned him
to poverty in exile. And that is what his book is about, as James puts it: "the
writing of this noble man" describes how he

> in himself the full recover wan
> Of his infortune, povert, and distresse,
> And in tham set his verray sekernesse. (33–35)

> in himself achieved full recovery
> From his misfortune, poverty and distress,
> And in them [i.e., fortune, wealth, and happiness] set his true security.

Boece's restoration is recorded in the past tense ("full recover *wan*") but
also in the "historical present" a few lines later ("And so aworth he *takith*
his penance," 41): this Boece occupies a past that is ongoing. Even if James's
"scole is over yong" [*learning is too young, i.e., insufficient*] (46) to convey
adequately *Boece*'s accomplished Latinity, both writers, in their different
temporalities (young and old), coexist happily in this *now*, which James says
leads to a future of "perfect joy." Fortune's "quhile" [*wheel*] (20), problematically associated with the depredations of time in the *Consolation*, is assimilated to the "quhile" [*while, interval, time*] (14) of the *Kingis Quair* itself,
which is structured by the "interdependence of present and past" — a positively valued condition in which James's mature self represents his youthful
experiences, as Gregory Kratzmann has seen, and learns from them.[64]

The poem consists of a long narrative of James's early sufferings in
prison, his falling in love at the sight of his lady in the adjacent garden,
his vision of Venus, Minerva, and Fortune, and his receiving a reassuring
token of the vision's happy meaning and eventual outcome. Its very end,
however, is what is most telling for my analysis. In a gesture of closure, in
the penultimate stanza, James wraps things up by acknowledging God as
an all-powerful poet who has written our lives in the sphere of the heavens:

> And thus endith the fatall influence
> Causit from Hevyn quhare powar is commytt
> Of govirnance, by the magnificence
> Of Him that hiest in the hevine sitt.
> To quham we thank that all oure lif hath writt,
> Quho couth it red agone syne mony a yere:
> "Hich in the hevynnis figure circulere." (1366–72)

And thus ends the fateful influence
Derived from Heaven, where power is given
For governing, by the magnificence
Of Him that sits highest in heaven.
Whom we thank, who has written all our life,
Whoever could read it, many a year since,
High in the heaven's circular schema.

The divine temporality that Philosophie explicated in the *Consolation* is invoked here in the *Kingis Quair* to close the poem. God has written our life, says James, and it can be read later (as in a horoscope) high in the fixed stars, "in the hevynnis figure circulere." That last line repeats the poem's first line; God's eternal vision and his creation—his writing—are assimilated to James's poem, and the poem's time is absorbed into eternity. But what is left out of this celebration of poetry as eternal is what the poems in the *Consolation* express: the attachment to the earthly and the difficulty of transcendence—the figure, that is, of the prisoner Boethius. Philosophie's discourse of the eternal, invoked here, is haunted by the unacknowledged difficulties of living in mundane time.

The events of James's life—the chronology referred to in this poem—belong to the time of the patriarchal family and sovereign succession. Though sorely tried, he wins his love, Joan Beaufort ("princess of the blood royal of England," as Crayon put it [818]), who becomes queen, and he assumes his rightful throne as king. To return to my terms when discussing Washington Irving and Geoffrey Crayon: James is well inside the reproductive family, indeed the dynasty; in this sense he is anything but queer. He conjures away the haunting figure of nontranscendence and temporal distress. But as I read it now the gesture works against itself, serving to conjure that figure: beside James lurks Boethius; beside the triumphal king sits the cost of earthly subjection. Ironically, then, the *now* of this poem is queer in the way I have been arguing that all time potentially is—queer, that is, as a moving headstone.

LONG EDDY, NEW YORK

We return at last to that headstone in the Catskills. I called it a piece of the nineteenth century that was carried along to me in the twenty-first. Yet that story is in fact too simple. The stone itself is, of course, thousands of years old. But it is also new: this is not the original late-nineteenth-century headstone, as becomes clear in a second look at the image. It is a granite replacement, made, I am told, in the 1950s. After I found this stone among the river rocks on the banks of our stream, I called a local logger with a backhoe to dig it out — it was way too heavy for me to wrangle — and return it to the graveyard. It now sits next to a tree trunk, in the vicinity of the dead but no longer marking the exact spot where the dead man, David LeValley, lies. (If he indeed lies there still: a casket handle, perhaps from his own coffin, was found wandering along the banks of the stream.)

The past that made its way downstream to me was in fact new. I returned it to the eroded cemetery, to what was inevitably not the original spot but rather some other spot along that stream, in an act of responsibility to ghosts who populate the living present. And I am now one of those: my girlfriend and I no longer own that property, but the spirit of our life there lingers still. My act of restitution was not merely symbolic, the headstone functioning as a marker for something long gone. It created a new kind of time: it opened up a new moment in the inexhaustible past, and offered yet another new past for the *now*.

The Lay of the Land

Amateur Medievalism and Queer Love
in A Canterbury Tale

A Canterbury Tale, the brilliant and baffling 1944 film, pushes to a bizarre and criminal point the implications of my discussion heretofore. If, as I have been maintaining throughout this book, the experience of a *now* shot through with different times is a wondrous possibility in the everyday, and if this possibility has ethical potential because it enables the rendering of justice that might have been absent in the past—if all this is the case—it could be thought that merely hypothesizing the concept of a more heterogeneous *now* is not enough. Suppose that some lunatic enthusiast decided that people must be compelled, by force if necessary, to engage such a *now*. Something like this is the startlingly peculiar premise of *A Canterbury Tale*: more specifically, a "loony English squire" insists that people must be forced to desire the past.

A Canterbury Tale depicts these attempts at temporal compulsion in a strange tale of an amateur medievalist gone haywire. The film's weird plot can be understood in terms of the film's production in a time of war, and the film ultimately indicts the squire as backward and outmoded. But the film is ambivalent, for it also represents positive social effects of the squire's temporally asynchronous experiences. The Middle Ages conjured up by this film conjures away the violence, disease, dirt, and other dark elements of the period's conventional depiction, but the film is not naively nostalgic: any positive view of noncontemporaneous contemporaneity is derived, strangely, from the squire's obsession and criminal acts. Rendering the film even more interesting for my final purposes here, it continues to push my exploration of the *now* to experience beyond the human realm. The film helps us broaden our understanding of what kinds of interrelations can make up the *now*, what "more life" might consist of, what can constitute the "collective" — the term is Bruno Latour's, to be distinguished from merely human "society" — of a more attached life.[1] In this way, the film does not simply yearn for some sanitized past but, in its vision of the breached boundaries between present and past and between human and nonhuman — offered to us by an amateur — it suggests expansive possibilities for a very queer *now*.

STICKY SITUATIONS

To the plot, and then to fuller discussion: the magistrate of a small village, located along the pilgrims' route to Canterbury, loves his rural habitat, the home of his ancestors, very much. This love makes him want to share his knowledge of the area with others; he'll try anything, in fact, in his campaign to inculcate local history in the minds of the populace but finds, to his dismay, that Englanders are unmoved by the past of rural Kent. Their indifference is not due to more immediately pressing concerns, even though the war effort pervades their lives (it's 1943 in the film); they just don't care. The magistrate, Thomas Colpeper, describes his vain efforts to teach people the history of their homeland: even before the war, he bitterly reflects, they had no interest. "I've written articles that didn't get further than the county papers. I rented a hall in London to speak from but nobody came to listen. I even held a meeting in Hyde Park."[2] He recalls that his frustration with the failure of his personal mission grew and grew — until, as he puts it, "a miracle happened": the English army established a camp near his village. Suddenly he had a potential captive audience! Still he found that no one was interested in the history of the area; as the commanding officer explained to the downhearted antiquarian, after a day's work the soldiers want to meet up with girls, or go to the movies to see girls on screen, or go to dances, rather than attend a historical lecture. *All they care about is girls!* the magistrate inwardly seethes: "They were always with girls, or after girls."

Despite the manifest indifference of his intended audience, though, he becomes even more determined to "pou[r] knowledge into people's heads — by force if necessary." So Colpeper, who is something of a loner living with his mother, fanatically devises a solution: in silent, anonymous strikes, in the blackout, he will pour *glue* onto the heads of village girls who go out at night, to keep them inside so as not to distract the soldiers from attending his lectures. Soon cases of icky, sticky hair multiply, and the anonymous perpetrator of these odd assaults becomes known as the Glueman. After an attack in the dark on the film's female protagonist, the identity of the Glueman is finally uncovered. Despite initial indignation and outrage, all seems to be forgiven by the end of the film — yet even though the protagonists at last admit that they like him, at the film's finale in Canterbury Cathedral Thomas Colpeper stands alone.

Unsurprisingly, given that bewildering plot, *A Canterbury Tale*, written and directed by Michael Powell and Emeric Pressburger — hot from their box-office triumph in *The Life and Death of Colonel Blimp* — was neither "understood" nor "enjoyed" when released in 1944, as Powell later reflected in his autobiography, and Powell acknowledged that "the story of *A Canterbury Tale*" was "a frail and unconvincing structure."[3] The sheer oddness of the Glueman plot — its "impossible premise," Powell called it — is exacerbated by the film's refusal to take a clear stand on the Glueman himself.[4] The full narrative of the film follows three young people who have alighted from a train in the fictional village of Chillingbourne; they are an American soldier, an English soldier, and an English Land Girl who has volunteered with the Women's Land Army to work in this rural setting where many men have gone off to war. The three stop at Chillingbourne for different reasons, but each must eventually get to Canterbury, which is the next stop on the train, and each ultimately finds a blessing there. During their brief sojourn in Chillingbourne these "modern pilgrims" become acquainted with one another and are drawn into the Glueman mystery; indeed, together they solve the puzzle of his identity and confront the magistrate. When confronted, Colpeper mystically, or at least mysteriously, implies that he is subject to a "higher cour[t]," where he clearly believes he will be exonerated. And strangely, even though the English soldier strenuously insists that he will denounce Colpeper to the police, he gets distracted and the matter is finally just abandoned in the film.[5] Is Colpeper, aka the Glueman, good or bad? Is his view of the past uselessly outdated or a beacon for the future? Is his idea of justice defensible before God? Is he just a demented homo who hates women? It was Powell who referred to him as "a loony English squire," but played with brilliant inscrutability by Eric Portman, himself (most probably) a gay man, his character is very difficult to pin down completely.[6]

The glue plot has been dismissed by critics as part and parcel of the "eccentric" nature of Powell and Pressburger's oeuvre, or, more negatively, as evidence of their "bad taste" and "perversity."[7] (When *Peeping Tom* was released in 1960 and effectively ended Michael Powell's career, *A Canterbury Tale* was held up as a creepy antecedent.)[8] The glue itself, according to Ian Christie, was a substitute for the original plot device of slashing girls' dresses, abandoned because it was thought to be too "sexually suggestive." But glue in the hair is hardly less sexually suggestive, as the infamous hair gel scene from *There's Something about Mary* makes perfectly clear.[9] And though Pressburger, responsible for the script, brushed off any inference of a "sexual connotation," Powell eventually confirmed it.[10] What is it about local history—amateur medievalism—that marks it here as both potentially redemptive and decidedly perverse?

PROPAGANDA AND PERVERSION

A Canterbury Tale is in fact a war film, and the context of war helps to explain Thomas Colpeper's preoccupations. War pervades every aspect of the movie, from the everyday mimetic detail of the blackout (creating a noir look in the first twenty minutes or so) to the construction of sets (the windows of Canterbury Cathedral had been boarded up, so the nave was reconstructed in perspective at Denham Studios) to the music (the organ at Canterbury had been "dismantled," so the organ music was recorded at Saint Albans), to characters, plot, and thematics.[11] Powell and Pressburger's commercial production company, The Archers, which produced this film, had worked with the British government's Ministry of Information on earlier films; *A Canterbury Tale* was not a government commission, but the ministry nonetheless played a role in its casting.[12] And *A Canterbury Tale* had in fact a specifically patriotic mission: "We were explaining to the Americans," Powell wrote, "and to our own people, the spiritual values and the traditions we were fighting for." This makes the film akin to "orientation films" made by the Ministry of Information to acquaint Britons and Americans with each other in view of the influx of American soldiers into England.[13] Thus in *A Canterbury Tale* there are be-mused comments by the American protagonist, Sgt. Bob Johnson, about tea drinking, for example — but the major English national characteristic depicted and celebrated by the film is the love of the English countryside, the homeland of their ancestors. The cinematography, showing scenes of a radiant Kent landscape in summer, was in particular widely admired. (This heightened "Englishness" was produced by many non-Englishmen, including the German-born cinematographer Edwin Hillier and the Hun-garian Pressburger himself, who was not even allowed to the filming in Kent because of his alien status.)

One way of beginning to explain Thomas Colpeper, then, is to see him as a personification of an idealized national character trait. Indeed, repre-sentation of English character was part of the "Programme for Film Pro-paganda" outlined in an early 1940 memo out of the Ministry of Informa-tion; Colpeper's fixation on "mythical old England" can be seen as State co-optation of "traditional, romantic values as part of mythologising pro-paganda."[14] Other English characters in the film may not be interested in local history, but they should be, the film teaches: Colpeper's High Tory investment in traditional English values disciplines English viewers as well as educates their allies. Appreciation for the local as part of a glorious shared national history is one of the "spiritual values and the traditions we were fighting for." Colpeper, isolated and peculiar, is nonetheless a tradi-tionalist through and through; Alexander Doty argues in a provocative article on this film that Colpeper is an extreme example of a "queer con-servative," a traditionalist whose sexual queerness is co-opted for nation-alistic use in a time of war. Doty points out the very high concentration of queer (i.e., sexually indeterminate or nonconformist) characters and jokes in the film and analyzes them with regard to the film's overall patriotic purpose: they pop up all over (presumably made especially visible in the homosocial and at times gender-inverted worlds produced by the war), but because of what he calls the "pervasive narrative and cultural forces at work in *A Canterbury Tale* to de-sexualize queerness as part of a conservative ideological programme," Doty finds that the message of the film to queers was "Close your eyes and think of England!"[15]

The nationalistic agenda is certainly powerful in the film — the finale shows the protagonists proceeding to Canterbury, where English soldiers march in preparation for deployment for D-Day — but I don't think the conservatism of the film functions quite as unambiguously as Doty suggests.[16] The utter fanaticism of Colpeper and the sheer bizarreness of his glue plot here, to my mind, suggest that this film cannot be completely understood in terms of patriotic purpose. The glue is an unsavory excess, as Michael Powell confirmed ruefully later: the "orientation" message was outdated by the time the film was released (since the film's opening was delayed until after D-Day), so "if you weren't interested in the theme of the film, there was something unnecessary and even unpleasant about the activities of Mr Culpepper [sic]." That bad aftertaste lingered among early reviewers.[17] But the nasty excessiveness was not merely an effect of the film's delayed opening; indeed, the character of the Glueman was difficult even to cast because of its perceived distastefulness.[18] A Canterbury Tale undertakes a propagandistic mission but manages to make something harder to characterize — let alone use — in the end.[19]

IN ONE ERA AND OUT THE OTHER

What is it, then, that this local historian, this amateur medievalist, desires? Thomas Colpeper's belief in traditional values may have been "a bit too conservatively old-fashioned for war-time England," Doty remarks; he is out of sync even with the war effort.[20] One can see this in his obsession relative to the range of attitudes toward the past charted by the film, from the soldiers' modernist desire to break with the past, to the Land Girl's fear of the past as a time of loss, to the rural villagers' relaxed sense of living with but not privileging the old. Colpeper stridently prefers the past: Chaucer is his point of reference, not only for the history of his home but also for his sense of daily life in the present. For Colpeper, the Canterbury Tales is a document of local history, of lives that passed through this area on pilgrimage, and those lives (including "doctors and lawyers, clerks and merchants," as he puts it) are just like those of present-day travelers, soldiers in their peacetime occupations, and "modern pilgrims" today.[21]

The film begins in fact with the opening page of the General Prologue to Chaucer's Canterbury Tales: the famous first eighteen lines are spoken in voice-over while the camera follows the printed page (see epilogue figure 1). The Middle English is what we see (it looks like W. W. Skeat's

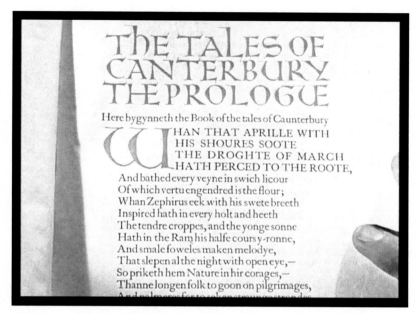

THE TALES OF
CANTERBURY
THE PROLOGUE

Here bygynneth the Book of the tales of Caunterbury

WHAN THAT APRILLE WITH
HIS SHOURES SOOTE
THE DROGHTE OF MARCH
HATH PERCED TO THE ROOTE,
And bathed every veyne in swich licour
Of which vertu engendred is the flour;
Whan Zephirus eek with his swete breeth
Inspired hath in every holt and heeth
The tendre croppes, and the yonge sonne
Hath in the Ram his halfe cours y-ronne,
And smale foweles maken melodye,
That slepen al the night with open eye,—
So priketh hem Nature in hir corages,—
Thanne longen folk to goon on pilgrimages,

Epilogue 1. The General Prologue to the Canterbury Tales, with voice-over in modern pronunciation. *From* A Canterbury Tale *(1944)*.

text, which would have been an available school edition), but what we hear is a twentieth-century version of Middle English, with modern pronunciation and hard words translated into modern English but other archaisms retained. That disjunction between the past language and the present adaptation of it immediately opens the question of how this past is related to the lived present. When the voice-over reaches the fifth line — "Whan Zephirus eek with his swete breeth" — the image track, having scrolled through to the end of the passage, shifts to a map of England, tracing the route to Canterbury from Winchester. Again there is a disjunction, for the route traced is not the route of Chaucer's pilgrims, who travel from Southwark (across the Thames from London) to Canterbury. And, oddly, the last word in the text, "seeke" in the final printed line, is read aloud as "weak" (rather than the literally proper "sick").

The Archers were notoriously fanatical about their production design: in the credits that immediately precede this opening, for example, the bells in the Bell Harry Tower in Canterbury Cathedral were painstakingly re-created in fiberglass miniature and then actually rung by "expert bellringers" in sync with the recorded peal, so that their movements would be synchronized to the soundtrack.[22] Considering such minute attention to detail I doubt that any of these changes to the Chaucer text came about by mere happenstance. (Besides, more than a few of their viewers would know those first eighteen lines by heart from school.) It could be that the present moment of war had put pressure on the film's dealings with Chaucer's text: an aerial view tracing a route out of Southwark toward the west might have prompted fearful memories or thoughts of aerial bombardment of London, so Winchester is made the starting point and the route runs south of that of Chaucer's pilgrims. And better to be weak than sick, since a weak nation could prevail alongside strong allies, but there was no cure for a sick nation besides defeat.[23] So the cinematic approach to the period here raises questions about the relationship between past and present and, consequently, about access to that past: this medievalized opening iconographically imposes the present day's distance from the past even as it quietly accommodates that past to the present.

From the map of the pilgrims' route the picture shifts briefly to a drawing of the pilgrims, reminiscent of manuscript illumination or early book illustration, and then to live action with music suggestive of the Middle Ages. The action is the bawdy-Chaucer-in-merrie-old-England type, intensely stereotypical: the use of live action alone nostalgically suggests that our technological age can recover the past, can bring it back in its fullness in ways that out-medieval the flat and schematic medieval manuscript or early printed book.[24] Moreover, Powell and Pressburger's Chaucer presents an idealized world in which humans live in tune with or even subordinate themselves to natural environments and rhythms. The pilgrims here — the Wife of Bath, the Miller with his bagpipes, the Clerk with his book, and other personnel — make their leisurely, pleasurable way to Canterbury in the spirit of companionability and aliveness. In this version of pastoral, the pilgrims ride through the lush, verdant countryside, deep in the summer landscape, not masters of it.[25] It's a very horizontal representation of the pilgrimage, with fairly tight shots of the pilgrim company, before a falcon is launched on its upward flight.[26]

The last two lines of the opening text ("The hooly blisful martir for to seke, / That hem hath holpen when that they were seeke" [or "weak," as in the film's voice-over]) are especially interesting here because they introduce into the mix the temporal complexities and material powers of a saint, Thomas Becket. Contact with a saint, alive or dead, transforms not only people — heals them, strengthens them — but also places: the saint makes specific locales spiritually significant and powerful across time. (In the vernacular life of *Seinte Margarete*, for example, the Holy Spirit says to the martyr: "Ant tu art eadi ant te stude thet tu on restest" [*And you are blessed, and the spot you stand on*].)²⁷ Though the saint's powers are of course believed in Chaucer's text to come from the divine, the film's interest is secular; I will get to that in a moment, but for now, suffice it to say that what the film reads in Chaucer is a sense that the touch of human life animates place. The Chaucerian text, in the film, paints an enchanted view of the pilgrim landscape that Colpeper wants to recover.²⁸

In voice-over a modern-day poem of archaized rhyming couplets follows the Chaucerian poetry, marking some continuities in the landscape as it appears in the image track but mostly stressing changes between the Middle Ages and now: "What would they see, Dan Chaucer and his goodly company today? / The hills and valleys are the same; / Gone are the forests since the enclosures came. / ... / The Pilgrim's Way still winds above the weald, / Through wood and brake and many a fertile field." It's raining in the present day; these are the same showers, presumably, as in Chaucer's day, transposed from April to August. But suddenly, shockingly, one and then another tank irrupts into the visual frame and sound track, emphasizing the huge impact war has had on the landscape: tanks roll all over the hill, digging up the Pilgrim's Way. As Thomas Colpeper avers later, the war is "an earthquake." Torn up by ugly martial machines, this whole area remains nonetheless in his view a place where humans, past and present, interrelate with non-human nature, and the latter itself is animated by the touch of humans past. In a bold match cut from medieval falcon to World War Two Spitfire we get a succinct image of Colpeper's asynchronous world: the falcon, from the supernatural romance world of the *Squire's Tale*, is supplanted by the fighter plane, but the film insists on the continued presence of the Chaucerian bird in that modern technological apparatus of war.²⁹

Colpeper's Middle Ages is indeed not the age of wars or uprisings, heretic burnings or the Black Death, but of peaceful pilgrimages and gratifying miracles.³⁰ True to pastoral form, the Middle Ages are the basis of the film's emphatically "anti-materialist" message.³¹ Shots of Canterbury Cathedral, accompanied by choral music, punctuate the narrative of the three "modern pilgrims"; the Cathedral synecdochically represents the medieval era and its persistence in the present, yet the spirituality endorsed by the film is not exactly medieval English Christianity or its modern-day descendant, Roman Catholicism, nor is it present-day Anglicanism.[32] Peter Conrad describes it as pantheism or nature-worship in the British Romantic tradition, but I would shift the emphasis a bit, to say, rather, that the film's spirituality is a celebration of the enduring human spirit, most perceptible (as we shall see) in the communion that results from Colpeper's absorption in his locale.[33] Miracles, repeatedly invoked in the film — "Miracles still happen, you know," insists Colpeper — all turn out in the end to be rationally explicable in terms of human action; it's the *idea* of miracles that the film clings to, effectively spiritualizing human agency itself. Indeed, the spiritual significance of Canterbury Cathedral emerges in Sgt. Bob Johnson's epiphany as he surveys the nave, having reached the end of his pilgrimage, and that significance turns out to hinge on the sweat of human labor: Bob appreciates the cathedral's grandeur and senses a link between this medieval structure and the church built by his grandfather back in Johnson County, Oregon — "Oregon red cedar, cedar shingles. 1887." Both structures have been created from natural elements and animated by the touch of people, and their disparate histories are joined in Bob's perception of shared labor. Bob's epiphany realizes the continuous temporality of human effort: of the Oregon Baptist building he remarks as he gazes up at the glorious nave of Canterbury Cathedral, "Well, that was a good job, too." Momentarily at least, in this pastoral, not only an abstract human spirit but physical labor in the landscape links the American and the English, connecting the deep past of the medieval to the more recent past and to the present in a very capacious *now*.

THE LAY OF THE LAND

Colpeper's version of this transtemporal communion of human and non-human nature is explicated in his lecture at the Colpeper Institute in Chillingbourne, where he has finally managed to drum up a soldier audience. From the soldiers' point of view — as an audience, they are for the most part bored and rowdy — the past is dead, manifest only in random antiquities beached on the strands of the forward-rushing stream of chronological time. "What have we got to do with this old road, and the people who traveled along it six hundred years ago?" blurts one of the impatient soldiers. But Colpeper smoothly replies in terms of the personal history of each of his listeners: "Isn't the house you were born in the most interesting house in the world to you? Don't you want to know how your father lived, and his father?" "That's all right, but how do we know it really happened?" another soldier protests. "Well, there are more ways than one of getting close to your ancestors," Colpeper responds. "Follow the old road," he tells the restive audience, "and as you walk think of them and of the old England. They climbed Chillingbourne hill, just as you do. They sweated and paused for breath just as you did today. And when you see the bluebells in the spring and the wild thyme, and the broom, and the heather [*music swells*] you're only seeing what their eyes saw. You ford the same rivers, the same birds are singing." As he speaks, the slide projector casts a round light on the screen behind him and only his eyes are illuminated.[34] The audience quiets and a kind of spell is cast by Colpeper's words:

> When you lie flat on your back, and rest, and watch the clouds sailing as I often do, you're so close to those other people that you can hear the thrumming of the hooves of their horses, and the sound of the wheels on the road, and their laughter, and talk, and the music of the instruments they carried. And when I turn the bend in the road, where they, too, saw the towers of Canterbury, I feel I've only to turn my head, to see them on the road behind me.

With his commonsense references to houses and fathers he links knowledge of the distant past to the more recent past and the present of each soldier, while his incantatory description of his sensory experience entrances the protagonists Bob and Alison with its suggestion of the copresence of past and present in the *now* (though, notably, the past is still "behind"). "Like it?" asks the English soldier, Sgt. Peter Gibbs, of Alison, the English Land Girl, who responds with a nonverbal and ever-so-slightly eroticized "Mmmm."

Colpeper's desire to experience the continued presence of the medieval pilgrims on the way to Canterbury, and thus to "get close to [his] ancestors" and gain understanding of them, can only be fulfilled by direct contact with the land—by lying "flat on [his] back."[35] For him the earth is imbued with the spirit of human life. Michael Powell, who grew up in Kent and felt a deep "loyalty to [that] place," as he put it, writes in his autobiography that "perhaps, besides kinship in blood, there is a kinship of place."[36] Not only shared blood but also shared place makes family, Powell implies, and love of place, love of the land itself, is like love of your kin, love of a relation. It's not just that a place *connects* you to your ancient kin, Powell is suggesting; the place *itself* becomes kin. In the very materiality of the land is the familiar body.

The idea of the land as a medieval ancestral body received precise expression by G. K. Chesterton in his 1932 book *Chaucer*.[37] In that volume Chesterton limns Chaucer himself as an "elemental and emblematic giant, alive at our beginnings and made out of the very elements of the land. . . . with our native hills for his bones and our native forests for his beard"; if we look down on England from above, he says, we can "see for an instant a single figure outlined against the sea and a great face staring at the sky."[38] Chesterton speaks metaphorically and analogically here as he concludes his chapter on "Chaucer as an Englishman": Chaucer is a giant, England is a giant, Chaucer is a giant that is England. Powell and Pressburger might be understood to be visualizing this kind of thinking in their depiction of Thomas Colpeper's love of Kent. And they add a queer twist: the land, this medievalized body, is his affectional, maybe even his erotic, preference. The land is the medium of the bond between him and his ancestors — "You ford the same rivers, the same birds are singing," as he says — but it is more than just a conduit: the land has been touched by his forebears, and the land is what remains, animated by that human touch. Colpeper loses himself in it.

His sudden and strangely disheveled appearance when Alison Smith, the Land Girl, comes upon him on Chilmans Downs, along the Pilgrim's Way, makes sense when viewed in this light: he's just experienced *locus interruptus*. And as we subsequently learn, this landscape has affective and erotic resonance for her as well as for Colpeper. As Alison reaches the bend and Canterbury Cathedral emerges into view, she suddenly hears the sound of pilgrims laughing, horses' bells jingling, and musical instruments playing. She is astonished at this, then is startled anew when she hears a voice declaring, "Glorious, isn't it?" Thomas Colpeper makes this out-of-the-blue observation, rising out of the tall grass with his hair and clothes oddly askew (see epilogue figure 2). "Is anybody there?" Alison asks. "It's a real voice you heard; you're not dreaming," Colpeper replies, intuiting that she has heard something — something that exactly conforms to his own experience as he described it earlier in his lecture. "I heard sounds," she confirms now. "Horses' hooves, voices, and a lute, or an instrument like a lute. Did you hear anything?" She is unable to specify precisely what musical instrument it is because it indexes a desire that is, as Helen Dell would put it, inchoate and ineffable.[39] This Colpeper immediately confirms in turn:

"Those sounds come from inside, not outside." He then remonstrates her for "disturb[ing]" him as he was "feeling the air, smelling the earth, watching the clouds." They go on nevertheless to have an intimate talk, touching on her previous trip there with her fiancé, now presumed dead in the war: "Do you see that clump of trees? I spent thirteen perfect days there in a caravan," she dreamily recalls. The caravan holiday would have been "both rather trendy and rather shocking," Ian Christie notes, because of its participation in the "back to nature" movement of the 1930s, on the one hand, and its "unchaperoned" character, on the other. Michael Powell refers to "her passionate love of the landscape where she had lost her virginity."[40] The intimacy of the conversation is sustained as they go on to talk about her long engagement to her fiancé, Geoffrey, and about miracles.

This love experience of the land infused by medieval people is not individual and isolating. It is shared; it is even intersubjective: Colpeper seems to be commenting on *her* inner experience when he greets Alison with "Glorious," as Ian Christie also sees. Colpeper is less interrupted in his moment of love of the past in the land than joined in it by Alison. This scene has been read as functioning to heterosexualize Colpeper or at least to affirm his "empathy with heterosexuality," and it is true that the two characters are definitely drawn closer together in this scene.[41] Each professes to have been initially mistaken about the other: Colpeper substitutes himself for Alison's Geoffrey as she asserts, "He loved this hill so much" and Colpeper instantly responds, "I love it too"; Alison appears to be leaning on his shoulder through a trick of perspective as the camera angle shifts to the right (see epilogue figure 3). But if Colpeper is straightened by contact with Alison here, Alison is touched by this queer, and the two become bonded in what Michael Powell called a "mystic relationship."[42]

These bonding effects are not lasting. Colpeper remains isolated from others in the film — unblessed and on his own in the final scene, even as the three protagonists receive blessings in various forms. Alison experiences a miracle in the form of news that fiancé Geoffrey is in fact alive, and she is firmly reabsorbed back into the ordinary hetero world. Colpeper's deep misogyny does not seem to be tempered by his contact with Alison, either. The narrative is in fact bracketed by instances of Colpeper's unwavering contempt for women. The ducking stool that hangs in his office was for punishing garrulous women, he approvingly remarks in an early scene. At the film's end, on the train to Canterbury, when he defends his Glueman strategy of keeping women inside in order to attract an audience, Alison

Epilogue 2. Thomas Colpeper experiencing locus interruptus.
From A Canterbury Tale *(1944)*.

Epilogue 3. Alison Smith and Thomas Colpeper, "mystically" united.
From A Canterbury Tale *(1944)*.

asks whether he ever thought to invite the women to his lectures; Colpeper replies immediately and forcefully, "No." ("Pity," is Alison's undaunted reply.) On her side, Alison's connection to the land originates in her own personal history of love and loss, which seems entirely different from Colpeper's queer connection with the land. Because of his influence on her she is able to connect her own personal trauma to a longer, public history—she donates some Roman coins found by her fiancé to the Colpeper Institute—and thus she can move from individual melancholy toward a more social appreciation of the living past; this whole experience leads her to vibrant and temporally expansive historical knowledge. She is appreciative of Colpeper's rural rootedness, but her future will be mobile: she clearly intends eventually to restore the moth-eaten caravan in which she spent that perfect holiday three years ago and which Colpeper derides as "impermanent." In that remark he collides with her energized form of living on, and the film, I think, marks him at that moment not only as out of sync but also, finally, as an impediment to a vital, historically engaged life.

Still, I want to return to that intersubjective moment on the Pilgrim's Way, for this shared queer love of the past in the land is not only perverse but also potentially redemptive, and not only in a nationalistic sense. I read this love against the grain of the propaganda mission of the film, a mission it obviously didn't accomplish very well in the first place. Powell and Pressburger may have, indeed, intended to represent here the experience of a common national history, but their linking that to queer pleasure takes the film beyond the realm of the propagandistic. It would be pointless, of course, to deny that a shared feeling about and understanding of the past in the land can work wonders for a nationalistic cause. The Nazis certainly knew this, and only a decade or so earlier Ernst Bloch had recognized how canny they were in deploying the feeling, shared among some Germans, of being left behind by modernity. Bloch theorized asynchrony in relation to socioeconomic factors and political power strategies: in *Heritage of Our Times*, written during the rise of the Nazis in Germany, he analyzed the appeal of the Nazis by noting how they exploited the existential nonsynchrony of young people, of the rural peasantry, and of the petite bourgeoisie. Bloch demonstrated that the Nazis exploited the felt connection of these groups to blood, to so-called primitive, nonmodern life, and—crucially here, for my analysis—to the earth.[43] Powell and Pressburger took as their goal the reinforcement of England's strength through pride in its heritage in a time of war.

But *A Canterbury Tale*, in all its strange excess, effectively suspends that goal. The queer temporal feeling shared by Colpeper with Alison is, well, just *weirder* than anything that could energize a collective national effort. Colpeper urgently wants to pass on "knowledge," and he has an entire institute in which to do so, where he displays cases of artifacts, drawings, and photographs of recent excavations. This "knowledge" is the practical result of his affective experiences; it has been enabled by his love of the land, but the film is much less interested in dwelling on these artifacts as data (only one photograph is actually shown, and it's very blurry) than in exploring that amorous temporal experience of the land he has had and the "miracles" that happen in his asynchronous world. These are the enabling conditions of his research, and they form the luminous heart of the film. The contrast with drearily detached conventional knowledge production is made particularly acute by the ironic title of Powell and Pressburger's next film, *I Know Where I'm Going!* with its unappealing connotations of being driven ever forward by some preconceived notion; of progressing toward a single defined goal; of ignoring one's surroundings on a blinkered journey.[44] But desire for the past leads Colpeper and Alison into a different way of experiencing where they are and how time moves, and it animates the drier, more objective pursuit of historical data at the Colpeper Institute. Moreover, it can lead us—if not the original audience of the film— further outside the modernist settlement, to extend our thinking further beyond the human/nonhuman divide as we reflect on Colpeper's particular vision of an animate earth in a densely populated *now*, a more attached world.

THE QUEER AMATEUR

Colpeper's odd enthusiasm is not only fairly useless for propaganda purposes. It is an inextricable blend of historical knowledge and profound passion and therefore characterizes him as a lowly, flailing antiquarian, an amateur in the era of professionals: not only struggling to get his message out without an official forum but also undeveloped relative to the historian's profession, frozen in a stage on the way to fully serious historicism, still and only loving that from which the historian detaches and analyzes. Moreover, precisely because he is seen as undeveloped and stuck in a phase, his characterization as amateur is of a piece with his characterization as queer. Loony squire, amateur medievalist, queer—I want finally to think about Thomas Colpeper as a concentrated figure of both failure and hope.

In my analysis Colpeper's particular love redefines his homeland as a body animated by medieval lives; this body of the land accepts and engulfs him as he rests in the long grass. In sad contrast in the film is his isolation back in village life: he lives with his mother and pursues his tacky, nocturnal activities alone. "A man alone, always alone, so alone," incanted Powell about Colpeper in an interview.[45] The magistrate's abjectness is palpable: he wants to "pass on" facts about his ancestral home, he wants to reproduce in this way, but no one will have him. Even when he has finally succeeded in gathering a crowd of soldiers to hear him lecture, he opens with a self-effacing account of previous failures to find a willing listener.

> The last time I was to speak ... there was an audience of one. He was reading his evening paper. I waited for a bit, then I asked him, "Ah, should I start?" He said, "Start what?" I said, "Didn't you come to hear me lecture?" He said, "No, I'm waiting for the pub to open." Well, we waited until 5:30, then we adjourned the lecture and both went to the pub.

And though he hopes to bring men to love — to love this place — the way he does, his glue plot is a far cry from the adhesiveness of which Walt Whitman sang; at the film's end he has garnered no more than the puzzled, vague affection of the protagonists.[46]

With his lean, hard face and his relentless misogyny, Colpeper is certainly unattractive: he disciplines men even as he punishes women. ("I'd Glueman him!" snaps one local woman fed up with his nighttime reign of sticky terror.) The title of my epilogue here, "The Lay of the Land," echoes the title of Annette Kolodny's groundbreaking feminist analysis of literal and figurative territorial domination in American letters even as it punningly describes Colpeper's queer love: misogyny and queerness are inextricable here.[47] Further, he's convinced that his actions are useful to the war effort. When confronted finally by the trio of protagonists, Colpeper explains that as Glueman he's just keeping women safe and sound while their men are at war: "You have a girl at home, haven't you?" he asks Bob. "Would you like her to go out with strangers when you're 3,000 miles away?" Co-opted by the state, antifeminist and abject, this magistrate is not a likely candidate to be redeemed by the queer scholar, Doty argues, in search of a queer in the past to love.[48]

Moreover, to anyone who has ever earnestly prepared to give a talk only to find at the appointed time a room of mostly empty chairs, Colpeper's abject self-image of the too-eager lecturer without an audience hits close to home. It makes me cringe in embarrassment. Not only for him but also,

and mostly, of course, for myself. His desperate, criminal attempt to create an audience by throwing glue could serve to distance him because of
its outrageousness: It could make me laugh, and I do laugh, sort of, in in-
credulity at the plot. But my laugh is less a confident distancing than a re-
coil at my own implication in this image: with his pathetic lonely eagerness
to share his enthusiasm about the Canterbury pilgrims, he's my personal
nightmare version of the Chaucerian — me — trying to interest an indifferent audience in the *Canterbury Tales*.

That is, I think, my particularly queer response to this queer figure. My
reaction is typical because the issue here is desire — both his and mine, to
share a love of the medieval with others — and desire, as Heather Love has
powerfully demonstrated in her book *Feeling Backward*, is so thoroughly
marked for queers with loss, isolation, and shame.[49] Thomas Colpeper
is a failure — in terms of modern productivity or reproductivity, a total
loser. "Within straight time the queer can only fail," observes José Esteban Muñoz.[50] Yes, Colpeper's failure, the failure of a queer in reproductive time, the failure of an amateur in professionalism's modernity, is inevitable, but that foregone conclusion is the least interesting thing we can
say about it. Colpeper's queer love, quite inexplicable in everyday modernist frameworks — he loves a *hill*? — can nonetheless rouse us to look for
other ways of world making, for other ways of knowing, doing, being. It
can move us to revalue such failures, amateurisms, nonmodern temporalities, and the attachments they foster. Think back on the amateurs in this
book, bathrobe clad, tardy and unruly: among them, Furnivall gives the
cold shoulder to the academy and offers medieval texts to readers so they
might connect with people from the past; Longfellow both studies and
inhabits asynchrony; M. R. James never forgets the uncertainty of historicist methods of recovering the past, characterizing it hauntingly as ghosts
and demons in his playful and menacing stories; Hope Emily Allen finally
prefers an unlimited web of connections to Margery Kempe over the narrowness of scholarly argument; Geoffrey Crayon, in his re-enactment and
its failure at Windsor Castle, leads us to face the necessity of being willing
to be haunted.[51] In their own inimitable ways urging us toward a disorderly
and asynchronous collective, they might be heard to murmur: "Find the
time, find your time." And that time is, after all, now.

PREFACE

1 See Hartley, *Mediaeval Costume and Life*, who catego-
rizes Tobit here as an invalid and comments on the modern look of the medieval invalid's setting (128, 130).

2 Chakrabarty, *Provincializing Europe*, 251. See also Serres:
"We are always simultaneously making gestures that are
archaic, modern, and futuristic" (*Conversations on Science, Culture, and Time*, 60).

3 Fradenburg, *Sacrifice Your Love*, 56; "'So That We May
Speak of Them,'" 209, on "the importance of passion to
rigorous practices of knowledge." See also Prendergast
and Trigg, "What Is Happening to the Middle Ages?"
esp. 224–26.

4 See Barnet and Wu, *The Cloisters*, 15, 19.

5 Hoving, *King of the Confessors*, 56, 58. The recent reno-
vation brings out the temporal heterogeneity even further: replacement stones had to be "medievalized,"
of course, made to look as if they had weathered in a
thirteenth-century Normandy garden, but replacement
mortar had to be made to look as if it were a 1930s imitation of the medieval; see Eve M. Kahn, "Cloisters Un-
veiled," *Traditional Building*, April 2006. http://www
.traditional-building.com/Previous-Issues-06/April
Project06cloisters.html.

6 Geary, "What Happened to Latin?" 872, 861, 873.

INTRODUCTION

1   This persona is remarkably consistent across the songs and so identified with the lead singer himself that I am compelled to refer to it simply as Morrissey. "Morrissey is a record to be played, never a life to be lived," writes Mark Simpson in explaining the singer's presence in the songs (*Saint Morrissey*, 15). I have used Goddard, *The Smiths*, 124–33, as my guide to the production and afterlife of this song. Also helpful has been Rogan, *Morrissey*. On the shifting reputation of the band, see Campbell and Coulter, "'Why Pamper Life's Complexities?'"

2   As Benveniste puts it, "the essential thing . . . is the relation between the indicator (of person, time, place, object shown, etc.) and the *present* instance of discourse." *Problems in General Linguistics*, 219. And in Morrissey's question, the present is exactly what is at stake.

3   The band's American record label Sire put together an unauthorized video for MTV in order to promote the single's United States release. Morrissey called it "degrading" and went on: "It need hardly be mentioned that they also listed the video under the title 'How Soon Is Soon?' which . . . where does one begin, really?"; Goddard, *The Smiths*, 132. As my students put it, who cares when soon is? Morrissey wants *now*.

4   See Heidegger, *The Basic Problems of Phenomenology*, 231–64.

5   Even the promise of some kind of meaningful passage from the past into the future that is offered by the song's declarative first words — "I am the son and the heir" — proves barren; no robust reproductive future for Morrissey, the inheritor only "of a shyness that is criminally vulgar, / And son and heir of nothing in particular." The echo of George Eliot's *Middlemarch* is hollow. This *now* offers only the impossibility of continuing the family line.

6   Goddard, *The Smiths*, 126–27. Goddard also describes the sound as "quivering" and "oscillating."

7   "Purposes and activities": Polt, *Heidegger*, 108. I have relied on Polt's illuminating explanation here.

8   "Faux lesbian Russian pop sensation" is Goddard's phrase for t.A.T.u.; *The Smiths*, 131. Jon Savage, on the song's interpretation of the late '70s and early '80s Manchester gay club scene, in *Village Voice Rock & Roll Quarterly*, 1989: "It captures that experience exactly, except the last line: home and sleep were not upsetting but a relief"; qtd. in Goddard, *The Smiths*, 128.

9   See William E. Jones, *Is It Really So Strange?*. Jones profiles the largely Latino Los Angeles–area Morrissey fans who created an intense scene before Morrissey's "comeback" in 2004. The film explores, among other things, the particular appeal that Morrissey has to Latinos, while some of the fans wrestle with their sense of Morrissey's relationship to racism.

10 Thanks to Tavia N'yongo for these observations about the temporalities here — and for his prompting me to consider more broadly in this chapter amateurism's implication in late capitalism.

11 Janice Whaley, The Smiths Project, http://thesmithsproject.blogspot.com/.

12 These are all other "attitudes to time" than what Gurevich identifies as modern "awareness of its swift and irreversible onward flow and . . . the identification of only one present"; Gurevich, "What Is Time?," 102.

13 Heidegger, The Basic Problems of Phenomenology, 237.

14 Coope, Time for Aristotle, 2. My account of Aristotle relies on Coope's crystal clear analysis. See also Sachs, Aristotle's Physics, esp. 131–33.

15 Inwood, "Aristotle on the Reality of Time," 151–52, usefully breaks down the logic of the problems Aristotle states in 217b32–218a30. I follow Coope's general outline of the problems, esp. p. 17.

16 See Hussey's introduction to Aristotle's Physics, xxxviii, xi, ix.

17 Coope, Time for Aristotle, 38. Time is "something of change" (31).

18 Aristotle, Physics, ed. and trans. Hussey, 218b21. All quotations of the Physics are from this translation unless otherwise noted.

19 219a3–6. Though the logic and the presentation of the passage are obscure, the general point is clear. Hussey believes that there is a missing premise: "that all lapse of time is perceptible" (142). Coope argues against this hypothesis, basing her analysis on the theory that Aristotle is arguing from our "ordinary judgments" about time; Time for Aristotle, 38–39.

20 Coope, Time for Aristotle, 38.

21 As a number, time depends on the consciousness of someone to do the numbering or measuring: "no time can exist without the existence of a soul" (223a26). Here I quote the translation of Hippocrates G. Apostle and refer to his notes speculating on Aristotle's meaning; Physics, trans. Apostle, 88, 267. Richard Sorabji notes that Aristotle elsewhere took another view about "perceptibles and knowables without any perceivers or knowers"; Sorabji, introduction to Simplicius, On Aristotle's Physics, 4.

   Time, moreover, is "both continuous, by virtue of the now, and divided at the now" (220a4–5, trans. Hussey). The present has "a two-fold character of a beginning and an end — a beginning, that is to say, of future and an end of past time" (Aristotle, Physics, VIII.1, 251b19–23, from Wheelwright's translation in "Natural Science," 49). Hussey calls this the "unity-in-variety of the now" (152); Heidegger refers to it as "spannedness"; I see it as part and parcel of asynchrony.

22 Simplicius, On Aristotle's Physics, 116. See also Philoponus on the relevant passage in Huber, Die Wanderlegende von den Siebenschläfern, 384–85, (Greek); for a Latin translation by Guilelmus Dorotheus, see Johannis Philoponi Commentaria, 106v.

23 Serres, Conversations on Science, Culture, and Time, 57–62.

24 Simplicius, On Aristotle's Physics, 115–16.

25 Ibid.

26 Indeed, Simplicius's treatment of the fable suggests that the story might have been believable as fact. According to him, Alexander of Aphrodisias, a second-century Greek commentator on Aristotle, "seems to have claimed that

the uncorrupted bodies of the heroes were still to be seen in his time"; Ross, *Aristotle's* Physics, 597.

27 Here I must indicate my indebtedness to Large, *Heidegger's* Being and Time, esp. 83–97; the quoted phrase is from 87.

28 Large, *Heidegger's* Being and Time, 87.

29 Polt, *Heidegger*, 107.

30 This is the way Large puts it in *Heidegger's* Being and Time, 85–86.

31 Both Simplicius and Aquinas painstakingly comment on the text and its phraseology, but Simplicius adds arguments for and against other commentators and philosophers in a way that the "literal" Thomas does not. On Thomas's "literalism" in regard to his *Expositio* on the *Physics*, see Helen S. Lang, *Aristotle's* Physics *and its Medieval Varieties*, 161–62.

32 "Sicut patet in iis qui in Sardo, quae est civitas Asiae, dicuntur fabulose dormire apud *heroas*, idest apud deos. Animas enim bonorum et magnorum heroas vocabant, et quasi deos colebant, ut Herculis et Bacchi et similium"; Aquinas, *Commentaria in octo libros Physicorum, lectio* 16; English translation in *Commentary on Aristotle's* Physics, trans. Blackwell, Spath, and Thirlkel, 255.

33 See Bourke's introduction to Aquinas, *Commentary on Aristotle's* Physics, xvii.

34 "Per incantationes enim aliquas, aliqui insensibiles reddebantur, quos dicebant dormire apud heroas; quia excitati, quaedam mirabilia se vidisse dicebant, et futura quaedam praenunciabant. Tales autem ad se redeuntes, non percipiebant tempus quod praeterierat dum ipsi sic absorpti erant"; Aquinas, *Commentaria in octo libros Physicorum, lectio* 16; trans. Blackwell, Spath, and Thirlkel, 255.

35 Aristotle had in book 4 gone on to say of dreams (it seems), one *can* mentally perceive a change even in the dark and therefore know that time has passed. Tertullian, for example, seems to interpret Aristotle as meaning that the sleepers sleep dreamlessly: "Aristotle remarks of a certain hero of Sardinia that he used to withhold the power of visions and dreams from such as resorted to his shrine for inspiration" [*Aristoteles heroëm quendam [Iolaus?] Sardiniae notat incubatores fani sui visionibus privantem*]; *A Treatise on the Soul* (*De anima*), ch. 49, trans. Holmes; Latin qtd. in Huber, *Die Wanderlegende von den Siebenschläfern*, 385. On Galen's objections to Aristotle's analysis, see Simplicius, *On Aristotle's* Physics, 117. Aquinas names the unperceived time between the now of the sleepers' first falling to sleep and the now of their waking: he refers to it, twice, as *medium tempus*, the "middle time"; *Commentaria in octo libros Physicorum, lectio* 16; trans. Blackwell, Spath, and Thirlkel, 255.

36 Aquinas, *Commentaria in octo libros Physicorum, lectio* 16; trans. Blackwell, Spath, and Thirlkel, 255.

37 See Bourke's introduction to Aquinas, *Commentary on Aristotle's* Physics, xxii–xxiv, for a brief discussion of Thomas's Christianity vis-à-vis Aristotle as non-Christian philosopher. On the issue of locating marvels in a marginal space as opposed to finding prodigies in a central space, see Daston and Park, *Wonders and the Order of Nature*, esp. 60–66.

38 See Lears, *No Place of Grace*, 11.

39 Gross, "Time and Nature in Twelfth-Century Thought," 90. Augustine thus contrasts with what we've seen as an Aristotelian emphasis on an observable world of "ordered and temporal processes"; see Gross, "Time and Nature in Twelfth-Century Thought," 95, 94, 91. Gross convincingly argues that Aristotelian ideas of time and nature, developed in early-twelfth-century thinkers such as William of Conches and Thierry of Chartres, prepared the way for the reception of Aristotle and the emergence of the "new science." Though I appreciate Gross's historical argument, my discussion here does not require an argument about a direction of development away from the Augustinian and toward the Aristotelian.

40 Gross, "Time and Nature in Twelfth-Century Thought," 94. As Gross demonstrates, Augustine asserts in *De Genesi ad litteram* that the time of the created world is associated with "[change] according to the ordered successiveness of things established by God, who governs all he created"; "Augustine's Ambivalence about Temporality," 138, quoting Augustine, *De Genesi ad litteram*, 5.5.12.

41 *Ambivalence* is something of a scholarly catchword for Augustine and temporality; see Gross, "Augustine's Ambivalence about Temporality," which cites Henri-Irénée Marrou, *L'Ambivalence du temps de l'histoire chez saint Augustin*. Time as an image of eternity is a formulation Augustine derives from Plato in the *Timaeus* and expresses in his early writings; see Plato, *Timaeus*, 37c–e: time is "a moving image of eternity" (1167). See Gross, "Augustine's Ambivalence about Temporality," n. 22, for references and for discussion of Augustine's debt to Plotinus's thought.

42 Ricoeur, *Time and Narrative*, 1: 5, 7. Note that Gross, in "Time and Nature in Twelfth-Century Thought," corrects "some modern commentators" on their overstressing the psychological aspect of Augustine's discussion (92). My treatment here, following Ricoeur's account of time in the *Confessions*, emphasizes a dynamic of asynchrony and thus ultimately contrasts with Cohen's analysis of human temporality as relatively static in Augustine; see Cohen, "Time Out of Memory," esp. 43.

43 And experience "holds firm"; Ricoeur, *Time and Narrative*, 1: 9. Ricoeur has compellingly presented the step-by-step process in which Augustine in book 11 derives his thesis about the nature of time as multiple and interior — that is, the three-fold present as a distention of the mind. I need not rehearse that process by which one aporia is solved only to open another one, but I do want to underscore Ricoeur's main insights about Augustine's analysis.

44 Augustine, *Confessions* 11.14.15, 11.16.21; Ricoeur, *Time and Narrative*, 1: 9–10. I use the online reprint of *Confessions* edited by James J. O'Donnell. The English translation used is Pine-Coffin's *Confessions*, except where noted.

45 Ricoeur calls this "an extended and dialectical present"; *Time and Narrative*, 1:11.

46 Augustine, *Confessions* 11.20.26.

47 Carruthers, *The Book of Memory*, 193.

48 Ricoeur, *Time and Narrative*, 1: 19.

49 Ricoeur quotes the whole passage to show "the dialectic of expectation, memory, and attention." The present is a dialectic between the *intentio* [present attention] of the present, active mind and the *distentio* [distention] that arises "out of the *intentio* that has burst asunder"; *Time and Narrative*, 1: 20.

50 Augustine, *Confessions* 11.28.38: "dicturus sum canticum quod novi. antequam incipiam, in totum expectatio mea tenditur, cum autem coepero, quantum ex illa in praeteritum decerpsero, tenditur et memoria mea, atque distenditur vita huius actionis meae in memoriam propter quod dixi et in expectationem propter quod dicturus sum. praesens tamen adest attentio mea, per quam traicitur quod erat futurum ut fiat praeteritum. quod quanto magis agitur et agitur, tanto breviata expectatione prolongatur memoria, donec tota expectatio consumatur, cum tota illa actio finita transierit in memoriam."

51 The "combined action of expectation, memory, and attention . . . 'continues.' The *distentio* is then nothing other than the shift in, the noncoincidence of the three modalities of action"; Ricoeur, *Time and Narrative*, 1: 20.

52 Augustine, *Confessions*, trans. Chadwick, 230 n. 19.

53 Ibid., 11.29.39.

54 Augustine, *Confessions*, 11.31.41. The human is a "composite or mixture of two substances, spiritual and corporeal"; Gross, "Augustine's Ambivalence about Temporality," 139–40.

55 Gurevich, "What Is Time?," 114; Augustine, *Confessions*, trans. Chadwick, 240 n. 27.

56 Gross, "Time and Nature in Twelfth-Century Thought," 93. Gross refers to the example of Augustine's discussion in *De Genesi ad litteram*, 4.33.51–52.

57 Ricoeur, *Time and Narrative*, 26. Time both resembles and distances eternity; this framework reveals simultaneously the hope and the sorrow of human life.

58 Augustine, *Confessions*, trans. Chadwick, 240 n. 27. Chadwick goes on to note that "temporal successiveness is an experience of disintegration; the ascent to divine eternity is a recovery of unity" (244 n. 31).

59 Ricoeur, *Time and Narrative*, 1: 25.

60 In "Augustine's Ambivalence about Temporality," Gross draws an ultimately different value: "For it is precisely in perceiving its own temporality and dissimilitude that the soul turns and redirects itself toward God. Augustine's ambivalence about time gives time lasting value" (148).

61 Serres with Latour, *Conversations on Science, Culture, and Time*, 56.

62 See Zimmerman, "Temporary Intrinsics and Presentism," 212, qtd. in Oaklander, "Presentism, Ontology and Temporal Experience," a critique of presentist approaches to tenses and temporal relations (73); Tsing, *In the Realm of the Diamond Queen*, xiv, qtd. by Matti Bunzl in "Syntheses of a Critical Anthropology," his foreword to the reprint edition of Fabian's *Time and the Other* (xxv); Boyarin and Land, *Time and Human Language Now*. Giorgio Agamben, too, in *The Time That Remains*, takes up Benveniste's theory of enunciation, coordinating it with another linguistic concept—the "operational time" of Gustave Guillaume—and extending that to his own problem-

atic of messianic time (65–68). Cohen provides a useful compact survey of the abundant literature of "critical temporal studies" published before 2003, including works of philosophers, anthropologists, linguists, psychoanalysts, physicists, and social psychologists, in *Medieval Identity Machines*, 3–11; more recently he extends his own research to archaeology: see his "Time Out of Memory."

63 Boyarin and Land, *Time and Human Language Now*, 31.

64 Latour, *Pandora's Hope*, 1–23, esp. 14, 4.

65 Latour, "Time's Two Arrows," in *Politics of Nature*, 188–94, at 188, 189; this is a section that distills his argument about temporality in *We Have Never Been Modern*.

66 Latour, *Politics of Nature*, 188–94, and *We Have Never Been Modern*. For an analysis of the development of modern objective measurement away from the earlier means of measurement by human body parts and human relationships (both paradigms of attachment), see Zygmunt Bauman, *Globalization*, qtd. in Boym, *The Future of Nostalgia*, 10–11.

67 Chakrabarty, "The Time of History and the Times of Gods," 36, 37.

68 Ibid., 39. My own coedited volume, the *Cambridge Companion to Medieval Women's Writing*, includes my chapter contesting traditional historiography ("Margery Kempe," 222–39) as well as an introductory timeline ("Chronology," viii–xviii). For the history of the timeline as a specifically modern figure for history, see Rosenberg and Grafton, *Cartographies of Time*: "From the most ancient images to the most modern, the line serves as a central figure in the representation of time" (14).

69 Chakrabarty, "The Time of History and the Times of Gods," 37, 39, 40. "Empty and homogeneous" echoes Benjamin, "Theses on the Philosophy of History," 261.

70 Medievalists have long analyzed the problematics of periodization: Davis, *Periodization and Sovereignty*, offers an excellent bibliography in the notes to her introduction. That some of these arguments about medieval/modern periodization regard "the Middle Ages as a stubborn and inevitable remainder, obstinately irreducible in its own right" is due to what could be called their "non-modern" approach to time; see Strohm, "Historicity without Historicism?," 389. See also Davis, *Periodization and Sovereignty*, 5: "The topic of multiple temporalities cannot be usefully broached, I suggest, until the process and the effects of periodization have been taken into account. . . . For this reason, the pertinent question regarding periodization is not 'When was the Middle Ages?' but 'Where is the Now?'" This is, she goes on to note, the title of an essay by Dipesh Chakrabarty. In "The Sense of an Epoch," Davis problematizes the question itself as a lure to periodization, since any answer must propose "a particular content, and by extension a set of potential meanings, for the apparently global time of 'the now'" (39).

71 Holsinger, *The Premodern Condition*. Cole and Smith, in *The Legitimacy of the Middle Ages*, offer an intensive investigation of relationships between the "medieval" and the "premodern," on the one hand, and "modernist and post-

modern frameworks," on the other; in their introduction, "Outside Modernity," they strenuously delineate the paradoxical role or deployment of the Middle Ages in theories of modernity (e.g., that of Hans Blumenberg) and in philosophical modernist projects (e.g., Heidegger's later work), outlining the difficulties but also the rewards of "reckoning with 'the medieval'" in these and later theoretical undertakings.

72 Davis, *Periodization and Sovereignty*, 6.

73 The conversation between medieval studies and postcolonial studies is increasingly rich and complicated: for intensive early focus on temporality, see Cohen, *The Postcolonial Middle Ages*, 1–17; for problematization of the relationship between critique of periodization and historical specificity in the context of postcolonial studies, see Ingham and Warren, *Postcolonial Moves*, 1–15. For a focus on linguistic and material objects and the difference such an emphasis makes to the theoretical discourse, see Kabir and Williams, *Postcolonial Approaches to the European Middle Ages*. For an extension of the problematics into a wider geographical frame, see Davis and Altschul, *Medievalisms in the Postcolonial World*. Lampert-Weissig, *Medieval Literature and Postcolonial Studies*, offers a useful overview as well as analysis of the shaping force of medieval discourses of power on later ones.

74 Simpson, "Diachronic History and the Shortcomings of Medieval Studies," 26–27.

75 Davis, *Periodization and Sovereignty*, 5. A related scholarly discussion — a consequence of the pressure being put on periodization of the Middle Ages — concerns the necessity of exploring the relations between medieval studies, on the one hand, and medievalism studies, on the other — that is, studies of the Middle Ages and studies of the making of the Middle Ages, as the distinction is conventionally understood: see Prendergast and Trigg, "The Negative Erotics of Medievalism." Ultimately, when period boundaries are understood as destabilized and "the Middle Ages" acknowledged as a constructed phenomenon, there is no analytical distinction between medieval studies and medievalism itself; see David Matthews, "What Was Medievalism?" and "From Mediaeval to Mediaevalism," and Davis and Altschul, *Medievalisms in the Postcolonial World*, 7–8.

76 Jameson, *A Singular Modernity*, 29; Bartolovich, "Is the Post in Posthuman," esp. 29. Bartolovich here sharply critiques Latour's *We Have Never Been Modern* and those medievalists who follow Latour's "particular parody of epochal thought."

77 Summit, "Literary History and the Curriculum," 142; Chakrabarty, *Provincializing Europe*, 108.

78 Timothy Mitchell, *Rule of Experts*, looks at the constitutive interrelations between the modern state and expertise, analyzing among other things the ways in which expertise constitutes itself as such and how the expert becomes the spokesperson for progress and development.

79 Weber, *The Protestant Ethic and the Spirit of Capitalism*, 123. On the secularization debate as it impacts medieval studies now, see Cole and Smith, *The*

Legitimacy of the Middle Ages, 1–36; as it informs our current notions of sovereignty and governance, see Davis, *Periodization and Sovereignty*.

80 Weber, *The Protestant Ethic and the Spirit of Capitalism*, 123. See Dohrn-van Rossum, *History of the Hour*, 10, on Weber.

81 See Dohrn-van Rossum, *History of the Hour*. In his Marxist analysis, Raymond Williams writes that the conversion of activity into paid labor is due to "capitalist productive relations"; the distinction I am delineating between amateurism and professionalism draws on this historical materialist condition. The concept of reification (*vergegenständlichung*) — "broadly, making a human process into an *objective* thing," as Williams puts it — does get at this abstract, objectified quality of the time of work that I want to use to characterize the time of the expert or professional. Williams refers to "reification" in his chapter "Alienation" in *Keywords*, 35; he refers to "capitalist productive relations" in "Work," 335. I would like to discuss the culture of expertise in terms that are not, I think, entirely encompassed by the concepts of labor and its alienations: its specific relations to an idea of the scientific method are what I touch on here.

82 Weber, *General Economic History*, 365.

83 See Dohrn-van Rossum, *History of the Hour*, 10; Lears, *No Place of Grace*, 10–11.

84 As the quotation marks indicate, "scientific" is a polemical, mystified formation; Latour distinguishes between polemical Science, on the one hand, from the sciences or Research, on the other. And in contrast to closed expertise he proposes a concept of the "amateur de sciences," in his book *Chroniques d'un amateur de sciences*. Latour argues that scientific researchers must, as researchers, enter into public discussion. The "amateur de sciences" — a "science critic" — would act like an "art critic," helping as a mediator to form public opinion and taste. For we are all, Latour argues, as consumers and participants in living, embarked on the same collective experiments in scientific politics, as we decide whether or not to buy genetically engineered food, to get rid of our diesel cars, and so on. The "amateur de sciences" brings criteria beyond the truth/falsehood axis to the table.

85 Walsh, "That Withered Paradigm," 366. Susan Aronstein referred to Walsh in the context of Chaucer and new media technologies in her paper at the 2010 New Chaucer Society Congress. Walsh argues that "at its basic and most ancient form, the expert paradigm was an undifferentiated variety of what we now call religion" (365). I can entertain this hypothesis, but my real interest here is in the particular expert variety of the modern scientist, which I think goes hand in hand with Enlightenment temporality. Jenkins pushes Walsh's analysis further in *Convergence Culture*, 50–58.

86 Walsh, "That Withered Paradigm," 366; Latour, *Pandora's Hope*, 10–17, 216–35, esp. 234; Walsh, "That Withered Paradigm," 366.

87 Goffman, *The Presentation of Self in Everyday Life*. Walsh refers to Goffman's book in his first note.

88 The "soldier" metaphor resonates with a famous analysis of modernity — or

even postmodernity. Dwight D. Eisenhower, in his "Farewell Address" to the United States populace in 1961, pointed to a disturbing trend in the "conduct of research" due to what he dubbed the "military-industrial complex": "Today the solitary inventor, tinkering in his shop, has been overshadowed by task forces of scientists in laboratories and testing fields."

89   My description here resonates with John Cochran's analysis of professional and amateur cookery in "Object Oriented Cookery," and I borrow his example of making an omelet. Cochran observes that a key component of amateurism is the treatment of objects as actants in an open, rather than closed, system; he develops Object Oriented Cookery in the context of the Object Oriented Ontology of Graham Harman. Thanks to Jen Boyle for pointing out this essay in her contribution to the "crowd review" process at the journal *postmedieval* (see below, n. 151). Note the irony, by the way, of using cookery as an example of professional expertise, given the long tradition of banishing cookery from the realm of expertise (on this, see Latour, *Pandora's Hope*, 233).

90   Latour, *Pandora's Hope*, 10–17.

91   Jenkins, *Convergence Culture*, 52–53.

92   Barthes, "Longtemps, je me suis couché de bonne heure," 284, 290, 289. I was pointed to this essay by Ika Willis, "'Writers Who Put Themselves in the Story': Dante Alighieri, Roland Barthes, Lieutenant Mary-Sue and Me" (paper written for "Desiring the Text, Touching the Past: Towards an Erotics of Reception," symposium at Bristol University, July 2010).

93   Willis, "Keeping Promises to Queer Children," 167. Barthes uses this phrase in "Brecht and Discourse," 216. For a survey of the fecund category of gay men's medievalist historical fiction writing on the web, with bibliography on fan fiction, see Kruger, "Gay Internet Medievalism."

94   On various advances of the amateur, the mob, into the professional's domain, see below, n. 151. On the professionalism of the critique of professionalism, see Moten and Harney, who analyze the "studied negligence" of the professional academic's critique ("The University and the Undercommons," 112): this is a negligence of the labor of the Undercommons.

95   Moten and Harney, "The University and the Undercommons," 115.

96   Wilson, "#1 Fan: Petrarch's Letters to Classical Authors" (paper written for "Desiring the Text, Touching the Past: Towards an Erotics of Reception," symposium at Bristol University, July 2010), draws attention to overlapping populations and their day-to-day negotiations of their activities.

97   In his analysis of race in United States science fiction fandom, Carrington, in *Speculative Fiction and Media Fandom*, documents science fiction fans' amateurism as productive reading and criticism; he makes manifest its particular combination of love and critique. Carrington finds early amateur readers of science fiction who self-consciously assumed anachronistic positions.

98   Pearsall, "Frederick James Furnivall," 128. See also Brewer, "Furnivall and the Old Chaucer Society," 2.

99   Benzie, *Dr. F. J. Furnivall*, 27, 254.

100 Brewer, "Furnivall and the Old Chaucer Society," 3.

101 Benzie, *Dr. F. J. Furnivall*, 130–31.

102 Matthews, "Chaucer's American Accent," 767.

103 The contemporary Arnold Schröer commented in 1881 that Furnivall "seems to be independently wealthy"; qtd. in Utz, *Chaucer and the Discourse of German Philology*, 117. Pearsall elaborates on Furnivall's financial situation, noting that his inheritance dwindled in 1866 "in the collapse of the Overend and Gurney banks" and that Furnivall was granted a Civil List annual pension of £150 "in recognition of his valuable services to the literature of the country" ("Frederick James Furnivall," 128).

104 Levine, *The Amateur and the Professional*, 71; see also 38, 43–44, 60, 73, 98.

105 Ibid., 24; see 23–30 passim, 38. Gossman, "History as Decipherment," observes a shift in historical writing in France that resonates with my interests here: after the middle of the nineteenth century in France, a generation of historians embraced "an austere ideal of science" and withdrew from "the often turbulent public forum . . . to the stillness of the study and the quiet of the seminar room" (29). Fradenburg quotes Gossman here and on philology's "own history of salvific grandiosity" ("'So That We May Speak of Them,'" 226 n.13).

106 See Momma, *From Philology to English Studies*, for an account of John Mitchell Kemble's struggles in the 1830s to establish philology in England in the Germanic mold; Momma, moreover, takes seriously the imperial context of the development of English vernacular philology and analyzes the place of empire in the unfolding story. See also Biddick, *The Shock of Medievalism*, 90–96.

107 See Utz, *Chaucer and the Discourse of German Philology*, 118. Utz analyzes a conflict between "enthusiasm" and "philology" that he derives from Plato's works, especially the *Ion*. Utz argues that not only "increasing economic and military competition" between the two countries but also "a narrowly formal 'philologization' of studies in Germany" led to Germans' insistence on their own philological superiority and devaluation of "the antiquarianism and amateurism of their English counterparts" (116–17).

108 David Matthews, "What Was Medievalism?" esp. 10–14.

109 Levine, *The Amateur and the Professional*, 30, 116–17.

110 Ganim, *Medievalism and Orientalism*, 33.

111 See Pearsall, "Frederick James Furnivall," 133; Benzie, *Dr. F. J. Furnivall*, 124. See Utz's analysis of this remark in *Chaucer and the Discourse of German Philology*, 122, esp. n. 43.

112 This is Utz's argument: *Chaucer and the Discourse of German Philology*, 124.

113 Brewer, "Furnivall and the Old Chaucer Society," 2.

114 Biddick, *The Shock of Medievalism*, 93; Benzie, *Dr. F. J. Furnivall*, 37.

115 W. W. Skeat, qtd. in Matthews, *The Making of Middle English*, 142.

116 Furnivall, *The Minor Poems of William Lauder*, xxv.

117 Levine, *The Amateur and the Professional*, 117. The edition, Levine chronicles, "had been authorized on March 31 1865 but did not appear until 1887" (116–17).

118   Furnivall, *Trial-Forewords to My "Parallel-Text Edition of Chaucer's Minor Poems,"* 91–92. Qtd. in Brewer, "Furnivall," 6.

119   Matthews, "Chaucer's American Accent," 767, 768, 769.

120   Aranye Fradenburg has suggested that "it is possible that my perspective as a medievalist may make it easier for me to see the importance of passion to rigorous practices of knowledge than is the case for scholars in other fields" ("'So That We May Speak of Them,'" 209). She argues that this is because medievalism has a long history of discourses of desire and utility; it is because the Middle Ages has schooled us in thinking about need and love, and its teachings come down to us with a cultural intensity that is almost capillary. But not many professional medieval scholars are as finely attuned to the enjoyment of the Middle Ages as Fradenburg has been over the course of her many works; more often they lose touch with "the histories we love — for example, . . . what we read, play with, as children" (210), as well as with the fact that "the differences between academic and popular medievalism are of course *made*, and sometimes are made to occlude similarities" (209). Amateur medievalists, in contrast, have no other reason to engage the Middle Ages but enjoyment, and that clarity can work to shine a light on the hidden loves of professionals. On desire and turning toward the past, see also Finke and Shichtman, *Cinematic Illuminations*, esp. 11–15.

121   See contemporary witnesses to Longfellow's teaching, qtd. in Calhoun, *Longfellow*, 133.

122   Macdonald, *Emeric Pressburger*, 358–59.

123   Thanks to Elaine Freedgood for suggesting to me this line of thought. The phrase "arrested development" in relation to homosexuality, as Stockton, *The Queer Child*, notes, "stays alive largely in certain political and religious rhetoric on the right" (22); she chronicles the development and deployment of the term via Darwin and Freud (22–24).

124   Muñoz, *Cruising Utopia*.

125   Powell, *Million-Dollar Movie*, 153. On this queer collaboration, see Doty, "The Queer Aesthete, the Diva, and *The Red Shoes*."

126   Williams, "Hope Emily Allen Speaks with the Dead." Williams's well-researched article convincingly thematizes and historicizes Allen's ideas, beliefs, and practices around gender and sexuality.

127   See Pincombe, "Homosexual Panic and the English Ghost Story." Pincombe draws on Cox, *M. R. James*.

128   Haralson, "Mars in Petticoats," quoting Margaret Fuller on 331; 330; quoting Lauren Berlant on 331. Haralson also quotes Walt Whitman's reservations about gender in Longfellow's work (331).

129   This suspicion is expressed forthrightly by Smith in "The Application of Thought to Medieval Studies." Among his objects of suspicion my work in *Getting Medieval* figures largely, as do Nicholas Watson's "Desire for the Past" and Kathryn Kerby-Fulton's *Books Under Suspicion*. "[The] faith that affect allows us a means to access the past remains puzzling to me," Smith remarks,

elaborating on the problems as he sees them. My rationale for using affect should be clear in *How Soon Is Now?* In this book I explicitly problematize time, arguing not only that pasts are in the present, that the *now* moment is more temporally heterogeneous than linear time schemes allow us to recognize, but also that we need a nonmodern temporal orientation to perceive this heterogeneity. And that is where affect comes in: if modernity depends on (among other things) a subject-object split, then one approach to nonmodernity (which comprehends "the past") involves trying to explore subjective attachment rather than objective detachment. Longfellow's knowledge of the medieval past is gained from the inside, as it were, as I show in chapter 1; in chapter 3 I explicitly work out the hermeneutical paradigm that is implied in this treatment of Longfellow, positing a contemporaneity that breaks down an absolute divide between subject and object, reader and text; this is a prerequisite to historicist knowledge, as Chakrabarty argues. In chapter 4, the subject-object divide is deconstructed completely. I am interested in affect, therefore, as one rubric under which a subject/object divide is spanned, giving us access to multiple temporalities; if we wish we can go on to view medieval phenomena in their contextual relationships to whatever institutions deemed relevant, but of course, tutored by our own attachments, we will not imagine that these phenomena and institutions are completely separate from us. If there is a "telos" to my work here, with all my interest in nonlinearity, it is *more attachment*, as Latour would say. I have focused on particular amateur readers not only because of their intrinsic interest but because as individuals they are inimitable; while we appreciate their ways of encountering medieval texts, we cannot simply "identify" with them as we endeavor to articulate our own relationship to the *now*.

Nicholas Watson, in his follow-up article to "Desire for the Past," concludes that his focus there on "the individual scholar's personal investments in the past . . . has come to seem too personal to have much bearing on the larger challenge posed to our relationship with the past by modernity" — and he goes on to mine medieval writings on imagination for a useful hermeneutic paradigm with which to explore relations between past and present, "inseparably entangled" as they are ("Phantasmal Past," 2, 4, 5). He thus leaves behind his earlier empathetic approach that posited "a double movement of identification and repudiation" ("Phantasmal Past," 2). But it seems to me that some such double movement still can provide a useful model of relationship to the past; my approach to individuals here depends on some sense of connection to them as well as difference from them, and I am thus in broad agreement with some such dialectical strategy as is offered in "Desire for the Past." But more to the point, I aspire to address the general problem of "contemporary culture's relationship to history itself" looming so large in Watson's "Phantasmal Past" (2): with my focus on amateurs, even though they are necessarily individual, I hope nonetheless to help enlarge the sense of what counts as history and who gets to do it.

130 Halberstam, *In a Queer Time and Place*, 6, 162; "Introduction: Low Theory" in *The Queer Art of Failure*, 1–25; Edelman, *No Future*; Stockton, *The Queer Child*, 11.

131 Muñoz, *Cruising Utopia*, 1, 11.

132 Thus, for example, a book such as Snediker's *Queer Optimism* develops a critical concept of "queer optimism" that is not "promissory," not "attached to a future," but rather is "embedded in its own immanent present" and thus able to respond to and solicit serious thinking (2–3).

133 Dean, "Bareback Time," 76.

134 Kitchen, *Suburban Knights*, 77. See my review essay, "Nostalgia on My Mind."

135 Gopinath, "Archive, Affect, and the Everyday," 168. For some people considered culturally "eccentric" and for "many displaced people from all over the world," as Svetlana Boym writes, "creative rethinking of nostalgia" serves not merely as "an artistic device but a strategy of survival" (*The Future of Nostalgia*, xvii). Gopinath takes up and adapts Boym's taxonomy in "Archive, Affect, and the Everyday." For an urgent expression of the uses of nostalgia in a queer context, see Juhasz, "Video Remains."

Boym's reliance specifically on Reinhart Koselleck's *Futures Past* for her historical account of the development of modern time and temporality and the consequent rise of nostalgia guarantees a historical narrative that caricatures the medieval. Kathleen Davis has trenchantly analyzed the political and theoretical context and consequences of Koselleck's foundational exclusion of medieval temporalities in his analysis of political-historical conceptions of time: see her *Periodization and Sovereignty*, 87–95. While her chronicling of medieval and early modern temporalities thus needs nuancing (indeed, premodern temporal desires and experiences can now provide resources for resistance to modern time, as I argue in this book, but Boym's theoretical allegiance to Koselleck precludes her from seeing a temporally complex Middle Ages), Boym creates a useful typology of modern nostalgias: "reflective" nostalgia "explores ways of inhabiting many places at once and imagining different time zones" (xviii), and is differentiated from "restorative" nostalgia that has no reflective aspect but seeks to restore a singular truth of the past.

136 Levine, *The Amateur and the Professional*, 59, 69.

137 Boym, *The Future of Nostalgia*, 11, xv, xvii.

138 Dell, "Nostalgia and Medievalism," 118–19.

139 Fradenburg, "'So That We May Speak of Them,'" 209.

140 Here I share the project enunciated by Prendergast and Trigg in "What Is Happening to the Middle Ages?" See, in the same spirit, Finke and Shichtman, *Cinematic Illuminations*, esp. 11–15. The implications for practice are not only that scholars acceptably write scholarly treatments of pop culture, which has been happening for some time; they should include — most important, to my mind — genuine dialogue between amateurs and professionals.

141 Lynch, "Nostalgia and Critique," 202–3.

142 Seremetakis, *The Senses Still*, 4. The Greek term *nostalghia* "evokes the sensory

dimension of memory in exile and estrangement" and "the transformative impact of the past as unreconciled historical experience"; qtd. by Gopinath, "Archive, Affect, and the Everyday," 169–70.

143   See Boym, *The Future of Nostalgia*, xvi, 54–55. As does Boym, I draw on elements of both affects described by Freud in "Mourning and Melancholia."

144   "Habitually dwelling" is from Ruskin, *Modern Painters*, 6: 446.

145   See the Bruce High Quality Foundation, "Zombies Were Trying To Get in the Building," http://www.thebrucehighqualityfoundation.com/Site/more.html. The Bruce High Quality Foundation has started its own university to counter the problems they see produced by current art school pedagogies, beholden to the art market.

146   See Freccero, "Les chats de Derrida." I draw here also on Morton's "Queer Ecology," quoting Eve Kosofsky Sedgwick's resonant description of a queer world as an "open mesh of possibilities" (276); see her "Queer and Now," 8.

147   Latour, *Politics of Nature*, 191.

148   "No one knows everything, everyone knows something, all knowledge resides in humanity": Jenkins quotes Pierre Lévy here and explores the potentials of knowledge communities in *Convergence Culture*, 26–29 passim. To limit "all knowledge" to "humanity," however, seems now (from the perspective of the second decade of the twenty-first century) an unnecessary and even self-defeating boundary to draw, as recent work in animal studies demonstrates; for a short statement of the issues, see Wolfe, "Human, All Too Human." An inclusion of the nonhuman clarifies that the radical multiplication of knowers will inevitably alter the very concepts of knowing and knowledge.

149   Cochran, "Object Oriented Cookery," 328.

150   See Latour, *Politics of Nature*, 22–23. Halberstam, *The Queer Art of Failure*, inspires and enacts resistance to academic professionalism, invoking Foucault's subjected knowledges, drawing on Stuart Hall's "low theory," and joining in the spirit of Moten and Harney's "The University and the Undercommons."

151   Peer review — the development of which was "an outgrowth of the professionalization of disciplines from mathematics to history — a way of keeping eager but uninformed amateurs out," as Patricia Cohen observes — is undergoing intensive scrutiny and spawning alternatives in the digital age ("Scholars Test Web Alternative to Peer Review," *New York Times*, August 23, 2010). See Fitzpatrick, *Planned Obsolescence*, chapter 1, "Peer Review"; the production of Fitzpatrick's book itself included an experiment with an open review process. In 2010 *Shakespeare Quarterly* became "the first traditional humanities journal" to experiment with open review (Cohen, "Scholars Test Web Alternative"). *Postmedieval* conducted its first experiment in open review in mid-2011: guest editors Jen Boyle and Martin Foys, in "Editors' Vision Statement," draw attention to what I would call the nonmodern temporality of "webby" (World Wide Web–based) systems and state their particular interest in *crowd* review, noting the association between the crowd and amateurism, and proposing that the crowd offers "an opportunity to experiment with the re-structuring

of professional and disciplinary affiliation": http://postmedievalcrowdreview
.wordpress.com. See the important forum, edited by Holly A. Crocker, on
crowd review: http://postmedieval-forum.com/forums/forum-ii-states-of-
review/. Open reviewing has been pursued for edited books as well: see *Writing History in the Digital Age*, ed. Jack Dougherty and Kristin Nawrotzki.
For humanities crowdsourcing see the experiment undertaken by the University College London library project of transcribing Jeremy Bentham's papers:
Travis Kaya, "Crowdsourcing Project Hopes to Make Short Work of Transcribing Bentham," *Chronicle of Higher Education*, September 13, 2010.

152 For one particular thread of the development of gay and lesbian history, for
example, and its relationship to the emergence of queer studies, see John
D'Emilio and Estelle B. Freedman's account of Allan Bérubé's life and work,
in Bérubé's *My Desire for History*, 1–37, esp. 24–25.

ONE. ASYNCHRONY STORIES

1 For the folktale classification of the magical sleep type (no. 766), see Aarne,
The Types of the Folktale, 265. For narrative motifs of the supernatural passage of time, see Thompson, *Motif-Index of Folk-Literature*, nos. D.1960.1 and
D. 2011. Colker's "A Medieval Rip van Winkle Story" documents a story not
noted in Thompson that, while Christian, has interesting resonances with
the tale of the Sardinian sleepers, sleeping supernatural lengths of time next
to mythic bodies. See also the useful volume by Hansen, *Ariadne's Thread*,
esp. 397–402. The two dated but still useful guides to the Seven Sleepers
tale and related tales of supernatural sleep — including the Sardinian heroes,
"The Monk and the Bird," Epimenides, and numerous other narratives — are
Huber, *Die Wanderlegende von den Siebenschläfern*, and Koch, *Die Siebenschläferlegende*. Because of my interest in demonstrating the pervasive pressure of other kinds of time in the here and now, I combine in my analysis
tales using several related motifs, including supernatural lapses of time experienced with and without sleep, as well as tales in which the specific state of
consciousness (or unconsciousness) is unclear. I also combine different kinds
of tales — local legends, saints' legends — usefully anatomized and contrasted
to fairy tales in Lüthis, *Once Upon a Time*, 35–46. I am not engaging specific
fairy tales (Sleeping Beauty, for example), though supernatural temporality is
pervasive therein, because, again, I am interested in the relationship of asynchrony to mundane everydayness rather than in supernatural temporalities
for their own sake.

2 Helen Dell in "'Yearning for the Sweet Beckoning Sound'" observes that for
fantasy fiction authors and readers "fantasy and the medieval have a privileged
link or are even interchangeable" (172). This link is the result of a modernist
chronology; according to Arthur Lindley in "The Ahistoricism of Medieval
Film," "history" starts after the putative breaking of modernity out of premodernity, but before modernity it is all strictly "dreamland." (The classical

age, too, is understood to be "history," given modernity's rebirthing relationship to it.) Medievalized fantasy fiction thus has become a privileged site of
an exploration of temporalities: Dell ("'Yearning for the Sweet Beckoning
Sound,'" 173) notes the commonness of "temporal distortion" in fantasy fictions, including C. S. Lewis's *The Lion, the Witch and the Wardrobe*. At the
same time, my hypothesis about life's essential asynchrony leads me to see that
all time travel tales — and not just medieval time travel fantasy — are part of
the same phenomenon: as C. S. Lewis puts it, "In life and art both, as it seems
to me, we are always trying to catch in our net of successive moments something that is not successive" ("On Stories," 20–21; qtd. by Dell, "'Yearning for
the Sweet Beckoning Sound,'" 174).

3 Gurevich, "What Is Time?," 139. Note that while Gurevich asserts that "medieval man feels himself on two temporal planes at once," my emphasis falls less
on the putatively essential nature of this multiple temporality and more on
the potential for this multiplicity resulting from Christian doctrine. Compare
his generic analysis of temporal multiplicity in *Medieval Popular Culture*: in
the grotesque, "it was the meeting of the two [heaven and earth] that struck a
note of marvel: each of the worlds was made vicariously foreign to the other.
The paradox of medieval grotesque is rooted in this confrontation of both
worlds" (183).

4 For a broad overview in English, see Hartland, *The Science of Fairy Tales*, chapters 7–9, all three under the title "The Supernatural Lapse of Time in Fairy-
land." Temporally discrepant worlds are a prominent feature of Celtic materials: for examples of two stories that thematize temporal divergence between
the everyday world and the otherworld — *Annwfn* or *Annwn* in Welsh, *síd*
in Irish — see Carey, *Echtrae Nera* (The Adventure of Nera), and Bhreathnach, *Tochmarc Becfhola* (The Wooing of Becfhola). Thanks to Craig Davis
for these references. For Meriadoc, see Day, *The Story of Meriadoc*, analyzed
in Cross, "'Heterochronia' in *Thomas of Erceldoune, Guingamor*, 'The Tale of
King Herla,' and *The Story of Meriadoc, King of Cambria*."

5 Nevanlinna, *The Northern Homily Cycle*, 2:200–206. The version I use here is
in British Library MS Harley 4196 and is cited by line number; in quoting it
I have modernized obsolete letters throughout. The exemplum in the Vernon
manuscript (Oxford, Bodleian Library MS Eng. poet.a.1) is edited by Horstmann, "Die Evangelien-Geschichten der Homiliensammlung des Ms. Vernon," 277–78.

6 On the cycle's "passionate evangelical spirit," see Anne B. Thompson's introduction to her edition of *The Northern Homily Cycle*, 1. Hope Emily Allen did
not publish her extensive work on the Vernon manuscript, but see the discussion in Hirsh, *Hope Emily Allen*, 82–87.

7 Anne B. Thompson's introduction to *The Northern Homily Cycle* explains
simply: "Thus, the Christian year begins not on January 1 or March 25, but
with Advent, the season in which the birth of Christ is anticipated and which
begins four weeks before Christmas. The year moves through the seasons of

Epiphany, Lent, Easter, and Pentecost, bringing the year to a close with the Twenty-fourth Sunday after Trinity. Every one of the fifty-two Sundays in the year has a name and a place in the Christian calendar, and each Sunday has a Gospel reading which is assigned on the basis of its appropriateness to the occasion" (2).

8   For an explanation of the divisions of the year, correlating scriptural history with the seasons and the times of day, see Jacobus de Voragine, *Legenda aurea*, 1:1–2.

9   Christianity, pivoting on the incarnation of Christ, creates a unique kind of time: Christ's life is not only calibrated across the ecclesiastical year, ever repeated, year after year; it condenses all of history and all of the future into a timeless now. See Kruger on Christianity's "reorganization of history around the incarnational moment" and the consequences for Jews and Judaism. Kruger, *The Spectral Jew*, 2. Along these lines see also Biddick on the "supersessionary fantasies about temporality" she calls "the *Christian typological imaginary*." Biddick, *The Typological Imaginary*, 2. For the classic discussion of typology (also called figural or scriptural or salvation history), see Auerbach, "Figura." For a compelling description of two aesthetic uses of typology see Newman, "Redeeming the Time," on William Langland's *Piers Plowman* and Julian of Norwich's *Revelation of Love*.

10 De Certeau, *The Mystic Fable*, 92–93. De Certeau notes the effect of Ockhamism on such a realist trope; Cole and Smith trace the role of analogy, which draws on linguistic and philosophical realism, in modernist philosophy and critical theory. Cole and Smith, *The Legitimacy of the Middle Ages*, 4–11.

11 I take the rest of the verse from the Clementine Vulgate. Note that in the Clementine Vulgate the beginning of the verse reads, "Modicum, et iam non videbitis me." The Middle English sermon does not include such a temporal indicator as *iam* here.

12 The Latin text of John 16:18 makes it clear that *modicum* is the problem: "Quid est hoc quod dicit: Modicum? Nescimus quid loquitur" (What is this that he saith, A little while? we know not what he speaketh).

13 Coope, *Time for Aristotle*, 31.

14 Muñoz, *Cruising Utopia*.

15 Exempla are conventionally read in a rhetorical tradition of persuasion; thus Le Goff quotes a definition: "a brief narrative presented as truthful (that is, historical) and used in discourse (usually a sermon) to convince listeners by offering them a salutary lesson." Le Goff notes that exempla emerged into popularity in a time (late twelfth century to early thirteenth) in which changes in society included new attitudes toward time and space; he argues that exempla "bridge the gap between historical reality and the eschatological unknown" in sermon discourse. "The Time of the *Exemplum*," 78, 80. The content of the exemplum here, the tale of the monk and the bird, addresses exactly that gap. I will argue that this narrative deploys more complex temporalities, though, than Le Goff implies in his brief article. The classic study of exempla remains extraordinarily useful: Welter, *L'Exemplum dans la littérature religieuse et di-*

dactique du Moyen Âge; see also the more recent study by Bremond, Le Goff, and Schmitt, *L'"Exemplum"*; for the tradition in English, see Owst, *Literature and Pulpit in Medieval England*, 149–209, arguing that the form contributed to the development of literary realism. Olsson quotes Welter's citation of a medieval *ars praedicandi* recommending that preachers use both allegory and exemplum: "the profundity of the allegory may please the learned and the simplicity of the *exemplum* may edify the ignorant" ("Rhetoric, John Gower, and the Late Medieval *Exemplum*," 185).

16   Herbert, "The Monk and the Bird," 428. For a full account of the narrative's sources, see Gerould, "The North-English Homily Collection," 63–65. Gerould notes that the narrative seems to have originated in the annals of the Afflinghem Abbey in Brabant, in the time of the Abbot Fulgentius (late eleventh century). Taken out of the chronicle format, it was first used in a sermon by Maurice de Sully; it appeared shortly afterward in the sermons of Odo of Cheriton and then in collections by Jacques de Vitry, Nicole de Bozon, John Bromyard, and John Herolt, among others; for Jacques de Vitry's version, see Greven, ed., *Die Exempla aus den Sermones feriales et communes des Jakob von Vitry*, 18. For Alfonso X's version that transforms the tale into a miracle of the Virgin, see Kulp-Hill, *Songs of Holy Mary of Alfonso X*, no. 103, 128–29. For a list of known versions, see Tubach, *Index Exemplorum*, 263 (no. 3378, "Monk Felix," related to no. 780, "Bridegroom absent 300 years"). See also Hartland, *The Science of Fairy Tales*, 187–90, for sources and analogues.

17   See Dohrn-van Rossum, who warns that the monastic hours should not be understood too mechanistically or as overly disciplinary, given that "life according to the Rule was bound . . . to natural time givers, daylight and the seasons" (*History of the Hour*, 33–39, at 38).

18   See Friedman, "Eurydice, Heurodis and the Noon-Day Demon."

19   The monk's thought process confirms Simplicius's illustrative commentary on Aristotle, as discussed in my introduction.

20   The late-twelfth-century Bishop of Paris Maurice de Sully in his sermons used this very exemplum, in the version that is most likely the source (via Odo of Cheriton, though Gerould [see n. 16 above] thinks Sully and Odo are independent) of the Vernon version here; the Douce manuscript in particular emphasizes the increasing wonderment of the monk in vibrant, extensive dialogue with the porter and then with the abbot and prior. See especially the early-thirteenth-century Douce version, among the large number of other versions edited by Meyer in "Les Manuscrits des sermons français de Maurice de Sully," 473–74, 485.

21   Paul Meyer, in the supplement to his 1876 article "Les Manuscrits des sermons français de Maurice de Sully," prints the relevant parts of MS Corpus Christi College 36, fol. 12c, wherein the bird sings the psalm, which is given in both Latin and French translation. Meyer, "Les Manuscrits des sermons français de Maurice de Sully" supplement, 190. Herbert, "The Monk and the Bird," 429, quotes the Latin sermon whose birdsong is given in French.

22   See Meyer, "Les Manuscrits des sermons français de Maurice de Sully," 485:

"qu'il dedenz .iij. cenz anz n'est mie enveilliz ne sa vesteüre usée, ne lui soullier perciés."

23 Joy, "*The Seven Sleepers*, Eros, and the Unincorporable Infinite of the Human Person," 91.

24 For mention of this strand, see Gering, *Islendzk Æventyri* (Icelandic Fairy Tales), 2: 122.

25 See Schmidt, "Sleeping toward Christianity," 55–56. A related narrative is that of the magical sleep of a ruler who is buried in a hill and expected to return at some point in the future: Frederick Barbarossa is the most prominent medieval example, but King Arthur, too, in folklore versions lies buried under the hills, and other rulers also populate stories of subterranean dormition: see Hartland, *The Science of Fairy Tales*, 207–21. The Barbarossa legend was itself extraordinarily popular and long lasting: Irving refers to it in "Rip van Winkle," in *The Sketch Book of Geoffrey Crayon*, 784; Longfellow refers to it in his *Golden Legend*, in *The Poetical Works of Henry Wadsworth Longfellow* 5:224; and Bloch, *Heritage of Our Times*, 121, combines it with a reference to the Seven Sleepers.

26 Dundes, *Fables of the Ancients?*, 55–58; Hartland, *The Science of Fairy Tales*, 182, mentions another tale of supernatural time lapse in the Qu'ran.

27 Bynum, *The Resurrection of the Body in Western Christianity*, 10. For discussion in the context of the Seven Sleepers, see Joy, "*The Seven Sleepers*, Eros, and the Unincorporable Infinite of the Human Person," 72–73.

28 "Unde manifestum est, melius dici vitam patrum quam vitas, quia, cum sit diversitas meritorum virtutumque, una tamen omnes vita corporis alit in mundo." Gregory of Tours, *Liber vitae patrum*, 212; trans. Charles W. Jones, *Saints' Lives and Chronicles in Early England*, 62.

29 Reames, *The* Legenda aurea, 3.

30 Caxton, "The Golden Legend," the introduction to his translation of the *Legenda aurea*, 1: 2. Reames meticulously analyzes Jacobus's biases and limitations in his whole *Legenda* but notes Caxton's enthusiastic use of it. Reames, *The* Legenda aurea, 205. In the service of its hagiographical function — emphasizing the predicaments of the Seven, their terrors and confusions, and thus enhancing the reader's feelings of awe at the devotion of these martyrs and the desire to profit by their example — Jacobus's narrative draws out even more markedly than does the *Northern Homily Cycle* sermon the reader's experience of the clash of temporalities. The temporal drama is vigorously conveyed; Vitz analyzes the highly performative aspects of this version in "'The Seven Sleepers of Ephesus.'"

31 Here I follow Jacobus's legend as presented on the Internet Medieval Source Book, from the text edited by F. S. Ellis, http://www.fordham.edu/halsall/basis/goldenlegend/GoldenLegend-Volume4.htm#Seven%20Sleepers.

32 Hansen, *Ariadne's Thread*, 399. Note, furthermore, the end of the Seven Sleepers narrative, in which precise dates are debated: "It is in doubt of that which is said that they slept three hundred and sixty-two years, for they were

raised the year of our Lord four hundred and seventy-eight, and Decius reigned but one year and three months, and that was in the year of our Lord two hundred and seventy, and so they slept but two hundred and eight years." Jacobus de Voragine, "Lives of the Seven Sleepers."

33 Otter, *Inventiones*, 117. Otter argues convincingly that Walter did not produce a mere grab bag of tales.

34 Ibid., 123, analyzing "*nostra modernitas*" as a "jumble."

35 *De nugis curialium*, ed. and trans. James, 2–3.

36 Otter, *Inventiones*, 118, 125.

37 This is the passage much later in *De nugis curialium* in which the "troops engaged in endless wandering" are identified as "of Herlethingus," assumed by scholars to be related to "Herlechin, Herlekin, or Harlequin" of the Wild Hunt (*De nugis curialium*, 26 n. 1). King Herla is not mentioned in this passage, but his name is clearly related, and he is associated with hunting; see Newstead, "Some Observations on King Herla and the Herlething," for a discussion of the relationship between Walter Map's story and the traditions of the Wild Hunt and the Herlething.

38 Lewis, *The Discarded Image*, 122–38. In the late Middle English romance *Thomas of Erceldoune*, as Roseanna Cross has demonstrated, the otherworld is explicitly related to Christian realms of heaven, the earthly paradise, purgatory, and hell. Cross, "'Heterochronia.'" Cross cites Lewis on the parallelism of otherworldly temporality to Christian time frames. Note that Cross argues that Walter Map's version of King Herla's legend makes the idea of God's "eternal present" tangible (174) — she observes the slowness of the passage of time in this other world — and uses the otherworldly temporality to critique social ills of the present.

39 Joyce, *Oisin in Tirnanoge*. For further examples of Celtic tales that thematize asynchrony, see Carey, *Echtrae Nera* (The Adventure of Nera); and Bhreathnach, *Tochmarc Becfhola* (The Wooing of Becfhola), summarized in Dillon, "Wooing of Becfhola and the Stories of Cano, Son of Gartnán." Cross, "'Heterochronia,'" cites *Oisin in Tirnanoge*. Loomis, "*Sir Orfeo* and Walter Map's *De nugis*," likens the Celtic-inspired *Sir Orfeo* to Map's tale of King Herla. According to Newstead, Walter Map's tale "has its closest affinities with Celtic tales of similar type." Newstead, "Some Observations on King Herla and the Herlething," 108.

40 "By the twelfth century Germanic, Celtic, classical, and Eastern ideas all contributed to the general notion that the Other World was somewhere underground — wherever else it might also be found." Patch, *The Other World according to Descriptions in Medieval Literature*, 238.

41 In clearly racialized terms, the "pygmy" (*pigmeus*) is likened to Pan in Walter's narrative; his life is supernatural in the sense C. S. Lewis explains, that is, "*more* 'natural' — stronger, more reckless, less inhibited, more triumphantly and impenitently passionate — than ours." Lewis, *The Discarded Image*, 133.

42 Longfellow, *Golden Legend*, in *Works*, 5:139–292; the recounting of "The

Monk and the Bird" is on 158–63. Longfellow was professor of modern languages at Bowdoin and then Smith Professor of Modern Languages and
Belles Lettres at Harvard; he had facility with French, German, Italian, and
Spanish, in addition to "at least a working knowledge of, and reading com-
petence in, Danish, Swedish, Dutch, and Portuguese." Irmscher, *Longfellow
Redux*, 147. He wrote detailed academic essays on topics in the linguistic and
literary histories of numerous languages, including English. Medieval European and English literatures were constant sources, influences, and inspira-
tions for his own poetic creation: *Tales of a Wayside Inn*, for example, takes
its inspiration from Chaucer and Boccaccio; the *Golden Legend*, discussed
later, reveals his wide reading in medieval materials, from medieval drama to
the letters of Abelard and Heloise, to scholastic disputation, to Middle High
German narrative. He was the first American translator of Dante's *Commedia*
in its entirety. "I have also been trying to follow Dante in his exile—a hopeless
task," he wrote late in his life; Kirsten Silva Gruesz speculates that temporal
ambivalence is the key to Longfellow's imitation "exile" here ("*El Gran Poeta
Longfellow and a Psalm of Exile*," 405–6).

43 Lears studies the period beginning around the time of Longfellow's death,
and his general argument is that the medievalism of that period—one kind
of antimodernism—"helped ease accommodation to new and secular cultural
modes" of modernity (*No Place of Grace*, xv). This was, he goes on, "an ironic,
unintended consequence" of antimodernism. My discussion of Longfellow
emphasizes double vision or temporal copresence rather than an ironic under-
cutting of antimodernism by modernism, in this way trying to explore a *nonmodern* temporality that is not defined by an either-or paradigm.

44 Ruskin, *Modern Painters*, 6: 446. Ruskin here gives as examples of "great men
having certain sympathies for those earlier ages" both Henry Wadsworth
Longfellow and Robert Browning. Certainly Ruskin's own medievalism is
driving his analyses here, but I take Ruskin's comment as a shrewd analysis of
the structure of doubleness—a hermeneutic contemporaneity, as I shall suggest in chapter 3—obtaining in such medievalism.

45 Longfellow, *Christus: A Mystery*, in *Works*, volume 5. The general theme of
Christus was conceived as "the various aspects of Christendom in the Apostolic, Middle, and Modern Ages," as Longfellow put it in his journal entry for
November 8, 1841; the next year he correlated the three parts with the Christian
virtues, respectively, of hope, faith, and charity. *Works*, 5:7, 9. The *Golden Legend*
itself met with moderate success in terms of sales—see Charvat, *The Profession of Authorship in America*, 146, 150. It inspired several very popular musical
adaptations, including *Scenes from Longfellow's* Golden Legend, a symphonic
cantata by Dudley Buck (1880), described by Goodrich in *Complete Musical
Analysis*, 297–306; Longfellow initially was dubious about the libretto—which
does not include the exemplum of monk and bird (see Buck, *Scenes from Longfellow's* Golden Legend)—but ultimately supported the endeavor. And Arthur
Sullivan (of Gilbert and Sullivan fame) wrote an even more popular and en-

during cantata, *The Golden Legend* (1886), based on Longfellow's work. Long-fellow's version of the monk and bird exemplum familiarized Americans with the anecdote and thus may have prepared the audience for Richard Chenevix Trench's version, published in the United States in 1857. Charvat, *The Profession of Authorship in America*, argues that the whole *Christus* trilogy was received tepidly (150) and was an intellectual and artistic failure (149), a judgment with which Buell agrees. Buell, *New England Literary Culture*, 259.

46 See Gruesz, "*El Gran Poeta* Longfellow."

47 Longfellow, *Works*, 5:442, 11.

48 Arvin notes that Walter von der Vogelweide "fascinated" Longfellow: he wrote a poem about him and anthologized two others by him. See Arvin's thoughtful treatment, to which I am indebted, of the *Golden Legend* in his *Longfellow, His Life and Work*, 86–99 (quotation on 89).

49 Herbert (428) identifies the version of the fable used by Longfellow as the early German metrical version printed in Hagen, *Gesammtabenteuer*, 3:611–23. See also Huber, *Die Wanderlegende von den Siebenschläfern*, 397. Note that there are variations in details that Longfellow must have gotten from other versions of the legend.

50 Griffith argues that Longfellow in *The Courtship of Miles Standish* makes folk-lore "an integral part of the atmosphere of the poem, an essential quality of the way events are looked at and talked about." Griffith, "Longfellow and Herder and the Sense of History," 261. I would argue that in the *Golden Legend* Longfellow does the same thing with medieval legends.

51 Longfellow, *Works*, 5:11. Thanks to Scott Black for this point about reading here.

52 See Matthews, "Chaucer's American Accent," 763, 764, 770. Matthews considers Lowell's 1845 essay on Chaucer as well as his better-known 1870 essay, "Chaucer"; he also discusses Emerson's 1837 lecture, "The American Scholar." William Calin comments that Longfellow's medievalism is "in some respects, more genuinely modern than, say, Emerson" ("What *Tales of a Wayside Inn* Tells Us about Longfellow and about Chaucer," 208). Calin remarks on a certain doubleness in medievalism; for my discussion of doubleness, see below.

53 Longfellow, "History of the Italian Language and Dialects," 283. See Irmscher, *Longfellow Redux*, 159, who quotes and analyzes these passages.

54 See contemporary witnesses to Longfellow's teaching, qtd. in Calhoun, *Long-fellow*, 133. As Calhoun observes, Longfellow's hard-fought modern language curriculum victories at Harvard resulted in "a new kind of course . . . one in which foreign languages were not an end in themselves but a way of under-standing a culture"; such new courses were "ventures in comparative litera-ture, a very new field on either side of the Atlantic" (130–31).

55 In his review essay "Defense of Poetry" Longfellow writes, "Poetry is the spirit of the age itself, — embodied in the forms of language, and speaking in a voice that is audible to the external as well as the internal sense" (68). Qtd. in Grif-fith, "Longfellow and Herder and the Sense of History," 258.

56   Lengthy discussions of the medieval poetry of France and of Spain fill out the travel narrative of *Outre-Mer*, and a chapter on early English prose romances was added to the British edition. The model for Longfellow's sketches here is Washington Irving's *Sketch Book of Geoffrey Crayon*, which I shall consider on its own in chapter 4. Longfellow declared in 1859, upon the death of Irving, that that book was the "book among all others which in early youth first fascinate[d] his imagination, and at once excite[d] and satisfie[d] the desires of his mind." Moreover, it had strange temporal powers: "whenever I open its pages, I open also that mysterious door which leads back into the haunted chambers of youth." Samuel Longfellow, *The Life of Henry Wadsworth Longfellow*, 1:12. Irving's narrative persona, the amateur Geoffrey Crayon, is cheerfully belated and abject as he describes and lives out the derivative relationship between Old World and New; Longfellow is doubly belated as he follows Irving, and his several protestations in *Outre-Mer* that others have written perfectly well about the sights he sees, so he won't bother to describe them, contribute to the doubly dilettante, derivative quality of the narrative. See Irmscher, *Longfellow Redux*, 177; Charvat, *The Profession of Authorship in America*, 119–20.

57   Longfellow, *Outre-Mer*, 7. The epigraph to *Outre-Mer* reads, "I have passed manye landes and manye yles and contrees, and cherched manye fulle straunge places, and have ben in manye a fulle gode honourable companye. Now I am comen home to reste. And thus recordynge the tyme passed, I have fulfilled these thynges and putte hem wryten in this boke, as it woulde come into my mynde."

58   David Meredith Reese, *Humbugs of New-York* (1838), qtd. by Franchot, *Roads to Rome*, 218; see her illuminating chapter, "The 'Attraction of Repulsion,'" 197–220. For a discussion of the beginning of Longfellow's "complicated love affair with Catholicism," see Irmscher, *Longfellow Redux*, 178–81.

59   Gruesz details the politics and poetics of Longfellow's translations and documents his appeal to a broad range of "the originators of Latin America's national literary canons" in *Ambassadors of Culture* (79).

60   Complicating the Old World / Catholicism connection to the New World was Longfellow's fantasy of northern origins of the New World, expressed in his 1841 poem "The Skeleton in Armor": he was intrigued by "the first bold viking who crossed to this western world," as he put it in a 1838 journal entry; see Barnes, "Nostalgia, Medievalism and the Vinland Voyages," 145.

61   Thomas Gold Appleton, Longfellow's brother-in-law, called the frenzy of present-day America "wheels of activity." Qtd. in Irmscher, *Longfellow Redux*, 158. See also Griffith, "Longfellow and Herder and the Sense of History."

62   Ruskin, *Modern Painters*, 6: 446–47. The passage in question contrasts Shakespeare with Longfellow and Browning; Ruskin in fact identifies Browning as having "*seen* other things," but I think he is also making the claim for Longfellow as well. The passage continues to work out the contrast between creative (ancient, before the modern) and reflective (modern) poets that Ruskin developed extensively in volume 3 of *Modern Painters*. This distinction is similar, Jonathan Bate finds, to Schiller's distinction between naïve (classical) and

sentimental (modern) artistry—naive in the sense of "unmediated," sentimental in the sense of "self-conscious" (*Romantic Ecology*, 72). The specific
phenomenon I have isolated in Longfellow ("double vision") is related to the
reflectiveness of the moderns in *Modern Painters* in that the double vision
draws not just on what is there to be seen but also on what the poet has experienced for himself. See Bate, *Romantic Ecology*, 62–84.

63 What I am getting at here with "double vision" is usefully explicated by Duncan in " 'Reactionary Desire,' " 73: "Ruskin's own historical stage . . . is defined
on the one hand by a total saturation of the conditions of modernity . . . and
on the other by the Gothic revivalist's—Ruskin's—accession to a full, alien-
ated consciousness. This critical consciousness . . . is formed in the act of reading—an act which is not simply a motion but a *discipline*, an exegesis, the
imagination's induction into a symbolic order of types and correspondences
from which it has become historically estranged."

64 Haralson, "Mars in Petticoats," 329, 336. Arvin reads in Henry, akin to a Pre-
Raphaelite "beautiful, melancholy, somewhat epicene figure," a "vacillation
between this fear [of death] and the intense *longing* for death." Arvin, *Longfellow, His Life and Work*, 91, 92. On the feminization of American literature
during this period see Pattee, *The Feminine Fifties*, esp. his characterization of
Hiawatha as "a feminized Indian, a Victorian gentleman" (169).

65 Gruesz, *Ambassadors of Culture*, 97, notes the same responses to the ending of
Evangeline.

66 Here I lean heavily on Calhoun's provocative description and analysis of the
scene in *Longfellow*, 1–3; on Longfellow's dandyism, see 134.

67 Qtd. in Calhoun, *Longfellow*, 3.

TWO. TEMPORALLY ORIENTED

1 Uebel, *Ecstatic Transformation*, 20. On the status of the author and narrator, see (among many others) Higgins, who refers to the former, because unknown, as "the *Mandeville*-author," and the latter as "Sir John," because he is
thus self-named in the book. Higgins, *Writing East*, 8. For simplicity I refer to
the author as "Mandeville," but, as will become explicit in this chapter, I don't
assume that a person called Sir John Mandeville actually authored the text.

2 *The Book of John Mandeville*, ch. 1, p. 108, lines 1–2. Unless otherwise noted,
quotations from the text are taken from the 1919 edition by Paul Hamelius
(titled *Mandeville's Travels*) for the Early English Text Society. I have modernized obsolete letters throughout. Hamelius edits the Cotton Titus manuscript, which I have chosen not only because it is one of the three early English
translations but also because of the specificity and expressiveness of its ending,
which does not include the later interpolation. My glosses draw on Hamelius's
notes as well as on Moseley, *The Travels of Sir John Mandeville*, and Letts,
Mandeville's Travels.

3 Tzanaki writes that Sir John's "tongue-in-cheek humour has obviously sur-
faced again" in the fountain passage; other instances include his trumping

the exotic existence of a vegetable lamb with his own report of home-grown barnacle geese. Tzanaki, *Mandeville's Medieval Audiences*, 103–6, at 106. Note that Odoric of Pordenone, the source of this passage about barnacle geese, reports that they grow in Ireland; Sir John claims them in his own country.

4 I am developing a description of the book's particular "chronotope," to use Bakhtin's term that expresses the inextricability of time from space. See *The Dialogic Imagination*, 84–258. My discussion thus revises a reading of the book that claims that time is generally a function of space in the book. See, e.g., Higgins, *Writing East*, 233–34; the very word "iorneye," often used in this text as a measure, suggests this analytical subordination of time to space: it is the spatial distance of one day's travel (see, e.g., ch. 5, p. 18, l. 31), or the temporal span of a day's travel (ch. 12, p. 65, l. 31). My reading also seeks to broaden critical emphasis beyond the travel-east/travel-backward-in-time scheme.

5 Hamelius, in the article from which I quote, is bewildered by what he sees as the contradictory doubleness of Mandeville's text itself, at once reverent and flippant. Hamelius, "The Travels of Sir John Mandeville," 351–52.

6 Howard, *Writers and Pilgrims*, esp. 72, 68.

7 Kohanski and Benson, "Introduction" to *The Book of John Mandeville*, 10.

8 Howard acknowledges this fully: see *Writers and Pilgrims*, particularly 67–69.

9 Akbari, *Idols in the East*, 24. Akbari goes on to demonstrate compellingly that there are "shifting centers" in the *Book of John Mandeville* that "supplement Jerusalem without displacing it."

10 See Scafi for a concise discussion of the *mappamundi*'s "strong intuition for the 'space-time' character of reality" ("Mapping Eden," 64). The thirteenth-century Ebstorf world map makes this vibrantly clear: the whole earth is represented "within the embrace of a gigantic Christ, whose head is in the east, near paradise, whose feet are in the west, and whose outstretched arms encompass the middle of the earth along a north-south axis." Scafi, *Mapping Paradise*, plate 9; see also the Hereford world map (c. 1300, plate 7 in *Mapping Paradise*), and Higgins, "Imagining Christendom from Jerusalem to Paradise." Christ's incarnation is the fulcrum of a kind of temporality unique to Christianity, as we have seen in earlier chapters; *mappaemundi* express this complex reality.

11 Thanks to Suzanne Akbari for help with this point. See Lampert-Weissig, *Medieval Literature and Postcolonial Studies*, for an incisive discussion of the function of the Jews in this text.

12 Kohanski and Benson, "Introduction" to *The Book of John Mandeville*. Indeed, Kohanski and Benson maintain in the introduction to their edition that "Old and New Testament events are yoked together not because (like the sacrifice of Isaac and the crucifixion of Christ) they have an important allegorical relationship to one another or any other interpretive significance, but simply because they happen to have taken place on the same physical spot" (10).

13 Lochrie, "Provincializing Medieval Europe," 597.

14 See Dohrn-van Rossum, *History of the Hour*, 84–88, on Chinese clocks, which may have some relevance with regard to the "Oriloges" here.

15 British Library MS Royal 17 C. xxxviii includes a fanciful clock in Prester John's Land: automata in the shape of "bryddes and beestis that turned aboute by gynne in an orlage" have been ordered made by "a ryche man that men called Catholonabeus." Kohanski and Benson, *The Book of John Mandeville*, lines 2479–80, 2473. Such automata might have been heir of Islamic clocks from the tenth century on, "toys used for entertainment at the courts and in wealthy homes and to amaze visitors." Dohrn-van Rossum, *History of the Hour*, 74. Catholonabeus (also known as the Old Man of the Mountain) has also ordained a false paradise. The proximity here of a clock to a false paradise is fascinating; since, as we shall see, time in Paradise is not the ordinarily measurable earthly time, the clock here might signal the falseness of this paradise.

16 See Yule, "The Travels of Friar Odoric," 1: 142–43.

17 Lochrie, "Provincializing Medieval Europe," 597.

18 Lochrie has commented on positive cosmopolitan outcomes of shame in "Provincializing Medieval Europe."

19 "But thei seye not so manye thinges at the messe as men don here, For thei seye not but only that that the APOSTLES seyden, as oure lord taughte hem, Right as Seynt PETER & seynt THOMAS & the other APOSTLES songen the mess, seyenge the PATER NOSTER & the wordes of the sacrement. But wee haue many mo [*more*] Addiciouns that dyuerse POPES han made that thei ne knowe not offe [*of*]" (ch. 33, p. 199, l. 34–p. 200, l. 4).

20 Higgins, "Imagining Christendom from Jerusalem to Paradise," 104; "consoling" in my previous sentence is his word. More generally, Higgins argues that Sir John's more significant "personal" moments "suggest that the *Mandeville*-author is interested in Saracen Otherness not merely in itself, but also so as to flatter and criticize the cultural Self of his projected audience by reconfirming Christianity's universal superiority, exposing the laxness of Latin Christian practice, and offering the consoling hope of re-expansion as a motive for religious reform." Higgins, *Writing East*, 110. In accepting Higgins's argument here I am diverging from Lochrie's reading of Mandeville's "cosmopolitan utopianism," his project to "provincialize Europe"; her analysis, Lisa Lampert-Weissig has shown, depends on excepting Mandeville's treatment of the Jews, which Lampert-Weissig argues is impossible to separate out from his larger goals. Lampert-Weissig, *Medieval Literature and Postcolonial Studies*, 86–105.

21 Higgins, "Imagining Christendom from Jerusalem to Paradise," 102–3. Such a Christian ordering of the world "frames territorial expansion as a process of salvation (as in saving the Christian within the pagan), in fulfillment of scripture. . . . Christian domination over the East appears nothing less than inevitable." Burgwinkle, "Utopia and Its Uses," 555. Burgwinkle is writing specifically about twelfth-century texts, but as Higgins points out, the emotions prompted by memory of the Crusades ran deep, and Mandeville "clearly seeks to benefit from them." Higgins, *Writing East*, 31.

22 In the Egerton version his fellows drink as well, but the effects of the fountain on them are not specified. See Letts, *Mandeville's Travels*, 1:121–22.

23 Understatement is his wont, and caution always limits his claims: see Howard,

Writers and Pilgrims, 63–64. Further, Howard notes Mandeville's "penchant" for anticlimax (65). See also Moseley, *The Travels of Sir John Mandeville*, 17, on Sir John's tone.

24 See chapter 18 in George F. Warner's edition: "I, Iohn Maundeuille, sawe this well and drank theroff thrys and all my felawes, and euermare sen that tyme I fele me the better and the haler and supposez for to do till the tyme that Godd of his grace will make me to passe out of this dedly lyf." *The buke of John Mande-uill*, 84. E. Washburn Hopkins notes the differences between the Fountain of Youth and the Water of Life, which were merged as Fountain of Youth legends developed to include the well's origin in Paradise ("The Fountain of Youth").

25 Hopkins, "The Fountain of Youth," 36.

26 Herrtage, *The Early English Versions of the* Gesta romanorum, 343–45; Hopkins, "The Fountain of Youth," 16.

27 For Herodotus, see Hopkins, "The Fountain of Youth," 29n1. Peter Martyr notes the invigoration by a healing fountain: an islander drank and bathed in the well in Florida, after which "hee is reported to have brought home a manly strength, and to have used all manly exercises, and that hee married againe, and begatt children." Hopkins, "The Fountain of Youth," 22–23. See the reversal of time's forward movement in *Huon de Bordeaux*, where eating the fruit of a tree beside the well makes an eighty- or one-hundred-year-old man as young as thirty again. Hopkins, "The Fountain of Youth," 8. The promise of the Fountain of Youth is the promise of the extension of the prime of life, the age of manly power and reproductivity; Hopkins, "The Fountain of Youth," 10, comments on the age of "youth."

28 See Sanok, "*The Lives of Women Saints of Our Contrie of England*," for mention of miraculous wells and springs in England at the sites of female English martyrs.

29 For example, the *Gesta* allegorizes this well as Christ himself, thus linking the idea of the immortal water of life to resuscitation.

30 Picking up from and extending Christian exegetical tradition, the *Letter of Prester John* says the Fountain of Youth is located in India, "ad radicem montis Olimphi, unde fons perspicuus exoritur, in se specierum saporem retinens. Variatur autem sapor eius per singulas horas diei et noctis, et progreditur itinere dierum trium non longe a paradiso, unde fuit Adam prothoplastus expulsus. Si quis autem ieiunus de ipso fonte ter gustaverit, ex tunc nullam pacietur infirmitatem, et semper erit iuvenis in etate triginta annorum, dum vixerit." [at the foot of Mt. Olympus, whence springs a clear fountain which has within itself every kind of taste. It changes its taste every hour by day and night, and is scarcely three days' journey from Paradise, whence Adam was expelled. Anyone who tastes of this fountain thrice, fasting, will suffer no infirmity thereafter, but remains as if of the age of 32 years as long as he lives.] Latin text in Wagner, *Die "Epistola presbiteri Johannis" lateinisch und deutsch*, 359; English translation in Letts, *Mandeville's Travels*, 2:505.

Uebel, *Ecstatic Transformation*, 119, situates the fountain within the utopian imaginings of the *Letter*, arguing that in the *Letter* "the constant oscillation of the familiar and the alien"—such as we've seen in the *Book of John Mandeville* as well— "was effected across a field of perpetual desire, the insistent wish to bring the two together. Thus . . . a pattern appears in the *Letter*: what was lost once gets figured as that which is desired forever": perpetual youth, linked to the lost Garden of Eden.

31 Hopkins, "The Fountain of Youth," 19.

32 Michelant, *Li Romans d'Alixandre*, 348, lines 15–16.

33 See the 1534 translation by Lord Berners of the thirteenth-century French prose text: Lee, *The Boke of Duke Huon of Burdeux*, 433–39. Only the exploits at the fountain of Ogier the Dane, a rebellious peer of Charlemagne, in Jean d'Outremeuse's *Myreur des Histors* prove the well to be as limited as in the *Book of John Mandeville*, which makes sense: the *Book of John Mandeville* is Jean's direct source. Borgnet, *Ly myreur des histors*, 3:58; see Hamelius's note in his edition of *Mandeville's Travels* 2:100.

34 Letts, *Mandeville's Travels*, 2:505; Wagner, "*Epistola presbiteri Johannis*," 359.

35 Scafi, *Mapping Paradise*, 62, on the present absence that is Eden; see also 149, on separation and connection of Paradise to the rest of the world.

36 See Augustine, *City of God*, 12.11 and 14.26. Discussed in Scafi, *Mapping Paradise*, 65–66.

37 Dante, *Paradiso*, 26.139–42, with commentary by Singleton; *The Book of John Mandeville*, ch. 10, p. 44, lines 15–17.

38 Scafi, *Mapping Paradise*, 160.

39 Ibid., 47–48, citing *Etymologiae* 14.3.2–4.

40 See Scafi, *Mapping Paradise*, 65.

41 Derrida, referring to temporality in Eden—specifically, the temporality of "God's exposure to surprise" in bringing the animals to Adam for naming—admits that "this time before time has always made me dizzy." Derrida, *The Animal That Therefore I Am*, 17.

42 See Coulton, *Life in the Middle Ages*, 4:272–79. The Italian is found in Del Lungo, *I Padri del Deserto*, 489–504. See also Huber, *Die Wanderlegende von den Siebenschläfern*, 397. Discussed in Patch, *The Other World according to Descriptions in Medieval Literature*, 165–66. See also Hartland, *The Science of Fairy Tales*, 193, for tales in which travelers go to Heaven or Paradise.

43 Coulton, *Life in the Middle Ages*, 4:276.

44 Ibid.

45 Ibid., 4:277. Recall the allegorical as well as literal meanings of forty days in the Gospel sermon discussed in chapter 1. Godfrey of Viterbo tells a related story; see Patch, *The Other World according to Descriptions in Medieval Literature*, 159–60.

46 Coulton, *Life in the Middle Ages*, 4:276–77.

47 Ibid., 4:274.

48 Tzanaki, *Mandeville's Medieval Audiences*, 99.

49 George F. Warner, *The buke of John Mandeuill*, 150. See the same syntax in the

Paris text, the earliest manuscript of the book: "De paradis terrestre ne vous saroie ie proprement parler, car ie ny fui onques. Ce poise moy, car ie ne fu mie digne de la aler." Letts, *Mandeville's Travels*, 2:405.

50   Scafi, *Mapping Paradise*, 241–42. Scafi paraphrases Mandeville at length here but does not include this comment ("that forthinketh me"); presumably he dismissed it as a throwaway.

51   See Connolly, "Imagined Pilgrimage in the Itinerary Maps of Matthew Paris," 616, and *The Maps of Matthew Paris*, esp. 28–39. Lori J. Walters referred to this article in "*A Map for Despairing Minds*: Real and Imagined Pilgrimages to Rome as Spiritual Consolation in a Gerson Anthology, Paris, BnF fr. 990" (paper presented at the Medieval Academy of America annual meeting, Chicago, March 2009).

52   Letts gives a straightforward account of the book's reception, noting that Hugh Murray in the early nineteenth century determined that the work contained much from Odoric, and then E. W. B. Nicholson in the 1870s "laid the foundations for a new approach to the whole subject." Letts, *Sir John Mandeville*, 37–38; 22. Yule and Nicholson in the *Encyclopaedia Britannica* entertain the possibility that the author traveled as far as the Holy Land and Egypt; George F. Warner in his 1889 edition of the book makes a case against even this much travel on the author's part.

53   Purchas, *Hakluytus Posthumus or Purchas His Pilgrimes*, 11: 188, 364; qtd. in Letts, *Sir John Mandeville*, 35.

54   Burton, *The Anatomy of Melancholy*, 2:40; Browne, *Pseudodoxia Epidemica*, 236. Both cited by Letts, *Sir John Mandeville*, 36–37.

55   Yule, "The Travels of Friar Odoric," 1: 28. See Kohanski and Benson, 2.

56   Yule, *The Book of Ser Marco Polo*, 1:109.

57   Ibid., 1:xv ("Preface to the Second Edition") and 1:lxvii ("Memoir of Sir Henry Yule" by Amy Frances Yule), which comments on Yule's complete identification with "his favourite traveller." Note also the echo of *Purgatorio* 4 in "*vôlti a levante*"; Yule thereby puts himself in Dante's place and Marco in Virgil's stead. For Amy Yule as "Mademoiselle Marco Paulovna," see 1:lxvii n. 70.

58   Cf. John Gross on Frederick James Furnivall: if Furnivall's "energies had taken another turn [he] might have covered a continent with railways." Qtd. in David Matthews, *The Making of Middle English*, 142.

59   Lang, *Letters to Dead Authors*, 110–11. Lang's language closely follows Yule's in the *Encyclopaedia Britannica* article. Some of the *Letters*, "exercises in the art of dipping," as he put it in his dedication to "Miss Thackeray," were originally written for the *St. James Gazette*. Lang also wrote parodic letters between various fictional characters: see his *Old Friends: Essays in Epistolary Parody* (1890).

60   See Yule, *A Narrative of the Mission Sent by the Governor-General of India to the Court of Ava in 1855*, 93–95 and plate 17. I was alerted to this passage by Rohayati Paseng Barnard's website about the Asia Collection at the University of Hawaii, Manoa, http://scholarspace.manoa.hawaii.edu/bitstream/101

25/14715/6/LibTreasuresExh.pdf.txt. The site points to the marked colonialist view of Maphoon, the "bearded" woman under scrutiny.

61 Fabian, *Time and the Other*. This British colonialist space–time scheme has been documented copiously and analyzed keenly. For a concise example of this space–time scheme see Maine, *Lectures on the Early History of Institutions*: in lecture 1, Maine sets up the historical argument for a common "Aryan" origin of Englishmen and Hindus via an analysis of analogies between the ancient laws of Ireland and current Hindu law. Lecture 10 details the relationship between the Law of Distress, a particular legal locus in ancient Irish law, and the current Hindu practice of "sitting dharná." Maine cites Whitley Stokes, an eminent Celtic philologist as well as Maine's right-hand man in India (see note 78 below), as having first noted the identical relationship. Maine had in 1871 published six lectures under the title *Village Communities in the East and West*, in which the parallel between the structure of communities in India and in ancient Germanic communities was drawn. When "we have learned not to exclude from our view of the earth and man those great and unexplored regions which we vaguely term the East; we find it to be not wholly a conceit or a paradox to say that the distinction between the present and the past disappears. Sometimes the past is the present; much more often it is removed from it by varying distances, which, however, cannot be estimated or expressed chronologically." Approvingly qtd. in Duff, *Sir Henry Maine*, 38. For a brilliant analysis of the discursive role of the Indian village community in colonial debate, see Kabir, "An Enchanted Mirror for the Capitalist Self." For another European medieval history deployed in the nineteenth-century imperial context, see Barnes's discussion of British Vinland narratives in Barnes, "Nostalgia, Medievalism and the Vinland Voyages."

62 In a letter quoted by his daughter, Yule is thanked by "a kindly Franciscan friar, who wrote: 'You may rest assured that the Beato Odorico will not forget all you have done for him.'" Yule, *The Book of Ser Marco Polo*, 1:lxxii n. 78.

63 Chakrabarty, "Response: Historicism and Its Supplements," 111, commenting on Kabir; Kabir, "An Enchanted Mirror for the Capitalist Self," 54, describing her term "Oriental Gothic."

64 Andrew Lang, impeccably educated at St Andrews and Oxford, left the academic life after his fellowship at Merton ended in 1876 and moved to London. During the 1880s in London, he wrote highly regarded journalism, literary criticism, fiction, poetry, and translations, and befriended Rider Haggard, Robert Louis Stevenson, and Rudyard Kipling, among many others. He championed many manuscripts that came into Longmans, where he was literary advisor. In the years following, his writing shifted toward myth and fairy tale—anthropological interests, broadly put—and the latter genre was defended for its realism and adult interest by J. R. R. Tolkien in a lecture in honor of Lang half a century later. Roger Lancelyn Green, *Andrew Lang*, 47. Green, on whose account I am relying here, calls him "the great scholar and the best-read man of his period" (76).

65 Lang, *Letters to Dead Authors*, 111. Further citations of this work are given in

parentheses in the text. On Mandeville as foolish, see Yule and Nicholson, "Mandeville, Jehan de," esp. 474.

66   For the phrase "divine amateur" applied to Andrew Lang, see Wilde, "English Poetesses" (1888): the context is a list of exceptional English prose stylists. Wilde laments that there are so few ("English prose is detestable"), going on to list Carlyle, Pater, Froude, Arnold, Meredith, Stevenson, and Ruskin as well as Lang, all with pithy epithets. Wilde, "English Poetesses," 105–6. For brief discussion, see Roger Lancelyn Green, *Andrew Lang*, 31–32. Lang implicitly identifies himself as an amateur in his introduction to Oskar Sommer's edition of *Le Morte Darthur*: "The learning about Malory has been so fully dealt with in this edition by an expert, that the comments of one who merely reads Malory for enjoyment may be confined to the enjoyable elements in his work." And Lang goes on to quote that consummate amateur Furnivall on Malory: "His, as Mr. Furnivall remarks, 'is a most pleasant jumble and summary of the legends about Arthur.'" Lang, "'Le Morte Darthur,'" in *Le Morte Darthur* 3: xiii.

67   Kabir, "An Enchanted Mirror for the Capitalist Self." Kabir has extended her analysis of medieval philology and empire, including affective dimensions, in "Reading between the Lines."

68   I rely here on Cox, *M. R. James*, 81–82. See also Pfaff, *Montague Rhodes James*, 79.

69   Cox, 71.

70   The first two of his four volumes of ghost stories are titled *Ghost-Stories of an Antiquary* (1904) and *More Ghost Stories of an Antiquary* (1911). The term "antiquary" or "antiquarian" here is not marked by its opposition to "professional," as we have seen it in Levine, *The Amateur and the Professional*; James is part of the academic establishment, and his protagonists tend to have academic credentials or have garnered academic recognition. But it is marked nonetheless by a sense of the forbidden (stirring up the past is dangerous), and thus has some relation to Levine's stigmatized term; if, for Levine, "pleasure" and "leisure" are dubious for the professional, they are downright dangerous for James's antiquaries.

71   S. T. Joshi comments that James's antiquarians are "stand-ins for himself." Joshi, "Introduction," xii. Joshi also reports James's early discovery of the wondrous stories of Walter Map; James in fact later edited and translated *De nugis curialium* (Joshi, viii). On the temporality of these stories written "at long intervals," see James, "Preface" to *Ghost-Stories of an Antiquary*, in Joshi, 254.

72   Rogers, introduction to the reprint of *Athens in the Fourteenth Century* in *The Legacy of M. R. James*, 230.

73   M. R. James, *Athens in the Fourteenth Century*, 237. Further citations of this work are given in parentheses in the text.

74   On Barker, see Cox, 82: "Barker could be almost anything Montague Rhodes James was not."

75   Cf. Cerquiglini, *In Praise of the Variant*, 34: "Medieval philology is the mourn-

ing for a text, the patient labor of this mourning. It is the quest for an anterior perfection that is always bygone." See also Finke and Shichtman, *Cinematic Illuminations*, 13–14, for discussion. Werner Hamacher emphasizes that philology's place is in the order of "the plea, the prayer, the desire." In its realm "affect stirs"; its dynamic is "the experience of drawing into withdrawal." Hamacher, "From '95 Theses on Philology,'" 994, 996, 995. For a contrasting account of philology—as engaging not loss and mourning but fullness and love—see Brown, "Love Letters." For the language of desire in classical philology see Constanze Güthenke, "The Unlikely Lover: Classical Scholarship, Empathy, and Wilamowitz' Plato" (paper written for the "Desiring the Text, Touching the Past: Towards an Erotics of Reception" symposium at Bristol University, July 2010).

76   "There is something not inanimate behind the Malice of Inanimate Objects": James, "The Malice of Inanimate Objects," 205.

77   Chabon, "The Other James," 131.

78   The amateur scholar phenomenon among British India officials has certainly been noted before. Those trained in or inspired by the new field of comparative philology were able to do scholarship in ancient languages of the British Isles even as their knowledge of ancient Indian languages prepared them to be colonial administrators on the subcontinent. As R. I. Best notes of Whitley Stokes (renowned Celticist and codifier of the whole body of Anglo-Indian law) and others, there existed the type of "high Indian officials" who continued "the studies and interests of their youth"; they were private scholars, "rare in Germany, where learning is professional, but then not uncommon in England." Best, "Whitley Stokes," 11. Thus the careers of philologist-administrators such as Stokes and Fitzedward Hall, both of whom served in India but eventually ended up living out their lives in England, took "no part in public or academic life, devoting [themselves] wholly to [their] favorite studies." (This is Best's comment on Stokes [Best, "Whitley Stokes," 10], which applies equally well to Hall.) They were trained and respected philologists; Stokes and his circle, in particular, trained in Dublin by a German philologist, distanced themselves shudderingly from mere "enthusiasts" of ancient Irish history and literature; yet these private scholars remained finally aloof from academic or professional philological study. Stokes Papers, box 2, University College London Library. On Stokes's melancholy and the intertwining of philology and empire in his oeuvre, see Kabir, "Reading between the Lines," esp. 92.

Fitzedward Hall, professor of the Sanskrit language and literature, and of Indian jurisprudence, at King's College, London, demonstrates a complex melancholy of the colonial amateur philologist. He was an American who had landed by happenstance in India; he stayed for more than fifteen years, mastering and then teaching languages, serving as inspector of public instruction, and then serving in the British military during the Mutiny, finally leaving the subcontinent in 1862 to join the faculty of King's College, London, and to become librarian at the India Office. Owen, "Hall, Fitzedward" in *Oxford Dictionary of National Biography*. A "furious dispute" (Winchester, *The Madman and the Professor*, 66) got him dismissed from the India Office and also the Philological Society; he went on to live a reclusive life in Norfolk, pursuing his philological passions — chiefly helping with the *Oxford English Dictionary*, in what Sir James Murray praised as "voluntary and gratuitous service to the history of the English language" (in the preface to volume 1 of the *Oxford English Dictionary*, 1888) — as an amateur to the end of his days. From the perspective of his later life in England, Hall complained of the constraints on his work time in India: "For many years, while there, spending a considerable part of every day in the saddle [in "laborious official positions"], I had little leisure for study. In fact, . . . I have rarely . . . had any hours for reading and writing, except such as would rightfully have been given to sleep. Scant opportunity, therefore, have I enjoyed of becoming a thorough scholar; and to thorough scholarship I lay no claim." Hall, *Modern English*, xv. A certain sorrow of the amateur seems to haunt him: in addition to this feeling ever incomplete, not "thorough," as he puts it here, it may also have had something to do with his sense that his Americanness was looked upon with "enmity" by the English. Knowles, "Making the *OED*," 29.

Interestingly for my analysis here, Whitley Stokes edited both the *Gaelic Maundeville*, an early Irish version of the travel narrative, and the *Gaelic Abridgement of the Book of Ser Marco Polo*, which Yule himself declared to be "certainly a great literary curiosity" — among a stunning number of other Celtic texts. Yule's comment about the *Gaelic Marco Polo* was made in his letter to Stokes dated March 2, 1889; Stokes had sent him a transcript of the work. Stokes Papers, University College of London Library.

79 Chabon, "The Other James," 130. See also Pincombe, "Homosexual Panic and the English Ghost Story," and Darryl Jones, "Introduction," xxi–xxix. I'm tempted to speculate that philology, as a pursuit that recognizes loss (as I've argued), is the acceptable way James found to act on such desire — to do his work, he apparently brought manuscripts back to his rooms at Kings — and keep it safely *unfulfilled*. Thanks to Christopher Cannon for prompting this speculation here.

80 Whitley Stokes (see note 78, above) also knew Carlyle. One of the two vacancies in the Honorary Fellows left by the deaths of Thomas Carlyle and Dean Stanley was filled by Henry Yule.

81 Carlyle, "The Hero as Poet," 68.

82 Trivedi, *Colonial Transactions*, 12, notes that Lord Macaulay, newly in India and soon to author the infamous "Minute on Indian Education" (1835), pronounced Dante inferior only to Shakespeare in European poetry.

83 Carlyle, "The Hero as Poet," 96.

84 Trivedi, *Colonial Transactions*, 12.

85 I owe this formulation to Paul Strohm. This "timelessness" is better understood, as Nicholas Watson's analysis of Carlyle suggests, as Shakespeare's modernity: Carlyle rejoices that "he lasts forever" in a present that is, accord-

ing to Watson, "separated from the past," its energies "redirect[ed]" toward the future. See Watson, "The Phantasmal Past," 7.

86 Luhrmann, *The Good Parsi*, 5.

87 Ibid., 85–86, 97.

88 Ibid., 97.

89 Ibid., 84, 100, 126, 102.

90 Chakrabarty, *Provincializing Europe*, 112 n. 27, acknowledges Ranajit Guha's role in the conception of "time-knots."

91 Chakrabarty, *Provincializing Europe*, 109, 108.

92 I note the theoretical influences here of Eng, "Out Here and Over There," and Gopinath, "Nostalgia, Desire, Diaspora."

THREE. IN THE NOW

1 *The Book of Margery Kempe*, ed. Sanford B. Meech and Hope Emily Allen, 147; hereafter this edition is referred to as *BMK* and cited by page number in parentheses; I have modernized obsolete letters throughout. Though there are more recent scholarly editions of the book, I choose this one because it bears the imprint of Hope Allen, whose editing activity is central to this chapter. My glosses throughout are informed by the modern English translation by B. A. Windeatt.

2 Hope Emily Allen Papers, Special Collections Department, Bryn Mawr College Library (hereafter HEA Papers, Bryn Mawr College Library); qtd. in Marea Mitchell, "'The Ever-Growing Army of Serious Girl Students,'" 20. Mitchell's article draws on her superb work with the minimally processed Bryn Mawr papers.

3 *Damsel* is a term used often to address Margery in her book. The first definition of *damsel* in the *Middle English Dictionary* (*MED*) is "an unmarried woman, a maiden or maiden lady, esp. one of noble or good family; also, any young woman or girl." *BMK*, ch. 12, p. 26, line 9, is listed as an example of this definition, but the sense of mismatch between Margery and the term is registered by Meech (who worked on the *MED*) in his glossary to *BMK*, where he writes that "damsel" is "a form of address to a burgess's wife probably unparalleled in printed [Middle English] literature" (393). If the priest's use of it here implies some sort of slight (his disparagement of her, as I argue, is temporal), its use in the book more generally might indicate a certain temporal aspiration on Margery's part: in its connotation of maidenly status the term as Margery rehearses it throughout the book might register her desire to turn back the clock on her loss of virginity.

4 See Wallace, "Mystics and Followers in Siena and East Anglia," and Dickman, "Margery Kempe and the Continental Tradition of the Pious Woman." Wallace in his recent work has located Margery in her own time, associating her book's project of "literary self-representation" with that of London chroniclers of the 1430s (Wallace, *Strong Women*, 132, 126–27).

5 For this latter formulation, see Watson, "The Making of *The Book of Margery Kempe*," 418. Watson demonstrates that the book is not as nonchronological as the priestly scribe in its prologue (*BMK* 5) avers. I am indebted to Watson's subtle and thorough analysis here.

6 Lavezzo, in "Sobs and Sighs between Women," has argued convincingly that bonds between women structure the book; her argument is supported by the intervention of this good lady in the scene between Margery and the priest.

7 Simplicius, commenting specifically on Aristotle's mention of the nine heroes of Sardinia, in *On Aristotle's* Physics, 115–16. See my discussion in the introduction.

8 Nevanlinna, *The Northern Homily Cycle*, 2:203.

9 In chapter 77, for example, Margery prays to God that he take away her crying during sermons so that she will not be thrown out of church for the disruption she causes, asking that he give her crying in private, but God refuses this request. In chapter 83 two priests who trusted in her manner of crying yet doubted whether it was "deceyuabyl er not" [*deceptive or not*] tested her to see whether she would cry when alone in a field.

10 Watson, "The Making of *The Book of Margery Kempe*," 420.

11 Millett and Wogan-Browne, *Hali Meidhad*, esp. pp. 4, 10.

12 Colledge and Walsh, eds., *A Book of Showings*, 2:566 (ch. 55, revelation 14); cited in Underhill, *Mysticism*, 68.

13 Gurevich, "What Is Time?," 139; Duffy, *The Stripping of the Altars*, 23. Duffy adds, "with the possible exception of the special case of Corpus Christi." I rely on Duffy's description of Palm Sunday here. Note also the prevalence at this time of the affective devotional style, in which works such as the *Meditations on the Life of Christ* invited the reader's imaginative participation in Christ's life. This was a very popular devotional mode: that work itself exists in three different forms and in many languages. Duffy states that the late medieval English version by Nicholas Love was "probably the most popular vernacular book of the fifteenth century" (235) in England. The work clearly influenced the style of Margery's Passion devotion in her book, ch. 79–81.

14 Rosamund Allen, "Introduction," *Eastward Bound*, 3.

15 For discussion of this contrast, see Kohanski and Benson, 9.

16 De Certeau, *The Mystic Fable*, 11.

17 Hirsh in *The Revelations of Margery Kempe* develops a concept of the "paramystical" to explain Margery's experiences. More recently there has been increased willingness to view Margery's as mystical experiences. I am not primarily concerned to distinguish Margery's experiences as mystical; indeed, my focus on temporality leads me to note a similarity between mundane time and Margery's experience of the eternal *now*.

18 Robson, ed., 30.

19 Recall that the same word he uses for time as an activity of mind — *distentio* — is used by Augustine in his *Confessions* to describe his life as a wasteful distraction: "The storms of incoherent events tear to pieces my thoughts, the

inmost entrails of my soul, until that day when, purified and molten by the fire of your love, I flow together to merge into you" [*tumultuosis varietatibus dilaniantur cogitationes meae, intima viscera animae meae, donec in te confluam purgatus et liquidus igne amoris tui*] (11.29.39). Latin text from O'Donnell's edition online; English trans. by Chadwick, 244. See my discussion in the introduction.

20 De Certeau's analysis, via Benveniste, of the performance of mystic speech, is related here: see de Certeau, *The Mystic Fable*, 163–64.

21 Ibid., 11.

22 In a similar passage in chapter 87, Margery remarks that her heavenly visitations and contemplations lasted for more than twenty-five years, "weke be weke & day be day, les than sche wer ocupijd wyth seke folke er ellys wer lettyd wyth other nedful occupasyon" [*week by week and day by day, except when she was occupied with sick folk or else prevented by other needful occupation*] (214). In chapter 57, she tells us the period of her extreme crying lasted for ten years, and on every Good Friday during that period her crying, her absorption into the *now*, lasted "v er vj owrys to-gedyr" [*five or six hours together*] (140).

23 Watson, "The Making of *The Book of Margery Kempe*," 418–19.

24 Gurevich, "What Is Time?," 139.

25 Watson, "The Making of *The Book of Margery Kempe*," 418.

26 I am here following Chakrabarty's analysis in "Minority Histories, Subaltern Pasts," chapter 4 of his *Provincializing Europe*.

27 Simpson, "Faith and Hermeneutics." Note that Simpson ends his analysis of the circular structure of interpretation by affirming the value of alterity and proposing means for sustaining it.

28 The phrase is from Davidse, "The Sense of History in the Works of the Venerable Bede," 657. Davidse explains the hermeneutic condition by explicitly arguing that our "understanding" or hermeneutic connection with the past *includes* — in fact is based on — distance: the fact that we attribute meaning to something in the past already links it to us in the present; such attribution, insofar as it preserves otherness even as it recognizes intelligibility, "turns the people inhabiting the past into contemporaries on the basis of the awareness that this is something that is really past and will stay past." In such an instance of "noncontemporaneous contemporaneity" Davidse thus insists on intelligibility *and* difference in the reading of historically distant works; he reckons hermeneutically with ambivalence in our experiences of time and history, including the past's own resistance, its intransigence (see esp. 657, 666). The phrase's echo of Reinhart Koselleck is duly noted, though Davidse remarks on the term's difference in meaning from Koselleck's *Gleichzeitigkeit der Ungleichzeitigen*. Note, too, the term's resemblance to Ernst Bloch's vocabulary of "non-contemporaneity" and "contemporaneity" in his *Heritage of Our Times*, which I cite in my epilogue.

29 Lorraine Code, translating the concept of Hans-Georg Gadamer's "fusion of horizons" into everyday conversation. "Why Feminists Do Not Read

Gadamer," 5. Gadamer in his *Truth and Method* defines a horizon as "the range of vision that includes everything that can be seen from a particular vantage point" (301). Code points out that there is a divergence of opinion as to the purpose of the hermeneutic caution against utter assimilation of the other's horizon to one's own: preserving alterity is one opinion, but "others propose that the purpose is more accurately represented as one of overcoming particularities in the synthesis that an achieved fusion of horizons can accomplish" (5). Clearly there is a range of theories and practices of hermeneutics; by adducing Gadamer's terminology I don't mean to imply that Gadamer stands in for all. While I have adopted his concept of the "horizon," I am mindful of the feminist hesitations about his project (see Code's introduction, as well as the rest of the book, *Feminist Interpretations of Hans-Georg Gadamer*); I have been stimulated as well by the work of Jeffrey J. Kripal in *Roads of Excess, Palaces of Wisdom*, who is influenced by Gadamer but moves in a different direction as he develops a "mystical hermeneutics" via Michael Sells and Elliot Wolfson.

30 Ruskin, *Modern Painters*, 6: 446–47; and see my chapter 1.

31 Gadamer, *Truth and Method*, 304.

32 Kripal, *Roads of Excess, Palaces of Wisdom*, 325.

33 Hirsh's excellent book *Hope Emily Allen* has substantially informed my work on Allen. See also his summary article, "Hope Emily Allen (1883–1960)."

34 Hirsh notes that the Victoria and Albert Museum had contacted M. R. James about the manuscript, but he was not available (*Hope Emily Allen*, 114). For "an element of haste": Hope Emily Allen to Rev. Paul Grosjean, S. J., April 4, 1938, HEA Papers, Bryn Mawr College Library.

35 Hope Emily Allen to Sanford Brown Meech, October 22, 1934, Oxford, Bodleian Library, MS Eng. Letters c. 212, f. 2.

36 Hope Emily Allen to Rev. Paul Grosjean, S. J., March 30, 1938, HEA Papers, Bryn Mawr College Library.

37 Deanne Williams, "Hope Emily Allen Speaks with the Dead," 150. Williams sees that Allen distanced herself from her collaborator Meech's professionalism (in ways that resonate with my emphasis on amateurism). Williams reads Allen's abandonment of BMK II as a loss of heart at the changes of life that came with the war; my own analysis is less historically specific, arguing (to use Williams's terms) that the model of "locating the self in the object of study" (138) that Allen developed could not facilitate a finished book.

38 Hirsh, *Hope Emily Allen*, 127; Hirsh, "Hope Emily Allen (1883–1960)," 235, 237 n. 6.

39 BMK, lvii.

40 Hope Emily Allen to Donald Goodchild, December 20, 1935, Oxford, Bodleian Library, MS Eng. Misc. c. 484, f. 151; Hirsh, "Hope Emily Allen and the Limitations of Academic Discourse."

41 Chakrabarty, *Provincializing Europe*, 112.

42 Barthes, *Sade, Fourier, Loyola*, 7–8.

43 Mabel Day to Hope Emily Allen, July 11, 1952, HEA Papers, Bryn Mawr College Library.

44 "Bud" [H. N. Milnes of Ohio State University] to Hope Emily Allen, January 20, 1948, HEA Papers, Bryn Mawr College Library.

45 Ruth J. Dean to Hope Emily Allen, July 23, 1939, HEA Papers, Bryn Mawr College Library.

46 Hope Emily Allen to Hester R. Gehring, April 19, 1947, HEA Papers, Bryn Mawr College Library.

47 Hope Emily Allen to Mabel Day, March 17, 1949, Oxford, Bodleian Library, MS Eng. Letters c. 212, f. 125.

48 Hope Emily Allen to Dorothy Ellis, April 18, 1941, Oxford, Bodleian Library, MS Eng. Letters d. 217, f. 113v.

49 Undated note (perhaps to E. I. Watkins?), HEA Papers, Bryn Mawr College Library.

50 R. Gordon Wasson to Hope Emily Allen, n.d., HEA Papers, Bryn Mawr College Library.

51 Hope Allen was born and raised, lived and died in the Oneida Community, about whose controversial past she expressed a careful ambivalence, simultaneously celebrating the community's controversial history and distancing herself from it. See especially Oxford, Bodleian Library, MS Eng. Misc. c. 484, ff. 97b–q. For further literary reflections on relations to the past, see also her "A Glut of Fruit" and "Ancient Grief."

52 "Relics," printed in Hirsh, "Past and Present in Hope Emily Allen's Essay 'Relics.'"

53 Hirsh, *Hope Emily Allen*, 127, describes Meech's narrow definition of mysticism as it constrained Allen's contributions to the edition: Allen had a broader understanding of mysticism and its relationship to the larger culture of *BMK*. I am suggesting that the dimensions of the work of the antiquarian, as Allen describes them in "Relics," might similarly exceed a narrower definition of the historian's work.

54 "Cycles of Time," Oneida Community Collection, Syracuse University Library. In this eight-and-a-half-page undated, typewritten essay Allen muses on the artificiality of time markers. Her own temporality, she suggests briefly at one point, links her to medieval people. Allen's connections to Native American culture were intimate and their relationship to her temporality is crucial to ponder; there are significant references to Native Americans in "Cycles of Time" and "Relics." She actively recorded Oneida Iroquois folklore narrated by primary informants who were domestic workers in her home: see Wonderley, *Oneida Iroquois Folklore, Myth, and History*. Marea Mitchell provocatively engages Allen's folklore work in a discussion of asynchronous temporalities in "Taking Time: Subjectivity, Time, and History in *The Book of Margery Kempe*'s Prayer and 'Where the Earth Opened'" (paper presented at the "Time and Temporalities" symposium, University of Tasmania, December 2007).

55 Hope Emily Allen [to Kenneth Sisam?], n.d., HEA Papers, Bryn Mawr College Library.

56 Albert C. Baugh to Hope Emily Allen, July 9, 1953, HEA Papers, Bryn Mawr College Library; Hope Emily Allen to P. M. Kean, April 30, 1956, Oxford, Bodleian Library, MS Eng. Misc. c. 484, f. 116.

57 "Advent of MK": Hope Emily Allen to Mabel Day, April 28, 1946, Oxford, Bodleian Library, MS Eng. Letters c.212, f. 80.

58 Hope Emily Allen to Mabel Day, July 27, 1949, Oxford, Bodleian Library, MS Eng. Letters c. 212, f. 128v; Hope Emily Allen to [J. S.?] Purvis, February 17, 1945, HEA Papers, Bryn Mawr College Library.

59 For discussion of Richardson's novel see Garrity, *Step-Daughters of England*, 85–139.

60 Hope Emily Allen (at Oneida) to Mabel Day, September 7, 1944, Oxford, Bodleian Library, MS Eng. Letters c. 212, f. 61v.

61 Hope Emily Allen to Mabel Day, April 28, 1946, Oxford, Bodleian Library, MS Eng. Letters c.212, f. 80.

62 Hope Emily Allen to Mabel Day, May 3, 1949, Oxford, Bodleian Library, MS Eng. Letters c.212, f. 127; Hope Emily Allen to Mabel Day, March 16, 1949, Oxford, Bodleian Library, MS Eng. Letters c.212, ff. 119–23; cf. Hope Emily Allen to Col. William Butler-Bowdon, March 26, 1936, HEA Papers, Bryn Mawr College Library: "When I spoke of Margery's 'killing' her son, I meant by overstimulating and over-tiring him, by talking (and perhaps writing) about her revelations."

63 Hope Emily Allen to Mabel Day, March 17, 1949, Oxford, Bodleian Library, MS Eng. Letters c. 212, f. 125.

64 All three passages qtd. in Marea Mitchell, "'The Ever-Growing Army of Serious Girl Students,'" 21; the latter two (including the letter to Mabel Day, from April 12 [no year]) are in the HEA Papers, Bryn Mawr College Library.

65 Hope Emily Allen to Helen [Cam?], August 21, 1956, HEA Papers, Bryn Mawr College Library.

66 Undated note, HEA Papers, Bryn Mawr College Library.

67 "Non-organised" notes: Hope Emily Allen to [J. S.?] Purvis, February 17, 1945, HEA Papers, Bryn Mawr College Library. The disorganization of her papers is in part an artifact of the minimally processed state of the Bryn Mawr collection, but see her letter to W. A. Pantin, May 22, 1956, there: "When my brother died, nearly two years ago, the mere state of confused papers in my own rooms was terrific."

68 On Ellis, see Hirsh, *Hope Emily Allen*, esp. 102–5.

69 Hope Emily Allen (at Oneida) to Dorothy Ellis, May 26, 1943, Oxford, Bodleian Library, MS Eng. Misc. c. 484, ff. 21, 23.

70 Kieckhefer explains the "valuable social function" that Margery might play as outsider: if she is recognized as an "exceptional individual with an extraordinary vocation," she can in the afterlife "serve Christian society all the more effectively as an intercessor." *Unquiet Souls*, 190–91.

FOUR. OUT OF SYNC IN THE CATSKILLS

1 Fabian, *Time and the Other*, 17.

2 Benjamin, "Theses on the Philosophy of History," 261; Chakrabarty, "The Time of History and the Times of Gods," 36.

3 Irving, "Rip van Winkle," from *The Sketch Book of Geoffrey Crayon, Gent.*, in the Library of America's edition of Irving's *History, Tales and Sketches*, 769– 85. Page numbers of this edition appear parenthetically in my text for citations of this and other selections from the *Sketch Book*.

4 At the "Time and Temporality" symposium at the University of Tasmania in Hobart, where I presented a version of this chapter in December 2007, Australian members of the audience mentioned their childhood familiarity with the legend.

5 See chapter 1, n. 25.

6 Pochmann, "Irving's German Sources in 'The Sketch Book'"; see also Young, "Fallen from Time," building on Pochmann's source study and adducing numerous other asynchrony stories. Hartland, *The Science of Fairy Tales*, 181, notes another time-lapse narrative in Washington Irving's oeuvre. Michael Warner mentions another possible source of "Rip van Winkle" in Louis-Sébastien Mercier's *L'An 2440*: see "Irving's Posterity," 798 n. 44. I am indebted to Warner's superb contextualization and analysis of "Rip van Winkle."

7 Pochmann, "Irving's German Sources in 'The Sketch Book,'" traces a general shift in Irving's works from classicism toward romanticism, from the publication of *Knickerbocker's History of New York* (1809) to the publication of the *Sketch Book* (1819–20), the volume in which "Rip van Winkle" appeared. Pochmann qualifies this periodization in terms that resemble those later applied to Longfellow by Ruskin: he talks of a transition to romanticism "in so far as it occurred (for Irving lived . . . always a little in the past tense)" (481). On Abbotsford's multiple temporalities, see Alexander, *Medievalism*, 68, and the 1940 essay "Gas at Abbotsford" by Virginia Woolf (who thought Abbotsford "perhaps the ugliest [house] in the whole Empire" [see Woolf, "Middlebrow," 178]).

8 Qtd. in Pochmann, "Irving's German Sources in 'The Sketch Book,'" 485–86.

9 See my introduction.

10 Qtd. in Pochmann, "Irving's German Sources in 'The Sketch Book,'" 486. Michael Warner comments on Irving's propensity, later in his career, to "put himself . . . in situations that could seem to echo those of his fiction" ("Irving's Posterity," 793). Another example, also noted by Warner, occurs in the "Author's Introduction" to the 1835 American edition of *A Tour on the Prairies*, where Irving's account of his return to America after his long absence resembles Rip's uncomprehending return to his former village ("Irving's Posterity," 793).

11 Thomas the Rhymer is also known as Thomas of Erceldoune (or Ercildoune); the Middle English romance of that name was noted in chapter 1, n. 38: see Murray, *The Romance and Prophecies of Thomas of Erceldoune*.

12   Irving elaborated on his 1817 Abbotsford experience years later in *The Crayon Miscellany*, whence these sentences are drawn (238–39). Discussed by Pochmann, "Irving's German Sources in 'The Sketch Book,'" 497. The version Scott recites is given in his own *Minstrelsy of the Scottish Border*, 4:86–90, and corresponds to Child Ballad 37C. In the Middle English romance, which Scott prints after the ballad, at 4:92–96, Thomas thinks he has stayed in the otherworld three days, but of course it has been three years and more (lines 282–86); in the Child Ballad, he stays for seven years, a number with mysterious associations. Scott reports (4: 83) that in popular legend Thomas returned to earth after the seven years only to rejoin his fairy mistress in her land once again, where he is still reputed to live; he is expected even yet to revisit earth. Thus the temporality of the otherworld, even if "seven years" seems scientifically measurable, is different from ordinary earthly temporalities. For a compelling analysis of Scott's medievalism in his own narrative fiction, which creates a certain timelessness bespeaking a complex critical nostalgia, see Lynch, "Nostalgia and Critique."

13   Scott, telling the tale of Thomas the Rhymer to Irving, which Irving recounts in "Abbotsford," in *The Crayon Miscellany*, 239.

14   "People in pain and distress or in need and want, thinking that such a change is great, think that the time also is great": Simplicius implies that people correlate the amount of time passed with their perception of the degree of change. See *On Aristotle's* Physics, 115.

15   See Young, "Fallen from Time," 466–67.

16   Here I differ from Michael Warner, who argues that Irving in "Rip van Winkle" invents "pirate time, . . . a temporality so alien to history that it eventually had to be declared a separate place: Never-Never Land." "Irving's Posterity," 798 n. 46. My argument is that time, nonlinear, produces a history that is noncontinuous, nonprogressive, a Benjaminian constellation of asynchronous moments, so that the fact that in "Rip Van Winkle" "markers of historicity do not move in progressive secular time," as Warner puts it, is precisely the point. Warner's description is perfectly apt as a description of the asynchrony that, I argue, reflects the nature of time and history: "Remnants of the past surface as uncanny interruptions, decay happens at uneven rates, and whole eras seem embalmed in parallel temporalities" (798 n. 46).

17   See Richardson, *Possessions*, esp. 65–66. Michael Warner notes that Irving "had been told, on a tour of Kaaterskill Falls . . . that he was witnessing the authentic haunts of Rip van Winkle." "Irving's Posterity," 793 and n. 50.

18   Chakrabarty, *Provincializing Europe*, 112.

19   Derrida, *Specters of Marx*, xvii.

20   Latour in *We Have Never Been Modern* criticizes deconstruction (metonymically represented by "Derrida" on pp. 5–6); it is "powerful itself," he admits, but cut off from epistemology and sociology it cannot, he maintains, take into consideration networks that are "neither objective nor social, nor are they effects of discourse, even though they are real, collective and discursive" (6).

Without performing a detailed analysis here I nonetheless want provisionally to suggest that Derridean deconstruction — in, for example, *Specters of Marx* as well as *The Animal That Therefore I Am* — addresses exactly the kinds of binary exclusions, particularly life/nonlife and human/nonhuman, that are of concern to Latour in *We Have Never Been Modern* and *Pandora's Hope*.

21 Wendy Brown, *Politics Out of History*, 145–46. I am using "ghostly" and "spectral" synonymously and thus more loosely than does Derrida, who distinguishes between specter and spirit (including the sense of "the ghost in general") on the basis of the *"non-sensuous sensuous* of which *Capital* speaks" as well as an asymmetry between the specter who sees us and whom we cannot see. *Specters of Marx*, 7. Though I do not engage the critique of materialism specifically, I draw on Derrida's deconstructive project in general.

22 For an explication and defense of this deconstructive view of queerness, see Freccero, "Always Already Queer (French) Theory," in *Queer/Early/Modern*, 13–30, and my *Getting Medieval*. See also Freccero, "Les chats de Derrida," on the queerness of theory after Derrida.

23 For Dame van Winkle, see Judith Fetterley's breakthrough analysis in *The Resisting Reader*.

24 Derrida, *Specters of Marx*, xix. For discussion, see Wendy Brown, *Politics Out of History*, 146–47, and Carla Freccero's excellent treatment in *Queer/Early/Modern*, esp. 75–78.

25 On the development of this narratorial voice see, e.g., Rubin-Dorsky, "Washington Irving and the Genesis of the Fictional Sketch," 217–18.

26 On Washington Irving's own status, see Pochmann, "Washington Irving: Amateur or Professional?" *The Sketch Book* marks Irving's shift from amateur to professional writer; see also Warner, "Irving's Posterity," 784: "If Irving began writing out of the bachelor practice of killing time merrily, by the time he wrote *The Sketch Book* he had begun to see his writing as 'literary property.'"

27 Manning specifically argues that Crayon's amateurism is nostalgic, and as such, "it is always already *passé*: nostalgia for a time that can never return is built into its self-expression." Manning, "Introduction," xvi, xiv. Manning's discussion has influenced my own reading of Crayon. Adding another, fascinating consideration that would help situate Geoffrey Crayon's persona in relation to the British colonial project in India is Ananya Jahanara Kabir's work on the relationship between the picturesque, the antiquarian, and the colonialist, in her "'Oriental Gothic.'"

28 Hazlitt, "Elia, and Geoffrey Crayon," 405–6, 405, 407. Susan Manning writes that Crayon's voice is "always a little nostalgic, and always more than a little ambivalent about his nostalgia." Manning, "Introduction," viii.

29 Michael Warner analyzes Irving's nostalgia as evidence of conflicts and ambivalence about historical times or structures, such as the "feudally guaranteed continuity of a family." "Irving's Posterity," 785.

30 Irving, "Westminster Abbey," 894 ("melancholy," "mournful"); 897 ("picturesque"). For the "literary catacomb," see "The Mutability of Literature," 855;

for the magi-like figures, see "The Art of Book-making," 809, from *The Sketch Book*. Contrast Jeffrey Rubin-Dorsky's reading of Geoffrey Crayon as "a dupe of his own desires" and Washington Irving as creating the tension between "Crayon's heightened desire to inhabit an ideal world imbued with poetic feeling and transcendent wonder" and "Irving's sober recognition that at its best reality affords little more than the commonplace" in "Washington Irving and the Genesis of the Fictional Sketch," 219.

31   *The Kingis Quair* had been relatively recently discovered when Washington Irving read it; the first edition of the poem was made in 1783 by William Tytler. At the time it was accepted that James wrote the *Kingis Quair* while in prison. Both the authorship and the dating of the *Kingis Quair* have subsequently been disputed. The poem is attributed to "Jacobus primus scotorum rex Illustrissimus" by the second scribe of the late-fifteenth-century manuscript, and most scholars now agree that James I was indeed the author. (Controversy was stirred up by J. T. T. Brown, *The Authorship of* The Kingis Quair [1896].) A later hand states that the poem was "maid quhan his majestee wes in Ingland." James was in English custody for eighteen years, from 1406 to 1424, moving around England (and crossing to France twice) with varying levels of freedom; see Balfour-Melville, *The English Captivity of James I*. James left England in spring 1424, having married Joan in mid-February and the treaty for his release (as well as a truce between England and Scotland) having been concluded on March 28. Debate over dating ranges from 1423, before James's marriage to Joan and while in prison (Skeat); to February 1424, after his marriage but still in England (Norton-Smith); to as late as 1435, well after both marriage and imprisonment (McDiarmid). See Mooney and Arn's introduction to their edition of *The Kingis Quair* for a succinct account of dating.

32   Note the use of the word "endeavoured" in a similar situation at the end of "The Mutability of Literature," where Crayon has returned to the library of Westminster Abbey, having had a dream of an animated book (864). Crayon's narrated experience at Windsor Castle blurs the boundary between categories in Austin's analysis of nineteenth-century British nostalgias in her article "The Nostalgic Moment and the Sense of History": it is specific in its cognitive understanding of the past's content (James I's love), and it also is affective. Thus Crayon's queer failure to meld with the past: he knows what he cannot have. His comments at the very beginning of the sketch about gazing on the likenesses of amorous beauties drawn by Sir Peter Lely — Crayon basks "in the reflected rays of beauty" (815) — are also perhaps to be understood in this light.

33   See Gordon, *Ghostly Matters*, 183.

34   Derrida, *The Animal That Therefore I Am*, 104. For explication, see Freccero, "Les chats de Derrida."

35   Geoffrey Crayon blurs the boundaries of the material and the immaterial as he refers to the *Consolation of Philosophy*: "It is the legacy of a noble and enduring spirit, purified by sorrow and suffering, bequeathing to its successors in

calamity, the maxims of sweet morality, and the trains of eloquent but simple reasoning, by which it was enabled to bear up against the various ills of life. It is a talisman, which the unfortunate may treasure up in his bosom, or like the good King James, lay upon his nightly pillow" (819). Boethius's text is the topic of these two sentences, but note how the referent of the pronoun "it" shifts around in this quotation: at first "it" refers to the book; the second "it" is Boethius's spirit; the third is the text again. Crayon picks up this very ambivalence from James's own way of speaking: for James in the *Kingis Quair*, both text and author are referred to by a single name, *Boece*.

36 Chaucer, *Boece*, in *The Riverside Chaucer*, ed. Larry D. Benson. References to this edition appear in parentheses in my text. Unless otherwise noted, Modern English translations are mine, drawing from and adapting Green's and Watts's translations from the Latin. Even if James specifically used John Walton's translation rather than Chaucer's, as has been speculated, Chaucer's presence still penetrates: Walton himself drew constantly on Chaucer's version. Walton, *Boethius*, xliv. By the time Chaucer rendered it as the *Boece* the text itself had become temporally complicated: several layers of commentary accompanied the Latin text(s) Chaucer worked with, and the anachronistic style of Boethius's text may have been modernized by the Vulgate manuscript tradition by the time Chaucer got to it. He was also using Jean de Meun's early-fourteenth-century French translation. See Machan, *Techniques of Translation*, and Machan and Minnis, *Sources of the* Boece. Concerning the speed of Elizabeth's translation, contemporary estimates by her clerk "range from twenty-four to thirty working hours," as Mueller and Scodel report (*Elizabeth I*, 53).

37 John Matthews, "Anicius Manlius Severinus Boethius," 16. He was executed sometime during the years 524–26. He had dedicated himself to institutions (especially the Roman Senate) that no longer had power, as John Marenbon remarks, and situates himself in the *Consolation* with particular references to Nero; Boethius thus places himself in a tradition of defenders of old "Roman principles" as against "Imperial tyranny." Marenbon, *Boethius*, 10, 149. Umberto Eco describes Boethius's temporality as more wily, seeing it as something craftily instrumental rather than sadly nostalgic in its multiplicity: "Boethius . . . is inventing a new way of culture, and, pretending to be the last of the Romans, he is actually setting up the first Study Center of the barbarian courts" (*Travels in Hyperreality*, 75). Note that Boethius, whose large oeuvre includes Aristotelian translation and commentary, was a contemporary of Simplicius.

38 Marenbon, *Boethius*, 157. Theoderic was a Christian, but an Arian Christian and therefore considered a heretic by Boethius and his like Catholic Christians. Danuta Shanzer reminds us that the "monolithic" term "Christian" is a blunt instrument; a "more nuanced view of spectrums of belief and practice that leave a place for people such as Boethius" is needed. "Interpreting the *Consolation*," 242.

39 Crabbe, "Literary Design in the *De Consolatione Philosophiae*," 240.

40   See Richard Green's introduction to his translation of *The Consolation of Philosophy*, ix–x.

41   Shanzer, "Interpreting the *Consolation*," 229.

42   Bk. 1, meter 1, lines 13–15. The Latin and French sources of Chaucer's version here: "Venit enim properata malis inopina senectus / Et dolor etatem iussit inesse suam"; "car viellece m'est venue plus tost que je ne cuidoie, hastee par mes maulz, et douleur a commendé que ses aages me soit venuz." Machan and Minnis, *Sources of the* Boece, 26, 27.

43   For the figure of Age in Charles of Orleans, see lines 2557–63 in Arn, ed., *Fortunes Stabilnes*, 228, and 5n9. "Heeris horre . . .": Bk. 1, meter 1, lines 15–17. "Intempestivi funduntur vertice cani / Et tremit effeto corpore laxa cutis"; "Chennes sont espandues par ma teste avant leur temps et tremble li lache cuirs en mon corps affoibli." Machan and Minnis, *Sources of the* Boece, 26, 27.

44   Bk. 1, meter 1, lines 28–29. "Protrahit ingratas imp[ia vita moras]"; "ma felonnesse vie m'aloigne la desagreable demeure de mort." Machan and Minnis, *Sources of the* Boece, 26, 27.

45   Sorrow, old age, and time had already been powerfully linked in another Chaucerian translation, *The Romaunt of the Rose*, a translation of the *Roman de la Rose*, where a portrait of Elde suggests the paradox of the present, of everyday time that I explored in my introduction: our experience is not at all linear, though our ordinary image of time is, precisely, a line. Time's aging function in the *Romaunt* works "ynly," that is, not only thoroughly and pervasively but also inwardly. There is a hint, expressed in that word "ynly" here, absent in the French (which has "durement") but shared by Chaucer's *Boece*, that time invades and settles into the body. See the *The Romaunt of the Rose*, pp. 690–91, lines 369–82, and 397.

46   Denny-Brown, *Fashioning Change*, 17–49.

47   The experiential relationship between living under Fortune and living in linear clock time is suggested by Richard of Wallingford's great fourteenth-century clock at Saint Albans, on which a wheel of fortune was installed during the abbacy of Wallingford's successor. See Mooney, "The Cock and the Clock," esp. 108. Fifteenth-century iconography, as Samuel C. Chew documents, confirms the relationship: Time himself turns Fortune's wheel. Chew, *The Pilgrimage of Life*, 26–27.

48   See the introduction.

49   This is not to assert that Boethius's treatment of time and eternity derives from Augustine's treatment in the *Confessions*. I am more modestly pointing out that the experience of earthly temporality is similar in both, and that time is discussed in relation to eternity in both, not that the structure of their relationship is necessarily similar. McTighe, "Eternity and Time in Boethius," insists that Boethius owed nothing on this score to Augustine; Boethius's description of time does not locate time in the mind, as does Augustine, and Augustine's discussion of the relationship between time and eternity differs

from Boethius's, which shows time to be less an "imitation of eternity" than its "expression" (53–54).

50 Epiphany, vision, and spirit are of course different phenomena. Shanzer argues that Philosophy in Boethius's Latin text makes an "epiphanic appearance," epiphany being the author Boethius's choice over dream or vision because of the long passages in dialogue needed for philosophizing, and because of "inevitable worries about *mise en abyme*" with dream or vision frames. "Interpreting the *Consolation*," 232. While in the sixth century Boethius may have had reservations about the dream or vision framework, by the fourteenth, when Chaucer's translation was made, there are not the same reservations; rather, a tradition of Boethian dream visions had become quite robust. Sarah Kay remarks that Boethius's "overall visionary framework in which a first-person subject, in the grip of melancholy meditation, conjures a personification promising enlightenment" was a resource for French poets of the "long fourteenth century." "Touching Singularity," 28, 21.

51 The Latin and French sources read "inexhausti vigoris, quamvis ita evi plena foret ut nostre nullo modo crederetur etatis"; "vigueur [telle] que nulz ne pot oncques espuisier, ja soit ce que elle fust plaine de si grant aage que on ne creoit en nule maniere que ele fust de notre temps." Machan and Minnis, *Sources of the* Boece, 26, 27. For temporality as the linchpin of Philosophie's epistemological analysis, see Elbow, *Oppositions in Chaucer*, 40–43.

52 This Neoplatonic Supreme Good is compatible with the Christian God.

53 Trans. Watts, *The Consolation of Philosophy*, 134.

54 "Eternitas igitur est interminabilis vite tota simul et p[er]fecta possessio"; "Pardurableté donques est parfaite possession et toute ensemble de vie nommie terminable." Machan and Minnis, *Sources of the* Boece, 216, 215. Marenbon, *Boethius*, 136, stresses that this conceptualization is different from understanding God's being as "timeless or atemporal": "God's eternity is a way of *living*."

55 "Nam quicquid vivit in tempore id presens a preteritis in futura procedit nichilque est in tempore constitutum quod totum vite sue spacium pariter possit amplecti. Set crastinum quidem nondum apprehendit, hesternum vero iam perdidit; in hodierna vero vita non amplius vivimus quam in illo mobili transitorioque momento"; "ne nulle chose n'est establie en temps qui puisse embracier ensemble toute l'espace de sa vie. Car certez elle ne tient pas encores le temps de lendemain et a ja perdu celui de hier; et certez en la vie de huy ne vivéz vous pas plus que en cest mouvable et trepassable moment." Machan and Minnis, *Sources of the* Boece, 216, 215.

56 "Infinitus ille temporalium rerum motus . . . illud quod inplere atque exprimere non potest, ita videtur emulari"; "cil non feniz mouvemens des chosez temporiex . . . il nous est avis qu'il ensuit et resemble en aucune maniere ce que il ne puet aconsuivre ne faire ne acomplir." Machan and Minnis, *Sources of the* Boece, 216, 217.

57 Marenbon, *Boethius*, 137.

58 Cf. the Latin ("Quod igitur temporis patitur condicionem . . .") and French ("La chose donques qui seuffre temporelle condicion . . ."). Machan and Minnis, *Sources of the* Boece, 216, 215.

59 Marenbon, *Boethius*, 163.

60 Kay, "Touching Singularity," 27.

61 See, in addition to bk. 5, meter 1, the chaotic waters churned by Fortune in bk. 2, meter 1, and the unruly seas in bk. 2, meter 8.

62 Lerer, *Boethius and Dialogue*. Sarah Kay sees something similar in the operations of a consuming Philosophy whose "success seems to be measured by the submergence of the Boethius-figure's voice in hers," though Kay's focus is on the verse passages that "represent a certain continuing opacity, or resistance, to Philosophy's blanket admonitions." "Touching Singularity," 24, 27. In contrast, see Marenbon, *Boethius*, esp. 163. Shanzer reviews arguments for and against the work's status as complete in "Interpreting the *Consolation*," 239–40.

63 *The Kingis Quair*, ed. Mooney and Arn. Line numbers appear parenthetically in my text, and my translations are informed by Mooney and Arn's glosses and notes, in addition to Skeat's notes (especially in reference to translating the penultimate stanza) in his edition, *The Kingis Quair*.

64 Kratzmann, *Anglo-Scottish Literary Relations*, 60.

EPILOGUE

1 Latour, *Politics of Nature*, esp. 32–41 and 238.

2 Powell and Pressburger, *A Canterbury Tale*. Quotations from the film are my own transcriptions from the 2006 Criterion Collection DVD.

3 Powell, *A Life in Movies*, 437, 447.

4 Powell, qtd. in Christie, *Powell, Pressburger and Others*, 33.

5 See the synopsis of the film, dated April 22, 1943, qtd. in Christie, "Another Life in Movies," 176.

6 Powell, *A Life in Movies*, 437. See Moor, "Bending the Arrow," particularly 212, noting that Eric Portman was among others on the Archers' productions who "may well have been gay or bisexual." Moor comments on the ways in which actors' gayness or queerness might have informed the playing of parts in the films; he also correlates this with Pressburger's exilic experience. Antonia Lant notes that Portman's previous Powell and Pressburger appearance as "an ardent Nazi" in *The 49th Parallel* "enhanced" the "perhaps even evil" quality of his Colpeper. *Blackout*, 199.

7 So reports film historian Ian Christie in the DVD commentary. I am much indebted to Christie's careful work on Powell and Pressburger in this commentary as well as in his numerous books and articles.

8 Press reviews of *Peeping Tom* included a discourse of "I told you so" about Powell in particular: see reviews in Christie, "The Scandal of *Peeping Tom*," in *Powell, Pressburger and Others*, 53–59, e.g., Derek Hill in the *Tribune*, April 29,

1960: "It is no surprise that this is the work of Michael Powell, who displayed his vulgarity in such films as *A Matter of Life and Death*, *The Red Shoes*, and *Tales of Hoffmann*, and the more bizarre tendencies of his curious mind in *A Canterbury Tale*" (55). Christie notes that the "trade" reviews were "uniformly favorable and for the most part highly appreciative" (53).

9   See Christie, "Another Life in Movies," 176–79, for discussion of this plot device, its origins and reception. Thanks to Arthur Lindley for the connection to *There's Something about Mary* and for numerous other sharp observations about *A Canterbury Tale* that have informed and influenced my view of the film.

10   Pressburger implied that it was completely plausible in the time of war but also admitted, "I think some other idea would probably have been better, but I just couldn't think of one — quite simply that." Later, Powell remarked on "this almost sexual idea of a man pursuing girls in the black-out and dropping glue on them. . . . It's a very simple Freudian idea." See Christie, "Powell and Pressburger," 128; Lant, *Blackout*, 201; and Fuller, "*A Canterbury Tale*," 34.

11   On the noir look of the film, see Fuller, "*A Canterbury Tale*," 36, and Christie, "Commentary"; on the nave and the organ music, see Powell, *A Life in Movies*, 448.

12   Ibid., 441–42.

13   Ibid., 437. On "orientation films," see Christie, "Commentary."

14   Moor, *Powell and Pressburger*, 95, 17. For the propaganda memo, see "Programme for Film Propaganda (1940)," in Christie, *Powell, Pressburger and Others*, 121–24.

15   Doty, "'An Instrument with a Flaming Sword,'" 57, 60.

16   Andrew Moor notes in Powell and Pressburger's films a range of features that can support a queerer reading of these characters, including "anti-classical" formal elements such as strangely arrested narratives and lack of conventional closure. Moor, "Bending the Arrow," 222–23.

17   Powell, *A Life in Movies*, 451. Andrew Moor reports that early reviews "were divided between praise of the cinematography and performances and, at best, suspicion of the storyline" and quotes one reviewer stating that "although the film 'is as good as a day in the country' he carried away from *A Canterbury Tale* 'an enjoyment that [he] was loath to examine too closely.'" *Powell and Pressburger*, 107.

18   Powell's first choice, Roger Livesey, passed on the role because "he didn't understand it" and therefore "found it distasteful." Powell, *A Life in Movies*, 440.

19   Moor in his excellent analysis contends that "the overarching ideological thrust of the film ultimately incorporates the paradoxical nature of its narrative"; while this point makes sense of the narrative's shape (its abandoning any effort to punish Colpeper), it does not adequately account for that lingering nastiness that even the film's first viewers experienced. Moor acknowledges the "tension between the iconoclastic or eccentric characteristics in [Powell

and Pressburger's] films and the conservative ideology which often informs them" and maintains that the incorporation of paradoxical elements cannot happen "smoothly," though he concludes that it does happen in the end in *A Canterbury Tale*. But while he allows that in their films "forms of national culture are subjected to an insightful interrogation" without "bland compliance" with "hegemonic ideals," I want to tip this delicate critical balance. See Moor, *Powell and Pressburger*, 107, 18.

20   Doty, "'An Instrument with a Flaming Sword,'" 49.

21   Conrad, *To Be Continued*, 23, states that Colpeper is an "expert on Chaucer" who lectures on "local history and *The Canterbury Tales*."

22   Powell, *A Life in Movies*, 448.

23   Peter Conrad notes these subtle alterations of the medieval, explicating them in terms of the film's context of the war and its "romantic revivalism." *To Be Continued*, 26–27.

24   For invigorating comments about remediation and the medieval film, see Richard Burt, "Getting Schmedieval," and Finke and Shichtman, *Cinematic Illuminations*.

25   The pastoral space is "a ludic space," as Moor puts it, "a place of potential, of development, of magic." *Powell and Pressburger*, 4.

26   In this it contrasts with several recent critical readings of Chaucer's poem. The first eighteen lines of Chaucer's General Prologue, various critics have argued, describe a seasonal landscape that is almost no landscape at all, it is so abstract; moreover, the personifications and anthropomorphizations in the lines and the syntax suggest that all the changes in non-human nature are finally subordinate to the stirrings in humans to get out and go on pilgrimage. That last point has been made recently by Gillian Rudd, who maintains that because these lines of the prologue absorb "the natural world into human value systems . . . this Prologue is not in the least interested in the world it apparently seeks to describe." *Greenery*, 43, 42. Peter Conrad concurs: "Chaucer's topography is meager" in the *Canterbury Tales*. *To Be Continued*, 29.

27   Millett and Wogan-Browne, *Seinte Margarete*, 80–81. For further discussion of this phenomenon, see Sanok, "*The Lives of Women Saints of Our Contrie of England*," 271.

28   And in this we might say that Colpeper follows the pilgrims themselves — specifically, the Wife of Bath — in his view of an organic whole in "th'olde dayes," lost to the present. Her *Tale* opens with remarks about "this land" once "fulfild of fayerye," as opposed to the disenchanted present of accumulation and alienation, when begging friars comb every corner for gain. The Wife describes a past "time of delighted absorption in the world," as Patricia Clare Ingham, adapting Raymond Williams, has noted in "Pastoral Histories," 35.

29   Ian Christie and others have suggested that this match cut may have inspired Stanley Kubrick in *2001: A Space Odyssey* with his famous cut from "prehistoric bone to a space station." See Christie, "Commentary," and *Arrows of Desire*, 49. See also the match cut in *Apocalypse Now*, and note Francis Ford Coppola's close relationship with Powell (*A Life in Movies*, 152, 324).

30 See Finke and Shichtman, *Cinematic Illuminations*, 48: "We would corre-late the amount of filth present in a medieval film with the film's view of the Middle Ages. Those films subscribing to the fantasy of the Middle Ages as a lost organic society will tend to be cleaner than those that see it as barbaric and uncivilized."

31 Moor, "Bending the Arrow," 216–17.

32 See Michael Alexander on Catholicism and medievalism, especially in the case of G. K. Chesterton. *Medievalism*, 209–13.

33 Conrad, *To Be Continued*, 29.

34 Christie, *Arrows of Desire*, 50: Colpeper is a "magus, or guardian of the spirit of place."

35 Conrad likens this to "Wordsworth the pantheist who lay in trenches in order to feel embedded in earth." *To Be Continued*, 29.

36 Powell, *A Life in Movies*, 78.

37 Ian Christie in his DVD commentary mentions echoes of Chesterton's *Chaucer* in Colpeper's lecture; Peter Conrad, too, mentions this work in rela-tion to *A Canterbury Tale*. *To Be Continued*, 24–25.

38 Chesterton, *Chaucer*, 204. Qtd. in Ellis, *Chaucer at Large*, 74.

39 On music, desire, and medievalism see Dell, "'Yearning for the Sweet Beckon-ing Sound,'" 177–80.

40 Christie, "Commentary"; Powell, *A Life in Movies*, 440.

41 Doty, "'An Instrument with a Flaming Sword,'" 51.

42 Powell, *A Life in Movies*, 440.

43 Bloch — whose writing Walter Benjamin identified as itself asynchronous, anachronistic — asserts, "Not all people exist in the same Now. They do so only externally, through the fact that they can be seen today. But they are thereby not yet living at the same time with the others." *Heritage of Our Times*, 97. For Benjamin's comment, see his letter to Alfred Cohn, February 6, 1935, qtd. in Rabinbach, "Unclaimed Heritage," 5: "The serious objection which I have of [*sic*] this book (if not of the author as well) is that it in absolutely no way cor-responds to the conditions in which it appears, but rather takes its place in-appropriately, like a great lord, who arriving at the scene of an area devastated by an earthquake can find nothing more urgent to do than to spread out the Persian carpets — which by the way are already somewhat moth-eaten — and to display the somewhat tarnished golden and silver vessels, and the already faded brocade and damask garments which his servants had brought."

44 Moor treats this "sister-film" alongside *A Canterbury Tale* in his chapter "Two Pastorals," in *Powell and Pressburger*, 85–125.

45 See Lacourbe and Grivel, "Rediscovering Michael Powell," a 1977 interview, 51.

46 Cf. Moor, "Bending the Arrow," who mentions Edward Carpenter in connec-tion to Colpeper: "He extolled Whitmanesque, manly comradeship and rural craftsmanship, finding a queer, anti-metropolitan home in the greenwood" (216).

47 Kolodny, *The Lay of the Land*.

48 This is Doty's overarching point in "'An Instrument with a Flaming Sword.'"
49 Love, *Feeling Backward*, esp. the introduction, 1–30.
50 Muñoz, *Cruising Utopia*, 173; see the whole chapter, "After Jack: Queer Failure, Queer Virtuosity," 169–83, for discussion of revaluing failure. See also Halberstam, *The Queer Art of Failure*.
51 Working off Derrida's notion of spectrality, Carla Freccero maintains that the "willingness to be haunted is an ethical relation to the world, motivated by a concern not only for the past but also for the future." *Queer/Early/Modern*, 75.

Aarne, Antti. *The Types of the Folktale: A Classification and Bibliography.* Translated and enlarged by Stith Thompson. 2nd ed. Helsinki: Academia Scientarum Fennica, 1964.

Agamben, Giorgio. *The Time That Remains: A Commentary on the Letter to the Romans.* Translated by Patricia Dailey. Stanford: Stanford University Press, 2005.

Akbari, Suzanne Conklin. *Idols in the East: European Representations of Islam and the Orient, 1100–1450.* Ithaca: Cornell University Press, 2009.

Alexander, Michael. *Medievalism: The Middle Ages in Modern England.* New Haven: Yale University Press, 2007.

Allen, Hope Emily. "Ancient Grief." *Atlantic Monthly* 131 (February 1923): 177–87.

———. "Cycles of Time." Hope Allen Papers. Oneida Community Collection, Box 40, file D. Special Collections Research Center, Syracuse University Library, Syracuse, N.Y.

———. "A Glut of Fruit." *Atlantic Monthly* 131 (September 1923): 343–52.

————. Papers. MSS. English Letters c. 212, d. 217, and MS. Engl. Misc. c. 484. Bodleian Library, Oxford.

————. Papers. Special Collections Department, Bryn Mawr College Library, Bryn Mawr, Pa.

Allen, Rosamund. "Introduction." In *Eastward Bound: Travel and Travellers, 1050–1550*, ed. by Rosamund Allen, 1–14. Manchester: Manchester University Press, 2004.

Aquinas, Thomas. *Commentary on Aristotle's* Physics. Translated by Richard J. Blackwell, Richard J. Spath, and W. Edmund Thirlkel. Introduction by Vernon J. Bourke. New Haven: Yale University Press, 1963.

————. *Commentaria in octo libros Physicorum*. Turin, 1954. Compiled by Enrique Alarcón for the Corpus Thomisticum. http://www.corpusthomisticum .org/cpy03.html.

Aristotle. *Physics*. Translated and with notes by Hippocrates G. Apostle. Bloomington: Indiana University Press, 1969.

————. *Physics, Books III and IV*. Edited, translated, and with an introduction by Edward Hussey. Oxford: Clarendon, 1983.

Arn, Mary-Jo, ed. *Fortunes Stabilnes: Charles of Orleans's English Book of Love: A Critical Edition*. Binghamton, N.Y.: Medieval and Renaissance Texts and Studies, 1994.

Arvin, Newton. *Longfellow, His Life and Work*. Boston: Little, Brown, 1963.

Auerbach, Eric. "Figura." In *Scenes from the Drama of European Literature*. Translated by Ralph Mannheim. New York: Meridian Books, 1959. First published 1944.

Augustine. *City of God*. Translated by Henry Bettensen. Harmondsworth: Penguin, 1984.

————. *Confessions*. Edited by James J. O'Donnell. Oxford: Clarendon, 1992.

————. *Confessions*. Translated by Henry Chadwick. Oxford: Oxford University Press, 1991.

————. *Confessions*. Translated by R. S. Pine-Coffin. London: Penguin, 1961.

Austin, Linda M. "The Nostalgic Moment and the Sense of History." In *The Medievalism of Nostalgia*, ed. Helen Dell, Louise D'Arcens, and Andrew Lynch. Special issue of *postmedieval: a journal of medieval cultural studies* 2 (2011): 127–40.

Bakhtin, M. M. *The Dialogic Imagination: Four Essays*. Translated by Caryl Emerson and Michael Holquist. Austin: University of Texas Press, 1981.

Balfour-Melville, E. W. M. *The English Captivity of James I, King of Scots*. London: G. Bell and Sons, 1929.

Barnes, Geraldine. "Nostalgia, Medievalism and the Vinland Voyages." In *The Medievalism of Nostalgia*, ed. Helen Dell, Louise D'Arcens, and Andrew Lynch. Special issue of *postmedieval: a journal of medieval cultural studies* 2 (2011): 141–54.

Barnet, Peter, and Nancy Wu. *The Cloisters: Medieval Art and Architecture*. New York: Metropolitan Museum of Art; New Haven: Yale University Press, 2005.

Barthes, Roland. "Brecht and Discourse: A Contribution to the Study of Discursivity." In *The Rustle of Language*, 212–22. Translated by Richard Howard. New York: Hill and Wang, 1986.

———. "'Longtemps, je me suis couché de bonne heure.'" In *The Rustle of Language*, 277–90. Translated by Richard Howard. New York: Hill and Wang, 1986.

———. *Sade, Fourier, Loyola*. Translated by Richard Miller. New York: Hill and Wang, 1976.

Bartolovich, Crystal. "Is the Post in Posthuman the Post in Postmedieval?" *postmedieval: a journal of medieval cultural studies* 1 (2010): 18–31.

Bate, Jonathan. *Romantic Ecology: Wordsworth and the Environmental Tradition*. London: Routledge, 1991.

Benjamin, Walter. "Theses on the Philosophy of History." In *Illuminations*, edited by Hannah Arendt, 253–64. Translated by Harry Zohn. New York: Schocken Books, 1969.

Benveniste, Émile. *Problems in General Linguistics*. Translated by Mary Elizabeth Meek. Coral Gables, Fla.: University of Miami Press, 1971.

Benzie, William. *Dr. F. J. Furnivall: Victorian Scholar Adventurer*. Norman, Okla.: Pilgrim Books, 1983.

Bérubé, Allan. *My Desire for History: Essays in Gay, Community, and Labor History*. Edited and with introduction by John D'Emilio and Estelle B. Freedman. Chapel Hill: University of North Carolina Press, 2011.

Best, R. I. "Whitley Stokes (1830–1909): A Memorial Discourse Delivered in the Graduates' Memorial Hall on Trinity Monday, 21st of May, 1951." *The Dublin Magazine* 32.2 (1957): 5–18.

Bhreathnach, Máire, ed. and trans. *Tochmarc Becfhola* (The Wooing of Becfhola). *Ériu* 35 (1984): 59–91.

Biddick, Kathleen. *The Shock of Medievalism*. Durham: Duke University Press, 1998.

———. *The Typological Imaginary: Circumcision, Technology, History*. Philadelphia: University of Pennsylvania Press, 2003.

Bloch, Ernst. *Heritage of Our Times*. Translated by Neville Plaice and Stephen Plaice. Berkeley: University of California Press, 1991. First published 1935.

Boethius. *The Consolation of Philosophy*. Translated by Richard Green. Indianapolis: Bobbs-Merrill, 1962.

———. *The Consolation of Philosophy*. Translated by V. E. Watts. Harmondsworth: Penguin, 1969.

Borgnet, A., ed. *Ly myreur des histors, chronique de Jean des Preis dit d'Outremeuse*. 6 vols. Brussels: Royal Academy, 1864–80.

Boyarin, Jonathan, and Martin Land. *Time and Human Language Now*. Chicago: Prickly Paradigm Press, 2008.

Boym, Svetlana. *The Future of Nostalgia*. New York: Basic Books, 2001.

Bremond, Claude, Jacques Le Goff, and J.-C. Schmitt. *L'"Exemplum."* Turnhout: Brepols, 1982.

Brewer, Derek. "Furnivall and the Old Chaucer Society." Annual Chaucer Lecture, New Chaucer Society. *Chaucer Newsletter* 1.2 (Summer 1979): 2–6.

Brown, Catherine. "Love Letters from Beatus of Liébana to Modern Philologists." *Modern Philology* (2009): 579–600.

Brown, J. T. T. *The Authorship of* The Kingis Quair: *A New Criticism.* Glasgow: James MacLehose and Sons, 1896.

Brown, Wendy. *Politics Out of History.* Princeton: Princeton University Press, 2001.

Browne, Thomas. *Pseudodoxia Epidemica.* In *The Works of Sir Thomas Browne,* edited by Simon Wilkin, 2:159–538. London: William Pickering, 1835. First published 1646.

Buck, Dudley. *Scenes from Longfellow's* Golden Legend: *Symphonic Cantata for Solos, Chorus and Orchestra.* New York: John Church, 1908.

Buell, Lawrence. *New England Literary Culture: From Revolution through Renaissance.* Cambridge: Cambridge University Press, 1986.

Burgwinkle, William. "Utopia and Its Uses: Twelfth-Century Romance and History." *Journal of Medieval and Early Modern Studies* 36 (2006): 539–60.

Burt, Richard. "Getting Schmedieval: Of Manuscript and Film Prologues, Paratexts, and Parodies." *Exemplaria* 19 (2007): 217–42.

Burton, Robert. *The Anatomy of Melancholy.* 3 vols. London: J. M. Dent, 1932. First published 1621.

Bynum, Caroline Walker. *The Resurrection of the Body in Western Christianity, 200–1336.* New York: Columbia University Press, 1995.

Calhoun, Charles C. *Longfellow: A Rediscovered Life.* Boston: Beacon Press, 2004.

Calin, William. "What *Tales of a Wayside Inn* Tells Us about Longfellow and about Chaucer." *Studies in Medievalism* 12 (2002): 197–213.

Campbell, Sean, and Colin Coulter, "'Why Pamper Life's Complexities?': An Introduction to the Book." In Sean Campbell and Colin Coulter, eds., *Why Pamper Life's Complexities? Essays on The Smiths,* 1–21. Manchester: Manchester University Press, 2010.

Carey, John, trans. *Echtrae Nera* (The Adventure of Nera). In *The Celtic Heroic Age,* edited by John T. Koch with John Carey, 117–22. Malden, Mass.: Celtic Studies Publications, 1995.

Carlyle, Thomas. "The Hero as Poet." In *On Heroes, Hero-Worship, and the Heroic in History,* with notes and introduction by Michael K. Goldberg, and text established by Michael K. Goldberg, Joel J. Brattin, and Mark Engel, 67–97. Berkeley: University of California Press, 1993. First published 1840.

Carrington, André M. *Speculative Fiction and Media Fandom through a Lens, Darkly.* Minneapolis: University of Minnesota Press, forthcoming.

Carruthers, Mary J. *The Book of Memory: A Study of Memory in Medieval Culture.* Cambridge: Cambridge University Press, 1990.

Caxton, William, trans. "The Golden Legend." In *The Golden Legend, or Lives of the Saints.* 1:1–5. Rev. ed. by J. M. Ellis for Temple Classics. London: J. M. Dent, 1900. First published 1483.

Cerquiglini, Bernard. *In Praise of the Variant: A Critical History of Philology.* Translated by Betsy Wing. Baltimore: Johns Hopkins University Press, 1999.

Chabon, Michael. "The Other James." In *Maps and Legends: Reading and Writing along the Borderlands*, 121–32. San Francisco: McSweeney's Books, 2008.

Chakrabarty, Dipesh. *Provincializing Europe: Postcolonial Thought and Historical Difference*. Princeton: Princeton University Press, 2000.

———. "Response: Historicism and Its Supplements: A Note on a Predicament Shared by Medieval and Postcolonial Studies." In *Medievalisms in the Postcolonial World: The Idea of "The Middle Ages" Outside Europe*, edited by Kathleen Davis and Nadia Altschul, 109–122. Baltimore: Johns Hopkins University Press, 2009.

———. "The Time of History and the Times of Gods." In *The Politics of Culture in the Shadow of Capital*, edited by Lisa Lowe and David Lloyd, 35–60. Durham: Duke University Press, 1997.

———. "Where Is the Now?" *Critical Inquiry* 30.2 (2004): 458–62.

Charvat, William. *The Profession of Authorship in America, 1800–1870*. Columbus: Ohio State University Press, 1968. Reprint with new postscript to preface, New York: Columbia University Press, 1992.

Chaucer, Geoffrey. *Boece*. In *The Riverside Chaucer*, edited by Larry D. Benson, 397–469. 3rd ed. Boston: Houghton Mifflin, 1987.

———. *The Romaunt of the Rose*. In *The Riverside Chaucer*, edited by Larry D. Benson, 685–767. 3rd ed. Boston: Houghton Mifflin, 1987.

Chesterton, G. K. *Chaucer*. New ed. London: Faber and Faber, 1948. First published 1932.

Chew, Samuel C. *The Pilgrimage of Life*. New Haven: Yale University Press, 1962.

Christie, Ian. "Another Life in Movies: Pressburger and Powell." In *The Cinema of Michael Powell: International Perspectives on an English Film-Maker*, edited by Ian Christie and Andrew Moor, 171–86. London: British Film Institute, 2005.

———. *Arrows of Desire: The Films of Michael Powell and Emeric Pressburger*. London: Faber and Faber, 1994.

———. "Commentary." *A Canterbury Tale*. Written and directed by Michael Powell and Emeric Pressburger. Irvington, N.Y.: Criterion Collection, 2006. DVD.

———. "Powell and Pressburger." In *Michael Powell: Interviews*, edited by David Lazar, 105–33. Jackson: University Press of Mississippi, 2003.

Christie, Ian, ed. *Powell, Pressburger and Others*. London: British Film Institute, 1978.

Christie, Ian, and Andrew Moor, eds. *The Cinema of Michael Powell: International Perspectives on an English Film-Maker*. London: British Film Institute, 2005.

Cochran, John. "Object Oriented Cookery." *Collapse* 7 (2011): 299–329.

Code, Lorraine. "Why Feminists Do Not Read Gadamer." Introduction to *Feminist Interpretations of Hans-Georg Gadamer*, edited by Lorraine Code, 1–36. University Park: Pennsylvania State University Press, 2003.

Cohen, Jeffrey Jerome. *Medieval Identity Machines*. Minneapolis: University of Minnesota Press, 2003.

———. "Time Out of Memory." In *The Post-Historical Middle Ages*, edited by Elizabeth Scala and Sylvia Federico, 37–61. New York: Palgrave, 2009.

Cohen, Jeffrey Jerome, ed. *The Postcolonial Middle Ages*. New York: Palgrave, 2001.

Cole, Andrew, and D. Vance Smith, eds. *The Legitimacy of the Middle Ages: On the Unwritten History of Theory*. Durham: Duke University Press, 2010.

Colker, Marvin L. "A Medieval Rip van Winkle Story." *Journal of American Folklore* 76 (1963): 131–63.

Colledge, Edmund, and James Walsh, eds. *A Book of Showings to the Anchoress Julian of Norwich*. 2 vols. Toronto: Pontifical Institute of Mediaeval Studies, 1978.

Connolly, Daniel K. "Imagined Pilgrimage in the Itinerary Maps of Matthew Paris." *The Art Bulletin* 81 (1999): 598–622.

———. *The Maps of Matthew Paris: Medieval Journeys through Space, Time and Liturgy*. Woodbridge, Va.: Boydell, 2009.

Conrad, Peter. *To Be Continued: Four Stories and Their Survival*. Oxford: Clarendon, 1995.

Coope, Ursula. *Time for Aristotle*: Physics *IV. 10–14*. Oxford: Clarendon, 2005.

Coulton, G. G. *Life in the Middle Ages*. 4 vols. in 1. Cambridge: Cambridge University Press, 1930.

Cox, Michael. *M. R. James: An Informal Portrait*. Oxford: Oxford University Press, 1983.

Crabbe, Anna. "Literary Design in the *De Consolatione Philosophiae*." In *Boethius, His Life, Thought, and Influence*, edited by Margaret T. Gibson, 237–74. Oxford: Blackwell, 1981.

Cross, Roseanna. "'Heterochronia' in *Thomas of Erceldoune, Guingamor*, 'The Tale of King Herla,' and *The Story of Meriadoc, King of Cambria*." *Neophilologus* 92 (2008): 163–75.

Dante. *Paradiso*. Vol. 3 of *The Divine Comedy*. Edited and translated by Charles S. Singleton. Princeton: Princeton University Press, 1991.

Daston, Lorraine, and Katharine Park. *Wonders and the Order of Nature, 1150–1750*. New York: Zone Books, 2001.

Davidse, Jan. "The Sense of History in the Works of the Venerable Bede." *Studi Medievali*, 3rd ser., 23.2 (1982): 647–95.

Davis, Kathleen. *Periodization and Sovereignty: How Ideas of Feudalism and Secularization Govern the Politics of Time*. Philadelphia: University of Pennsylvania Press, 2008.

———. "The Sense of an Epoch: Periodization, Sovereignty, and the Limits of Secularization." In *The Legitimacy of the Middle Ages: On the Unwritten History of Theory*, edited by Andrew Cole and D. Vance Smith, 39–69. Durham: Duke University Press, 2010.

Davis, Kathleen, and Nadia Altschul, eds. *Medievalisms in the Postcolonial World: The Idea of "The Middle Ages" Outside Europe*. Baltimore: Johns Hopkins University Press, 2009.

Day, Mildred Leake, ed. and trans. *The Story of Meriadoc, King of Cambria*. New York: Garland, 1988.

Dean, Tim. "Bareback Time." In E. L. McCallum and Mikko Tuhkanen, eds., *Queer Times, Queer Becomings*, 75–99. Albany: SUNY Press, 2011.

de Certeau, Michel. *The Mystic Fable*. Vol. 1: *The Sixteenth and Seventeenth Centuries*. Translated by Michael B. Smith. Chicago: University of Chicago Press, 1992.

Del Lungo, Isidoro, ed. *I Padri del Deserto*. Vol. 1 of *Leggende del Secolo XIV*. Florence: G. Barbèra, 1863.

Dell, Helen. "Nostalgia and Medievalism: Conversations, Contradictions, Impasses." Editor's Introduction to *The Medievalism of Nostalgia*, edited by Helen Dell, Louise D'Arcens, and Andrew Lynch. Special issue of *postmedieval: a journal of medieval cultural studies* 2 (2011): 115–26.

———. "'Yearning for the Sweet Beckoning Sound': Musical Longings and the Unsayable in Medievalist Fantasy Fiction." In *The Medievalism of Nostalgia*, edited by Helen Dell, Louise D'Arcens, and Andrew Lynch. Special issue of *postmedieval: a journal of medieval cultural studies* 2 (2011): 171–85.

Denny-Brown, Andrea. *Fashioning Change: The Trope of Clothing in High- and Late-Medieval England*. Columbus: Ohio State University Press, 2012.

Derrida, Jacques. *The Animal That Therefore I Am*. Edited by Marie-Louise Mallet. Translated by David Wills. New York: Fordham University Press, 2008.

———. *Specters of Marx: The State of the Debt, the Work of Mourning, and the New International*. Translated by Peggy Kamuf. New York: Routledge, 1994.

Dickman, Susan. "Margery Kempe and the Continental Tradition of the Pious Woman." In *The Medieval Mystical Tradition in England*, edited by Marion Glasscoe, 150–68. Cambridge: D. S. Brewer, 1984.

Dillon, Myles. "The Wooing of Becfhola and the Stories of Cano, Son of Gartnán," *Modern Philology* 43 (1945): 11–17.

Dinshaw, Carolyn. *Getting Medieval: Sexualities and Communities, Pre- and Postmodern*. Durham: Duke University Press, 1999.

———. "Nostalgia on My Mind." In *The Medievalism of Nostalgia*, edited by Helen Dell, Louise D'Arcens, and Andrew Lynch. Special issue of *postmedieval: a journal of medieval cultural studies* 2 (2011): 225–38.

Dinshaw, Carolyn, and David Wallace, eds. *The Cambridge Companion to Medieval Women's Writing*. Cambridge: Cambridge University Press, 2003.

Dohrn-van Rossum, Gerhard. *History of the Hour: Clocks and Modern Temporal Orders*. Translated by Thomas Dunlap. Chicago: University of Chicago Press, 1996.

Doty, Alexander. "'An Instrument with a Flaming Sword': Conservative Queerness in *A Canterbury Tale*." In *British Queer Cinema*, edited by Robin Griffiths, 47–60. London: Routledge, 2006.

———. "The Queer Aesthete, the Diva, and *The Red Shoes*." In *Out Takes: Essays on Queer Theory and Film*, edited by Ellis Hanson, 46–71. Durham: Duke University Press, 1999.

Duff, M. E. Grant. *Sir Henry Maine: A Brief Memoir of His Life*. New York: Henry Holt, 1892.

Duffy, Eamon. *The Stripping of the Altars: Traditional Religion in England c. 1400–c. 1580*. New Haven: Yale University Press, 1992.

Duncan, Ian. "'Reactionary Desire': Ruskin and the Work of Fiction." In *Ruskin and Modernism*, edited by Giovanni Cianci and Peter Nicholls, 67–81. New York: Palgrave, 2001.

Dundes, Alan. *Fables of the Ancients? Folklore in the* Qur'an. Lanham, Md.: Rowman and Littlefield, 2003.

Eco, Umberto. *Travels in Hyperreality: Essays*. Translated by William Weaver. San Diego: Harcourt Brace Jovanovich, 1986.

Edelman, Lee. *No Future: Queer Theory and the Death Drive*. Durham: Duke University Press, 2004.

Eisenhower, Dwight D. "Farewell Address," 17 January 1961. Final TV Talk, 1/17/61 (1). Box 38, Speech Series, Papers of Dwight D. Eisenhower as President, 1953–61, Eisenhower Library; National Archives and Records Administration. http://www.ourdocuments.gov/doc.php?flash=true&doc=90.

Elbow, Peter. *Oppositions in Chaucer*. Middletown, Conn.: Wesleyan University Press, 1975.

Ellis, Steve. *Chaucer at Large: The Poet in the Modern Imagination*. Minneapolis: University of Minnesota Press, 2000.

Eng, David L. "Out Here and Over There: Queerness and Diaspora in Asian American Studies." In "Queer Transexions of Race, Nation, and Gender." Special issue, *Social Text* 52–53 (Fall/Winter 1997): 31–52.

Fabian, Johannes. *Time and the Other: How Anthropology Makes Its Object*. New York: Columbia University Press, 1983. Reprint with a new foreword by Matti Bunzl, 2002.

Fetterley, Judith. *The Resisting Reader: A Feminist Approach to American Fiction*. Bloomington: Indiana University Press, 1978.

Finke, Laurie A., and Martin B. Shichtman. *Cinematic Illuminations: The Middle Ages on Film*. Baltimore: Johns Hopkins University Press, 2010.

Fitzpatrick, Kathleen. *Planned Obsolescence: Publishing, Technology, and the Future of the Academy*. New York: New York University Press, 2011.

Fradenburg, L. O. Aranye. *Sacrifice Your Love: Psychoanalysis, Historicism, Chaucer*. Minneapolis: University of Minnesota Press, 2002.

———. "'So That We May Speak of Them': Enjoying the Middle Ages." *New Literary History* 28 (1997): 205–30.

Franchot, Jenny. *Roads to Rome: The Antebellum Protestant Encounter with Catholicism*. Berkeley: University of California Press, 1994.

Freccero, Carla. "Les chats de Derrida." In *Derrida and Queer Theory*, edited by Michael O'Rourke. New York: Palgrave. Forthcoming.

———. *Queer/Early/Modern*. Durham: Duke University Press, 2006.

Freeman, Elizabeth. *Time Binds: Queer Temporalities, Queer Histories*. Durham: Duke University Press, 2010.

Freud, Sigmund. "Mourning and Melancholia." In *The Standard Edition of the Complete Psychological Works of Sigmund Freud*, edited by James Strachey, 14:237–58. London: Hogarth, 1957.

Friedman, John Block. "Eurydice, Heurodis and the Noon-Day Demon," *Speculum* 41 (1966): 22–29.

Fuller, Graham. "*A Canterbury Tale*." *Film Comment* 31.2 (March 1995): 33–36.

Furnivall, Frederick James. *Trial-Forewords to My "Parallel-Text Edition of Chaucer's Minor Poems."* Chaucer Society, 2nd ser., 6. London: N. Trübner, 1871.

Furnivall, Frederick James, ed. *The Minor Poems of William Lauder.* EETS 41. London: N. Trübner, 1870.

Gadamer, Hans-Georg. *Truth and Method.* Translated by Joel Weinsheimer and Donald G. Marshall. 2nd ed. London: Continuum Books, 2004.

Ganim, John M. *Medievalism and Orientalism: Three Essays on Literature, Architecture and Cultural Identity.* New York: Palgrave, 2005.

Garrity, Jane. *Step-Daughters of England: British Women Modernists and the National Imaginary.* Manchester: Manchester University Press, 2003.

Geary, Patrick J. "What Happened to Latin?" *Speculum* 84 (2009): 859–73.

Gering, Hugo, ed. *Islendzk Æventyri: Isländische Legenden Novellen und Märchen.* 2 vols. Halle, 1882–4.

Gerould, Gordon Hall. "The North-English Homily Collection: A Study of the Manuscript Relations and of the Sources of the Tales." B.A. diss., Oxford University, 1902.

Gibson, Margaret T., ed. *Boethius, His Life, Thought, and Influence.* Oxford: Blackwell, 1981.

Glasscoe, Marion, ed. *The Medieval Mystical Tradition in England.* Cambridge: D. S. Brewer, 1984.

Goddard, Simon. *The Smiths: Songs that Saved Your Life.* London: Reynolds and Hearn, 2006.

Goffman, Erving. *The Presentation of Self in Everyday Life.* New York: Anchor Books, 1959.

Goodrich, A. J. *Complete Musical Analysis.* Cincinnati: John Church, 1889.

Gopinath, Gayatri. "Archive, Affect, and the Everyday: Queer Diasporic Revisions." In *Political Emotions*, edited by Janet Staiger, Ann Cvetkovich, and Ann Reynolds, 164–92. New York: Routledge, 2010.

———. "Nostalgia, Desire, Diaspora: South Asian Sexualities in Motion." In "New Formations, New Questions: Asian American Studies." Special issue of *Positions* 5 (1997): 467–89.

Gordon, Avery. *Ghostly Matters: Haunting and the Sociological Imagination.* Minneapolis: University of Minnesota Press, 1996.

Gossman, Lionel. "History as Decipherment: Romantic Historiography and the Discovery of the Other." *New Literary History* 18 (1986): 23–57.

Green, Roger Lancelyn. *Andrew Lang.* London: Bodley Head, 1962.

Gregory of Tours. *Liber vitae patrum.* In *Gregorii episcopi Turonensis miracula et opera minora*, edited by Bruno Krusch. Monumenta Germaniae historica, scriptores rerum merovingicarum vol. 1, pt. 2. Hanover: Hahn, 1969. First published 1885.

Greven, Joseph, ed. *Die Exempla aus den Sermones feriales et communes des Jakob von Vitry.* Heidelberg: Carl Winter, 1914.

Griffith, John W. "Longfellow and Herder and the Sense of History." *Texas Studies in Literature and Language* 13 (1971): 249–65.

Gross, Charlotte. "Augustine's Ambivalence about Temporality: His Two Accounts of Time." *Medieval Philosophy and Theology* 8 (1999): 129–48.

———. "Time and Nature in Twelfth-Century Thought: William of Conches,
Thierry of Chartres, and the 'New Science.' " In *Reading Medieval Culture:
Essays in Honor of Robert W. Hanning*, edited by Robert M. Stein and Sandra
Pierson Prior, 89–110. Notre Dame: University of Notre Dame Press, 2005.

Gruesz, Kirsten Silva. *Ambassadors of Culture: The Transamerican Origins of
Latino Writing*. Princeton: Princeton University Press, 2002.

———. "*El Gran Poeta* Longfellow and a Psalm of Exile." *American Literary History* 10.3 (1998): 395–427.

Gurevich, Aron. *Medieval Popular Culture: Problems of Belief and Perception*.
Translated by János M. Bak and Paul A. Hollingsworth. Cambridge: Cambridge University Press, 1990.

———. "What Is Time?" In *Categories of Medieval Culture*, 93–152. Translated by
G. L. Campbell. London: Routledge, 1985.

Hagen, Friedrich Heinrich von der. *Gesammtabenteuer: Hundert altdeutsche Er-
zählungen*. Stuttgart: J. G. Cotta'scher, 1850.

Halberstam, Judith. *The Queer Art of Failure*. Durham: Duke University Press,
2011.

———. *In a Queer Time and Place: Transgender Bodies, Subcultural Lives*. New
York: New York University Press, 2005.

Hall, Fitzedward. *Modern English*. London: Williams and Norgate, 1873.

Hamacher, Werner. "From '95 Theses on Philology.' " *PMLA* 125 (2010): 994–1001.

Hamelius, P. "The Travels of Sir John Mandeville." *The Quarterly Review* 227.451
(April 1917): 331–52.

Hamelius, P., ed. *Mandeville's Travels*. 2 vols. EETS 153, 154. London: Kegan Paul,
Trench, Trübner, 1919–23.

Hansen, William. *Ariadne's Thread: A Guide to International Tales Found in Classical Literature*. Ithaca: Cornell University Press, 2002.

Haralson, Eric L. "Mars in Petticoats: Longfellow and Sentimental Masculinity."
Nineteenth-Century Literature 51 (1996): 327–55.

Hartland, E. S. *The Science of Fairy Tales: An Inquiry into Fairy Mythology*. London: Walter Scott, 1891.

Hartley, Dorothy. *Mediaeval Costume and Life: A Review of Their Social Aspects
Arranged under Various Classes and Workers with Instructions for Making Nu-
merous Types of Dress*. Introduction and notes by Francis M. Kelly. London:
B. T. Batsford, 1931.

Hazlitt, William. "Elia, and Geoffrey Crayon." In *The Spirit of the Age: or Contemporary Portraits*, 395–408. 2nd ed. London: Colburn, 1825.

Heidegger, Martin. *The Basic Problems of Phenomenology*. Translated by Albert
Hofstadter. Bloomington: Indiana University Press, 1988.

Herbert, J.-A. "The Monk and the Bird." *Romania* 38 (1909): 427–29.

Herrtage, Sidney J. H., ed. *The Early English Versions of the* Gesta romanorum.
EETS, e.s., 33. London: Trübner, 1879.

Higgins, Iain Macleod. "Imagining Christendom from Jerusalem to Paradise:

Asia in *Mandeville's Travels*." In *Discovering New Worlds: Essays on Medieval Exploration and Imagination*, edited by Scott D. Westrem, 91–114. New York: Garland, 1991.

———. *Writing East: The "Travels" of Sir John Mandeville*. Philadelphia: University of Pennsylvania Press, 1997.

Hirsh, John C. "Hope Emily Allen (1883–1960): An Independent Scholar." In *Women Medievalists and the Academy*, edited by Jane Chance, 227–38. Madison: University of Wisconsin Press, 2005.

———. *Hope Emily Allen: Medieval Scholarship and Feminism*. Norman, Okla.: Pilgrim Books, 1988.

———. "Hope Emily Allen and the Limitations of Academic Discourse." *Mystics Quarterly* 18 (1992): 94–102.

———. "Past and Present in Hope Emily Allen's Essay 'Relics.'" *Syracuse University Library Associate Courier* 24 (1989): 49–61.

———. *The Revelations of Margery Kempe: Paramystical Practices in Late Medieval England*. Leiden: Brill, 1989.

Holsinger, Bruce. *The Premodern Condition: Medievalism and the Making of Theory*. Chicago: University of Chicago Press, 2005.

Hopkins, E. Washburn. "The Fountain of Youth." *Journal of the American Oriental Society* 26 (1905): 1–67.

Horstmann, Carl. "Die Evangelien-Geschichten der Homiliensammlung des Ms. Vernon." *Herrigs Archiv* 57.31 (1877): 241–316.

Hoving, Thomas. *King of the Confessors*. New York: Simon and Schuster, 1981.

Howard, Donald R. *Writers and Pilgrims: Medieval Pilgrimage Narratives and Their Posterity*. Berkeley: University of California Press, 1980.

Huber, P. Michael. *Die Wanderlegende von den Siebenschläfern: Eine literargeschichtliche Untersuchung*. Leipzig: Otto Harrassowitz, 1910.

Ingham, Patricia Clare. "Pastoral Histories: Utopia, Conquest, and the *Wife of Bath's Tale*." *Texas Studies in Literature and Language* 44 (2002): 34–47.

Ingham, Patricia Clare, and Michelle R. Warren, eds. *Postcolonial Moves: Medieval through Modern*. New York: Palgrave, 2003.

Inwood, Michael. "Aristotle on the Reality of Time." In *Aristotle's Physics: A Collection of Essays*, edited by Lindsay Judson, 151–78. Oxford: Clarendon, 1991.

Irmscher, Christoph. *Longfellow Redux*. Urbana: University of Illinois Press, 2006.

Irving, Washington. *The Crayon Miscellany*. Author's rev. ed. New York: George P. Putnam, 1849.

———. *The Sketch Book of Geoffrey Crayon, Gent*. In *History, Tales and Sketches*, edited by James W. Tuttleton. New York: Literary Classics of the United States, 1983.

Jacobus de Voragine. *Legenda aurea*. Translated by William Granger Ryan and Helmut Ripperger. 2 vols. New York: Longmans, Green, 1941.

———. "Lives of the Seven Sleepers." In *Legenda aurea*. Vol. 4. Original English ed. by William Caxton, 1483. Rev. ed. by J. M. Ellis for Temple Classics. London: J. M. Dent, 1900. Electronic edition via the Internet Medieval Source

Book: http://www.fordham.edu/halsall/basis/goldenlegend/GoldenLegend-Volume4.htm#Seven%20Sleepers.

James I. *The Kingis Quair*. In *The Poetical Remains of James the First, King of Scotland*, edited by William Tytler, 53–162. Edinburgh: J. and E. Balfour, 1783.

James, M. R. *Athens in the Fourteenth Century: An Inedited Supplement to Sir John Maundeville's Travels. Published from the Rhodes MS. No. 17, by Prof. E. S. Merganser*. Cambridge: Macmillan and Bowes, 1887. Reprint with introduction by Nicholas Rogers in *The Legacy of M. R. James: Papers from the 1995 Cambridge Symposium*, edited by Lynda Dennison, 236–38. Donington: Shaun Tyas, 2001.

———. "Canon Alberic's Scrap-book." In *Count Magnus and Other Ghost Stories*, by M. R. James, 1–13. Vol. 1 of *The Complete Ghost Stories of M. R. James*. New York: Penguin, 2005.

———. "The Malice of Inanimate Objects." In *The Haunted Doll's House and Other Ghost Stories*, edited by S. T. Joshi, 201–5. Vol. 2 of *The Complete Ghost Stories of M. R. James*. New York: Penguin, 2006.

———. "Preface to *Ghost-Stories of an Antiquary*." In *Count Magnus and Other Ghost Stories*, by M. R. James, 254. Vol. 1 of *The Complete Ghost Stories of M. R. James*. New York: Penguin, 2005.

Jameson, Fredric. *A Singular Modernity: Essay on the Ontology of the Present*. New York: Verso, 2002.

Jenkins, Henry. *Convergence Culture: Where Old and New Media Collide*. New York: New York University Press, 2006.

Jones, Charles W. *Saints' Lives and Chronicles in Early England*. Ithaca: Cornell University Press, 1947.

Jones, Darryl. "Introduction." In *Collected Ghost Stories*, by M. R. James, ix–xxx. Oxford: Oxford University Press, 2011.

Jones, William E. *Is It Really So Strange?*, Culver City, Calif.: Strand Releasing, 2004. DVD.

Joshi, S. T. "Introduction." In *Count Magnus and Other Ghost Stories*, by M. R. James, vii–xviii. Vol. 1 of *The Complete Ghost Stories of M. R. James*. New York: Penguin, 2005.

Joy, Eileen A. "*The Seven Sleepers*, Eros, and the Unincorporable Infinite of the Human Person." In *Anonymous Interpolations in Aelfric's "Lives of Saints*,*"* edited by Robin Norris, 71–96. Kalamazoo, Mich.: Medieval Institute Publications, 2011.

Joyce, P. W., ed. and trans. *Oisin in Tirnanoge*. In *Old Celtic Romances*, 385–99. Dublin: Educational Co. of Ireland, 1920.

Juhasz, Alexandra. "Video Remains: Nostalgia, Technology, and Queer Archive Activism." *GLQ* 12 (2006): 319–28.

Kabir, Ananya Jahanara. "An Enchanted Mirror for the Capitalist Self: The *Germania* in British India." In *Medievalisms in the Postcolonial World: The Idea of "The Middle Ages" Outside Europe*, edited by Kathleen Davis and Nadia Altschul, 51–79. Baltimore: Johns Hopkins University Press, 2009.

———. "'Oriental Gothic': The Medieval Past in the Colonial Encounter." In *Re-*

orienting Orientalism, edited by Chandreyee Niyogi, 65–88. New Delhi: SAGE Publications, 2006.

————. "Reading between the Lines: Whitley Stokes, Scribbles and the Scholarly Apparatus." In *The Tripartite Life of Whitley Stokes (1830–1909)*, edited by Elizabeth Boyle and Paul Russell, 78–97. Dublin: Four Courts Press, 2011.

Kabir, Ananya Jahanara, and Deanne Williams, eds. *Postcolonial Approaches to the European Middle Ages: Translating Cultures*. Cambridge: Cambridge University Press, 2005.

Kay, Sarah. "Touching Singularity: Consolation, Philosophy, and Poetry in the French *Dit*." In *The Erotics of Consolation: Desire and Distance in the Late Middle Ages*, edited by Catherine E. Léglu and Stephen J. Milner, 21–38. New York: Palgrave, 2008.

Kieckhefer, Richard. *Unquiet Souls: Fourteenth-Century Saints and Their Religious Milieu*. Chicago: University of Chicago Press, 1984.

Kitchen, E. F. *Suburban Knights: A Return to the Middle Ages*. Brooklyn, N.Y.: PowerHouse Books, 2010.

Knowles, Elizabeth. "Making the *OED*: Readers and Editors. A Critical Survey." In *Lexicography and the* Oxford English Dictionary: *Pioneers in the Untrodden Forest*, edited by Lynda Mugglestone, 22–39. Oxford: Oxford University Press, 2000.

Koch, John. *Die Siebenschläferlegende, ihr Ursprung und ihre Verbreitung: Ein mythologisch-literaturgeschichtliche Studie*. Leipzig: Carl Reissner, 1883.

Kohanski, Tamarah, and C. David Benson, eds. *The Book of John Mandeville*. Kalamazoo: Medieval Institute Publications, 2007.

Kolodny, Annette. *The Lay of the Land: Metaphor as Experience and History in American Life and Letters*. Chapel Hill: University of North Carolina Press, 1975.

Koselleck, Reinhart. *Futures Past: On the Semantics of Historical Time*. Translated by Keith Tribe. New York: Columbia University Press, 2004.

Kratzmann, Gregory. *Anglo-Scottish Literary Relations, 1430–1550*. Cambridge: Cambridge University Press, 1980.

Kripal, Jeffrey J. *Roads of Excess, Palaces of Wisdom: Eroticism and Reflexivity in the Study of Mysticism*. Chicago: University of Chicago Press, 2001.

Kruger, Steven F. "Gay Internet Medievalism: Erotic Story Archives, the Middle Ages, and Contemporary Gay Identity." *American Literary History* 22 (2010): 913–44.

————. *The Spectral Jew: Conversion and Embodiment in Medieval Europe*. Minneapolis: University of Minnesota Press, 2006.

Kulp-Hill, Kathleen, trans. *Songs of Holy Mary of Alfonso X, The Wise: A Translation of the* Cantigas de Santa Maria. Tempe: Arizona Center for Medieval and Renaissance Studies, 2000.

Lacourbe, Roland, and Danièle Grivel. "Rediscovering Michael Powell." In *Michael Powell: Interviews*, edited by David Lazar, 44–66. Jackson: University Press of Mississippi, 2003.

Lampert-Weissig, Lisa. *Medieval Literature and Postcolonial Studies*. Edinburgh: Edinburgh University Press, 2010.

Lang, Andrew. *Letters to Dead Authors*. New York: Scribner's, 1886.

———. "'Le Morte Darthur.'" In *Le Morte Darthur by Syr Thomas Malory*, edited by H. Oskar Sommer, xiii–xxv. Vol. 3: *Studies on the Sources*. London: David Nutt, 1891.

———. *Old Friends: Essays in Epistolary Parody*. London: Longmans, Green, 1890.

Lang, Helen S. *Aristotle's* Physics *and its Medieval Varieties*. Albany: SUNY Press, 1992.

Lant, Antonia. *Blackout: Reinventing Women for Wartime British Cinema*. Princeton: Princeton University Press, 1991.

Large, William. *Heidegger's* Being and Time: *An Edinburgh Philosophical Guide*. Edinburgh: Edinburgh University Press, 2008.

Latour, Bruno. *Chroniques d'un amateur de sciences*. Paris: École des mines, 2006.

———. *Pandora's Hope: Essays on the Reality of Science Studies*. Cambridge: Harvard University Press, 1999.

———. *Politics of Nature: How to Bring the Sciences into Democracy*. Translated by Catherine Porter. Cambridge: Harvard University Press, 2004.

———. *We Have Never Been Modern*. Translated by Catherine Porter. Cambridge: Harvard University Press, 1993.

Lavezzo, Kathy. "Sobs and Sighs between Women: The Homoerotics of Compassion in *The Book of Margery Kempe*." In *Premodern Sexualities*, edited by Louise Fradenburg and Carla Freccero, 175–98. New York: Routledge, 1996.

Lears, T. J. Jackson. *No Place of Grace: Antimodernism and the Transformation of American Culture, 1880–1920*. Chicago: University of Chicago Press, 1994.

Lee, S. L., ed. *The Boke of Duke Huon of Burdeux*. EETS, e.s., 40, 41, 43, 50. London: Trübner, 1882–87.

Le Goff, Jacques. "The Time of the *Exemplum* (Thirteenth Century)." In *The Medieval Imagination*, translated by Arthur Goldhammer, 78–80. Chicago: University of Chicago Press, 1988.

Lerer, Seth. *Boethius and Dialogue: Literary Method in* The Consolation of Philosophy. Princeton: Princeton University Press, 1985.

Letts, Malcolm. *Mandeville's Travels: Texts and Translations*. 2 vols. London: Hakluyt Society, 1953.

———. *Sir John Mandeville: The Man and His Book*. London: Batchworth Press, 1949.

Levine, Philippa. *The Amateur and the Professional: Antiquarians, Historians and Archaeologists in Victorian England, 1838–1886*. Cambridge: Cambridge University Press, 1986.

Lewis, C. S. *The Discarded Image: An Introduction to Medieval and Renaissance Literature*. Cambridge: Cambridge University Press, 1964.

———. "On Stories." In *Of Other Worlds: Essays and Stories*, edited by Walter Hooper, 3–21. New York: Harcourt, Brace and World, 1966.

Lindley, Arthur. "The Ahistoricism of Medieval Film." *Screening the Past* 3 (1998). http://www.latrobe.edu.au/screeningthepast/firstrelease/fir598/ALfr3a.htm.

Lochrie, Karma. "Provincializing Medieval Europe: Mandeville's Cosmopolitan Utopia." *PMLA* 124 (2009): 592–99.

Longfellow, Henry Wadsworth. "Defense of Poetry." *North American Review* 34 (1832): 56–78.

———. "History of the Italian Language and Dialects." *North American Review* 35 (1832): 283–342.

———. *Outre-Mer: A Pilgrimage beyond the Sea.* 2 vols. New York: Harper and Bros., 1835.

———. *The Poetical Works of Henry Wadsworth Longfellow.* 6 vols. Boston: Houghton Mifflin, 1883–94.

Longfellow, Samuel, ed. *The Life of Henry Wadsworth Longfellow.* 3 vols. Boston: Houghton Mifflin, 1891.

Loomis, R. S. "*Sir Orfeo* and Walter Map's *De nugis.*" *Modern Language Notes* 51 (1936): 28–30.

Love, Heather. *Feeling Backward: Loss and the Politics of Queer History.* Cambridge: Harvard University Press, 2007.

Luhrmann, T. M. *The Good Parsi: The Fate of a Colonial Elite in a Postcolonial Society.* Cambridge: Harvard University Press, 1996.

Lüthis, Max. *Once Upon a Time: On the Nature of Fairy Tales.* Translated by Lee Chadeayne and Paul Gottwald. New York: Frederick Ungar, 1970.

Lynch, Andrew. "Nostalgia and Critique: Walter Scott's 'Secret Power.'" In *The Medievalism of Nostalgia*, ed. Helen Dell, Louise D'Arcens, and Andrew Lynch. Special issue of *postmedieval: a journal of medieval cultural studies* 2 (2011): 201–15.

Macdonald, Kevin. *Emeric Pressburger: The Life and Death of a Screenwriter.* London: Faber and Faber, 1994.

Machan, Tim William. *Techniques of Translation: Chaucer's Boece.* Norman, Okla.: Pilgrim Books, 1985.

Machan, Tim William, and Alastair J. Minnis. *Sources of the Boece.* Athens: University of Georgia Press, 2005.

Maine, Henry. *Lectures on the Early History of Institutions.* 7th ed. London: John Murray, 1914. First published 1875. http://oll.libertyfund.org/index.php?option =com_staticxt&staticfile=show.php%3Ftitle=2040&Itemid=27.

Manning, Susan. "Introduction." In *The Sketch-Book of Geoffrey Crayon, Gent.*, by Washington Irving, vii–xxix. Oxford: Oxford University Press, 1996.

Map, Walter. *De nugis curialium (Courtiers' Trifles).* Edited and translated by M. R. James with revisions by C. N. L. Brooke and R. A. B. Mynors. Oxford: Clarendon, 1983.

Marenbon, John. *Boethius.* Oxford: Oxford University Press, 2003.

Matthews, David. "Chaucer's American Accent." *American Literary History* 22 (Winter 2010): 758–72.

———. "From Mediaeval to Mediaevalism: A New Semantic History." *Review of English Studies* n.s. 62 (2011): 695–715.

————. *The Making of Middle English, 1765–1910*. Minneapolis: University of Minnesota Press, 1999.

————. "What Was Medievalism? Medieval Studies, Medievalism and Cultural Studies." In *Medieval Cultural Studies: Essays in Honour of Stephen Knight*, edited by Ruth Evans, Helen Fulton, and David Matthews, 9–22. Cardiff: University of Wales Press, 2006.

Matthews, John. "Anicius Manlius Severinus Boethius." In *Boethius, His Life, Thought, and Influence*, edited by Margaret T. Gibson, 15–43. Oxford: Blackwell, 1981.

McTighe, Thomas P. "Eternity and Time in Boethius." In *History of Philosophy in the Making: A Symposium of Essays to Honor Professor James D. Collins on his 65th Birthday*, edited by Linus J. Thro, S.J., 35–62. Washington, D.C.: University Press of America, 1982.

Meech, Sanford B., and Hope Emily Allen, eds. *The Book of Margery Kempe*. EETS 212. Oxford: Oxford University Press, 1940.

Meyer, Paul. "Les Manuscrits des sermons français de Maurice de Sully." *Romania* 5 (1876): 466–87. Supplement in *Romania* 23 (1894): 177–91.

Michelant, Heinrich, ed. *Li Romans d'Alixandre*. Stuttgart: Bibliothek des Literarischen Vereins, 1846.

Millett, Bella, and Jocelyn Wogan-Browne, eds. *Hali Meidhad*. In *Medieval English Prose for Women: Selections from the Katherine Group and Ancrene Wisse*, 2–43. Oxford: Clarendon, 1990.

————. *Seinte Margarete*. In *Medieval English Prose for Women: Selections from the Katherine Group and Ancrene Wisse*, 44–85. Oxford: Clarendon Press, 1990.

Mitchell, Marea. "'The Ever-Growing Army of Serious Girl Students': The Legacy of Hope Emily Allen." *Medieval Feminist Forum* 31 (Spring 2001): 17–29.

Mitchell, Timothy. *Rule of Experts: Egypt, Techno-Politics, Modernity*. Berkeley: University of California Press, 2002.

Momma, Haruko. *From Philology to English Studies: Language and Culture in the Nineteenth Century*. Cambridge: Cambridge University Press, 2012.

Mooney, Linne R. "The Cock and the Clock: Telling Time in Chaucer's Day." *Studies in the Age of Chaucer* 15 (1993): 91–109.

Mooney, Linne R., and Mary-Jo Arn, eds. *James I of Scotland*, The Kingis Quair. Originally published in *The Kingis Quair and Other Prison Poems*. Kalamazoo: Medieval Institute Publications, 2005. http://www.lib.rochester.edu/camelot/teams/kqintro.htm.

Moor, Andrew. "Bending the Arrow: The Queer Appeal of The Archers." In *The Cinema of Michael Powell: International Perspectives on an English Film-Maker*, edited by Ian Christie and Andrew Moor, 209–23. London: British Film Institute, 2005.

————. *Powell and Pressburger: A Cinema of Magic Spaces*. London: I. B. Tauris, 2005.

Morton, Timothy. "Queer Ecology." *PMLA* 125 (2010): 273–82.

Moseley, C. W. R. D., ed. and trans. *The Travels of Sir John Mandeville*. Harmondsworth: Penguin Books, 1983.

Moten, Fred, and Stefano Harney. "The University and the Undercommons: Seven Theses." *Social Text* 22 (2004): 101–15.

Mueller, Janelle, and Joshua Scodel. *Elizabeth I: Translations, 1592–1598*. Chicago: University of Chicago Press, 2009.

Muñoz, José Esteban. *Cruising Utopia: The Then and There of Queer Futurity*. New York: New York University Press, 2009.

Murray, James A. *The Romance and Prophecies of Thomas of Erceldoune*. EETS 61. London: Trübner, 1875.

Myers, Andrew B., ed. *A Century of Commentary on the Works of Washington Irving*. Tarrytown, N.Y.: Sleepy Hollow Restorations, 1976.

Nealon, Christopher. *Foundlings: Lesbian and Gay Historical Emotion before Stonewall*. Durham: Duke University Press, 2001.

Nevanlinna, Saara, ed. *The Northern Homily Cycle: The Expanded Version in* MSS *Harley 4196 and Cotton Tiberius E vii*. 3 vols. Helsinki: Société Néophilologique, 1972–84.

Newman, Barbara. "Redeeming the Time: Langland, Julian, and the Art of Lifelong Revision." *Yearbook of Langland Studies* 23 (2009): 1–32.

Newstead, Helaine. "Some Observations on King Herla and the Herlething." In *Medieval Literature and Folklore Studies: Essays in Honor of Francis Lee Utley*, edited by Jerome Mandel and Bruce A. Rosenberg, 104–10. New Brunswick, N.J.: Rutgers University Press, 1970.

Oaklander, L. Nathan. "Presentism, Ontology and Temporal Experience." In *Time, Reality and Experience*, ed. Craig Callender, 73–90. Cambridge: Cambridge University Press, 2002.

Olsson, Kurt O. "Rhetoric, John Gower, and the Late Medieval *Exemplum*." *Medievalia et Humanistica* 8 (1977): 185–200.

Otter, Monika. *Inventiones: Fiction and Referentiality in Twelfth-Century English Historical Writing*. Chapel Hill: University of North Carolina Press, 1996.

Owen, W. B. "Hall, Fitzedward (1825–1901)." Revised by J. B. Katz. In *Oxford Dictionary of National Biography*. Oxford: Oxford University Press, 2004. http://www.oxforddnb.com/view/article/33652.

Owst, G. R. *Literature and Pulpit in Medieval England*. Cambridge: Cambridge University Press, 1933.

Patch, Howard. *The Other World according to Descriptions in Medieval Literature*. Cambridge: Harvard University Press, 1950.

Pattee, Fred Lewis. *The Feminine Fifties*. New York: D. Appleton-Century, 1940.

Pearsall, Derek. "Frederick James Furnivall (1825–1910)." In *Medieval Scholarship: Biographical Studies on the Formation of a Discipline*, edited by Helen Damico, 125–38. Vol. 2: *Literature and Philology*. New York: Garland, 1998.

Pfaff, Richard William. *Montague Rhodes James*. London: Scolar Press, 1980.

Philoponus, John. *Johannis Philoponi Commentaria, 5A: In libros Physicorum*. Translated by Guilelmus Dorotheus. Commentaria in Aristotelem Graeca, Versiones Latinae 9. Frankfurt: Minerva, 1984. First published in 1554.

Pincombe, Mike. "Homosexual Panic and the English Ghost Story: M. R. James and Others." In *Warnings to the Curious*, edited by S. T. Joshi and Rosemary Anne Pardoe, 184–96. New York: Hippocampus Press, 2007.

Plato. *Timaeus*. Translated by Benjamin Jowett. In *The Collected Dialogues of Plato*, edited by Edith Hamilton and Huntington Cairns, 1151–1211. Princeton: Princeton University Press, 1961.

Pochmann, Henry A. "Irving's German Sources in 'The Sketch Book.'" *Studies in Philology* 27 (1930): 477–507.

———. "Washington Irving: Amateur or Professional?" In *A Century of Commentary on the Works of Washington Irving*, edited by Andrew B. Myers, 420–34. Tarrytown, N.Y.: Sleepy Hollow Restorations, 1976.

Polt, Richard. *Heidegger: An Introduction*. Ithaca: Cornell University Press, 1999.

Powell, Michael. *A Life in Movies: An Autobiography*. New York: Knopf, 1987.

———. *Million-Dollar Movie: The Second Volume of His Life in Movies*. London: Heinemann, 1992.

Powell, Michael, and Emeric Pressburger. *A Canterbury Tale*. 1944. Irvington, N.Y.: Criterion Collection, 2006. DVD.

———. *I Know Where I'm Going!* 1945. Irvington, N.Y.: Criterion Collection, 2001. DVD.

Prendergast, Thomas A., and Stephanie Trigg. "The Negative Erotics of Medievalism." In *The Post-Historical Middle Ages*, edited by Elizabeth Scala and Sylvia Federico, 117–37. New York: Palgrave, 2009.

———. "What Is Happening to the Middle Ages?" *New Medieval Literatures* 9 (2007): 215–29.

Purchas, Samuel. *Hakluytus Posthumus or Purchas his Pilgrimes, contayning a History of the World in Sea Voyages and Lande Travells, by Englishmen and others*. Vol. 11 of 20. Glasgow: James MacLehose and Sons, 1905–7.

Rabinbach, Anson. "Unclaimed Heritage: Ernst Bloch's *Heritage of Our Times* and the Theory of Fascism." *New German Critique* no. 11 (March 1977): 5–21.

Reames, Sherry L. *The* Legenda aurea: *A Reexamination of its Paradoxical History*. Madison: University of Wisconsin Press, 1985.

Richardson, Judith. *Possessions: The History and Uses of Haunting in the Hudson Valley*. Cambridge: Harvard University Press, 2003.

Ricoeur, Paul. *Time and Narrative*. 3 vols. Translated by Kathleen McLaughlin and David Pellauer. Chicago: University of Chicago Press, 1984.

Robson, John, ed. *Sir Amadace*. In *Three Early English Metrical Romances*, 27–56. London: Camden Society, 1842.

Rogan, Johnny. *Morrissey: The Albums*. London: Calidore, 2006.

Rosenberg, Daniel, and Anthony Grafton. *Cartographies of Time: A History of the Timeline*. New York: Princeton Architectural Press, 2010.

Ross, W. D., trans. *Aristotle's* Physics: *A Revised Text with Introduction and Commentary by W. D. Ross*. New York: Clarendon, 1936.

Rubin-Dorsky, Jeffrey. "Washington Irving and the Genesis of the Fictional Sketch." In *Critical Essays on Washington Irving*, edited by Ralph M. Aderman, 217–37. Boston: G. K. Hall, 1990.

Rudd, Gillian. *Greenery: Ecocritical Readings of Late Medieval English Literature*. Manchester: Manchester University Press, 2007.

Ruskin, John. *Modern Painters*. Vol. 4 part 5, "Of Mountain Beauty." Vol. 6 of E. T. Cook and Alexander Wedderburn, eds., *The Works of John Ruskin*. London: George Allen, 1904.

Sachs, Joe. *Aristotle's* Physics: *A Guided Study*. New Brunswick, N.J.: Rutgers University Press, 1995.

Sanok, Catherine. "*The Lives of Women Saints of Our Contrie of England*: Gender and Nationalism in Recusant Hagiography." In *Catholic Culture in Early Modern England*, edited by Ronald Corthell, Frances E. Dolan, Christopher Highley, and Arthur F. Marotti, 261–80. Notre Dame: University of Notre Dame Press, 2007.

Scafi, Alessandro. "Mapping Eden: Cartographies of the Earthly Paradise." In *Mappings*, edited by Denis Cosgrove, 50–70. London: Reaktion Books, 1999.

———. *Mapping Paradise: A History of Heaven on Earth*. London: British Library, 2006.

Schmidt, Claire. "Sleeping toward Christianity: The Form and Function of the Seven Sleepers Legend in Medieval British Oral Tradition." M.A. thesis, University of Missouri, Columbia, 2008.

Scott, Walter. *Minstrelsy of the Scottish Border*. Edited by T. F. Henderson. 4 vols. 1902. Reprint. Detroit: Singing Tree Press, 1968. First published 1802.

Sedgwick, Eve Kosofsky. "Queer and Now." In *Tendencies*, 1–20. Durham: Duke University Press, 1993.

Seremetakis, C. Nadia. *The Senses Still: Perception and Memory as Material Culture in Modernity*. Chicago: University of Chicago Press, 1996.

Serres, Michel, with Bruno Latour. *Conversations on Science, Culture, and Time*. Translated by Roxanne Lapidus. Ann Arbor: University of Michigan Press, 1995.

Shanzer, Danuta. "Interpreting the *Consolation*." In *The Cambridge Companion to Boethius*, edited by John Marenbon, 228–54. Cambridge: Cambridge University Press, 2009.

Simplicius. *On Aristotle's* Physics *4.1–5, 10–14*. Translated by J. O. Urmson. Introduction by Richard Sorabji. Ithaca: Cornell University Press, 1992.

Simpson, James. "Diachronic History and the Shortcomings of Medieval Studies." In *Reading the Medieval in Early Modern England*, edited by David Matthews and Gordon McMullan, 17–30. Cambridge: Cambridge University Press, 2007.

———. "Faith and Hermeneutics: Pragmatism versus Pragmatism." *Journal of Medieval and Early Modern Studies* 33:2 (2003): 215–39.

Simpson, Mark. *Saint Morrissey*. London: SAF Publishing, 2004.

Skeat, Walter W., ed. *The Kingis Quair: Together with A Ballad of Good Counsel: by King James I of Scotland*. Rev. ed. Edinburgh: William Blackwood, 1911.

Smith, D. Vance. "The Application of Thought to Medieval Studies: The Twenty-First Century." *Exemplaria* 22 (2010): 85–94.

Snediker, Michael D. *Queer Optimism: Lyric Personhood and Other Felicitous Persuasions*. Minneapolis: University of Minnesota Press, 2009.

Stockton, Kathryn Bond. *The Queer Child, or Growing Sideways in the Twentieth Century*. Durham: Duke University Press, 2009.

Stokes, Whitley. Papers. MSS Add. 300. Special Collections, University College London Library.

Stokes, Whitley, ed. *The Gaelic Abridgement of the Book of Ser Marco Polo*. Zeitschrift für celtische Philologie 1 (1896/97): 244–73, 362–438.

———. *The Gaelic Maundeville*. Zeitschrift für celtische Philologie 2 (1899): 1–63, 226–312.

Strohm, Paul. "Historicity without Historicism?" *postmedieval: a journal of medieval cultural studies* 1 (2010): 380–91.

Summit, Jennifer. "Literary History and the Curriculum: How, What, and Why." *Profession* (2010): 141–50.

Tertullian. *A Treatise on the Soul*. Translated by Peter Holmes. Buffalo: Christian Literature Publishing, 1885. Online edition by Kevin Knight. http://www.newadvent.org/fathers/0310.htm.

Thompson, Anne B., ed. *The Northern Homily Cycle*. Kalamazoo: Medieval Institute Publications, 2008. http://www.lib.rochester.edu/camelot/teams/tnhcintro.htm.

Thompson, Stith. *Motif-Index of Folk-Literature: A Classification of Narrative Elements in Folk Tales, Ballads, Myths, Fables, Medieval Romances, Exempla, Fabliaux, Jest-Books, and Local Legends*. Rev. ed. 6 vols. Bloomington: Indiana University Press, 1955–58.

Trivedi, Harish. *Colonial Transactions: English Literature and India*. Manchester: Manchester University Press, 1993.

Tsing, Anna Lowenhaupt. *In the Realm of the Diamond Queen: Marginality in an Out-of-the-Way Place*. Princeton: Princeton University Press, 1993.

Tubach, Frederic C. *Index Exemplorum: A Handbook of Medieval Religious Tales*. Helsinki: Academia Scientiarum Fennica, 1981.

Tzanaki, Rosemary. *Mandeville's Medieval Audiences: A Study on the Reception of the* Book *of Sir John Mandeville (1371–1550)*. Aldershot: Aldgate, 2003.

Uebel, Michael. *Ecstatic Transformation: On the Uses of Alterity in the Middle Ages*. New York: Palgrave, 2005.

Underhill, Evelyn. *Mysticism*. New York: Doubleday, 1990. First published 1930.

Utz, Richard. *Chaucer and the Discourse of German Philology: A History of Reception and an Annotated Bibliography of Studies, 1793–1948*. Turnhout: Brepols, 2002.

Vitz, Evelyn Birge. "'The Seven Sleepers of Ephesus': Can We Reawaken Performance of This Hagiographical Folktale?" In *Medieval and Early Modern Performance in the Eastern Mediterranean*, edited by Arzu Ozturkmen and Evelyn Birge Vitz. Turnhout: Brepols, Forthcoming, 2013.

Wagner, Bettina, ed. *Die "Epistola presbiteri Johannis" lateinisch und deutsch*. Tübingen: Max Niemeyer, 2000.

Wallace, David. "Mystics and Followers in Siena and East Anglia: A Study in Taxonomy, Class and Cultural Mediation." In *The Medieval Mystical Tradition in England*, edited by Marion Glasscoe, 169–91. Cambridge: D. S. Brewer, 1984.

——. *Strong Women: Life, Text, and Territory, 1347–1645*. Oxford: Oxford University Press, 2011.

Walsh, Peter. "That Withered Paradigm: The Web, the Expert, and the Information Hegemony." In *Democracy and New Media*, edited by Henry Jenkins and David Thornburn, 365–72. Cambridge: MIT Press, 2004.

Walton, John, trans. *Boethius: De Consolatione Philosophiae*. Edited by Mark Science. EETS 170. London: Humphrey Milford, 1927.

Warner, George F., ed. *The buke of John Maundeuill, being the travels of Sir John Mandeville, knight, 1322–1356: a hitherto unpublished English version from the unique copy (Egerton ms. 1982) in the British Museum*. Westminster: Nichols and Sons, 1889. http://name.umdl.umich.edu/acd9576.

Warner, Michael. "Irving's Posterity." *English Literary History* 67 (2000): 773–99.

Watson, Nicholas. "Desire for the Past." *Studies in the Age of Chaucer* 21 (1999): 59–97.

——. "The Making of *The Book of Margery Kempe*." In *Voices in Dialogue: Reading Women in the Middle Ages*, edited by Linda Olson and Kathryn Kerby-Fulton, 395–434. Notre Dame: University of Notre Dame Press, 2005.

——. "The Phantasmal Past: Time, History, and the Recombinative Imagination." *Studies in the Age of Chaucer* 32 (2010): 1–37.

Weber, Max. *General Economic History*. New Brunswick, N.J.: Transaction Books, 1981. First published 1927.

——. *The Protestant Ethic and the Spirit of Capitalism*. Translated by Talcott Parsons. New York: Routledge, 2001. First published 1930.

Welter, J.-Th. *L'Exemplum dans la littérature religieuse et didactique du Moyen Âge*. Geneva: Slatkine Reprints, 1973. First published 1927.

Wheelwright, Philip, trans. "Natural Science" (includes *Physics* I–II, III.1, VIII). In *Aristotle: Containing Selections from Seven of the Most Important Books of Aristotle*, 3–63. New York: Odyssey Press, 1935.

Wilde, Oscar. "English Poetesses." In *The Artist as Critic: Critical Writings of Oscar Wilde*, edited by Richard Ellmann, 101–8. Chicago: University of Chicago Press, 1982. First published 1888.

Williams, Deanne. "Hope Emily Allen Speaks with the Dead." *Leeds Studies in English* 35 (2004): 137–60.

Williams, Raymond. *Keywords: A Vocabulary of Culture and Society*. Rev. ed. New York: Oxford University Press, 1985.

Willis, Ika. "Keeping Promises to Queer Children: Making Space (for Mary Sue) at Hogwarts." In *Fan Fiction and Fan Communities in the Age of the Internet: New Essays*, edited by Karen Hellekson and Kristina Busse, 153–70. Jefferson, N.C.: McFarland, 2006.

Winchester, Simon. *The Madman and the Professor*. New York: HarperCollins, 1998.

Windeatt, B. A., ed. and trans. *The Book of Margery Kempe*. Hammondsworth: Penguin, 1985.

Wolfe, Cary. "Human, All Too Human: 'Animal Studies' and the Humanities." *PMLA* 124 (2009): 564–75.

Wonderley, Anthony. *Oneida Iroquois Folklore, Myth, and History: New York Oral Narrative from the Notes of H. E. Allen and Others*. Syracuse: Syracuse University Press, 2004.

Woolf, Virginia. "Gas at Abbotsford." In *The Moment and Other Essays*, 56–62. New York: Harcourt, Brace, and World, 1975. First published 1947.

―――. "Middlebrow." In *The Death of the Moth and Other Essays*, 176–86. San Diego: Harcourt Brace, 1970. First published 1942.

Young, Philip. "Fallen from Time: Rip van Winkle." In *A Century of Commentary on the Works of Washington Irving*, edited by Andrew B. Myers, 457–79. Tarrytown, N.Y.: Sleepy Hollow Restorations, 1976.

Yule, Henry. *The Book of Ser Marco Polo*. 3rd ed. 2 vols. London: John Murray, 1903.

―――. *A Narrative of the Mission Sent by the Governor-General of India to the Court of Ava in 1855, with Notices of the Country, Government, and People*. Kuala Lumpur: Oxford University Press, 1968. First published 1858.

Yule, Henry, ed. and trans. "The Travels of Friar Odoric." In *Cathay and the Way Thither*, 1:1–162. London: Hakluyt Society, 1866.

Yule, Henry, and E. W. B. Nicholson. "Mandeville, Jehan de." In *Encyclopaedia Britannica*, 15: 473–75. 9th ed. 1883.

Zimmerman, Dean. "Temporary Intrinsics and Presentism." In *Metaphysics, the Big Questions*, edited by Peter van Inwagen and Dean Zimmerman, 206–19. Oxford: Blackwell, 1998.

Note: Page numbers in *italics* indicate illustrations.

CAROLYN DINSHAW is a professor in the Departments of English and Social and Cultural Analysis at New York University. She is the author of *Getting Medieval: Sexualities and Communities, Pre- and Postmodern*, also published by Duke, and *Chaucer and the Text: Two Views of the Author* and *Chaucer's Sexual Poetics*. She is also a founding co-editor of the journal GLQ: *A Journal of Lesbian and Gay Studies* (also published by Duke University Press).

Library of Congress Cataloging-in-Publication Data

Dinshaw, Carolyn.

How soon is now? : medieval texts, amateur readers, and the queerness of time /

Carolyn Dinshaw.

p. cm.

Includes bibliographical references and index.

ISBN 978-0-8223-5353-9 (cloth : alk. paper)

ISBN 978-0-8223-5367-6 (pbk. : alk. paper)

1. Time in literature.

2. Time — History — To 1500.

3. Literature, Medieval — History and criticism.

4. Queer theory.

I. Title.

PN56.T5D56 2012

809'.93384 — dc23   2012011611